The Great Indoors

The Great Indoors

At Home in the Modern British House

Ben Highmore

P

PROFILE BOOKS

First published in Great Britain in 2014 by
PROFILE BOOKS LTD
3A Exmouth House
Pine Street
Exmouth Market
London ECIR OJH
www.profilebooks.com

1 3 5 7 9 10 8 6 4 2

Typeset in Caslon by MacGuru Ltd
info@macguru.org.uk

Printed and bound in Great Britain by
Clays, Bungay, Suffolk

A CIP catalogue record for this book is available
from the British Library.

ISBN 978 1 84668 183 7
eISBN 978 1 84765 346 8

The paper this book is printed on is certified by the © 1996 Forest Stewardship
Council A.C. (FSC). It is ancient-forest friendly. The printer
holds FSC chain of custody SGS-COC-2061

FSC
www.fsc.org
MIX
Paper from
responsible sources
FSC® C018072

In memory of my father
David Highmore, 1932–2013

CONTENTS

The regimental order of the terraced house.

WELCOME HOME

The delights of a well-appointed home are infinite, providing a launching-pad for nearly all the rich range of human activity that makes up life today.[1]

This book is about the ordinary spaces of household life. It describes the major rooms – the kitchen, the front room and bedroom – as well as those more obscure spaces such as the upstairs landing and the hallway. Its historical focus is the twentieth century – particularly the second half, the post-war period. But the book also creeps into the present, and now and again it takes a much longer historical view. I pay attention to domestic rooms because they have been the stage sets for seismic shifts in social and cultural life over the last hundred years or so. Some of these changes are now glaringly obvious: today, for instance, we can seem wholly dependent on technology for most of our indoor entertainment. Other changes are less pronounced but no less significant: we sit differently, eat differently and use our rooms with a different sense of purpose. Domestic change has sometimes been swift, but often it has been incremental and sometimes glacial in its movement. We can see the results of change, but often it is hard to say where and when a change took place: when did people first 'flop' down into settees rather than 'take their seat'? Did anyone ever simply decide overnight that from now on they would often eat meals while watching TV? Sometimes change appears dramatic – as if it happened overnight. The technological inventions that have left their indelible mark on the ordinary house are often presented like this. But anyone who has watched *Tomorrow's World* will know that just because something has been invented doesn't mean it will affect the lives of ordinary folk as they go about their daily routines. Even those inventions that do take off can be slow to gain a foothold in ordinary life, let alone become a ubiquitous part of it.

As well as drawing attention to change I am keen to notice the continuities of domestic life. In the Mass-Observation archive – a source that I will continually mine in this book – there are hundreds and hundreds of descriptions by ordinary men and women listing the items on their mantelpieces.[2] They are split into two sets. One is from the late 1930s, the other from the early 1980s. There are, as you might expect, differences between the two groups of description: in the 1930s there are more ashtrays and pipe-cleaners; in the 1980s there are more foreign coins waiting patiently for the next holiday abroad. Across the two moments there is continuity too: clocks seem as popular in the '30s as in the '80s – the same could be said for lone buttons, drawing pins, elastic bands and appointment cards. Other changes are more subtle: in the 1930s the lists are short, unfussy; by the 1980s they have become more elaborate, as if ordinary people have got more comfortable narrating their possessions and their lives. Other differences point to more fundamental changes: in the 1980s the mantelpiece doesn't necessarily sit above a fireplace. By the 1980s some of the shelves that maintain the role of the mantelpiece are now radiator shelves or the telephone shelf. For some the mantelpiece has transformed

into a fridge door and its surrounding surfaces. But the fact
that people have maintained a specific space for odds-and-ends
and precious objects as well as for general communication and
household reminders suggests that continuity sits alongside
change in our domestic lives.

For a Martian anthropologist eager to study human life on
the islands that make up Britain, the house would offer a natural
site for fieldwork. Houses are where these particular humans,
living as they do in a cold and wet climate, scurry back to in
the evening. It is where they invest their money, where they
keep their stuff. He or she (presuming that Martians follow such
coarse distinctions) might chance upon these mantelpieces and
might be forgiven for seeing them as sacred sites for collecting things that have little use but large symbolic value (why
else give them such a prominent position?). Knick-knacks of
all sorts would be found there: personal mementoes, household
reminders, assorted oddities. Here humans bring together the
precious, the peculiar and the haphazard. Returning home to
Mars, and asked to report on what was most important to these
humans, the Martian anthropologist will perhaps mention a list
of things that, according to the Mass-Observation archive, are
present on most mantelpieces across the century and across the
varieties of people who respond to the directives: coins, pins and
postcards. Perhaps this is our common culture at its most basic.
And perhaps it has survived for years and will continue to, just
as long as we need buttons.

This book will sometimes require the services of a Martian
anthropologist to make visible a world that is often hidden
from view simply by over-familiarity. Perhaps we don't see electric sockets any more because we take them so completely for
granted. The only surprise we might get from a sink today would
be if there wasn't gushing hot water 'freely' available – on tap,
so to say. Talking of his time working with Mass-Observation

in 1937, the photographer Humphrey Spender remembers visiting one particular house in the industrial town of Bolton: 'we found, on the mantelshelf of the front parlour the component parts, heavily chromium-plated and gleaming, of a Hoover [vacuum cleaner]. There was no electricity connected to that house, so clearly this new invention, this new-fangled thing had another kind of meaning – as a kind of status symbol.'³ Sociologists and others are quick to explain such oddities in terms of status-seeking, but would a working-class family in Bolton really spend what would have been a king's ransom just to seem upwardly mobile? Perhaps the machine had been won in some sort of lottery and was now lying dormant in its dysfunctional splendour. Perhaps someone in the family was moonlighting as a repairer of domestic appliances, and here was the machine cleaned and ready to be put back together. Perhaps the family knew that an electricity supply was just around the corner, and here was their leap into the future – their down payment on an energy-guzzling tomorrow.

The connections and interconnections between houses alter during the period I'm looking at. This 1937 Bolton house has no electricity, even though the National Grid has been fully operational for two years and Bolton is a bustling urban area. It probably doesn't have its own water supply and most likely shares a toilet with a number of other houses. Fuel for warmth and for cooking was presumably supplied through a weekly delivery of coal. If there was a radio set (and there might well have been), then this was because there was a wireless enthusiast in the house. Today we see it as essential that we are connected to an array of services: gas, electricity, water, sewage, telephone, television, radio, the internet. Today when we ask if a house is networked, we are simply asking if it has broadband – all the other services are just assumed.

This book, then, is partly an account of how British houses

and their households were changed by electricity, by the uneven spread of household gadgets and labour-saving devices: by telephones, radios, TVs, computers and by central heating. It is not a straightforward story of expensive appliances gradually becoming more affordable, of distribution trickling down from the well heeled to the masses, so to say. Our Bolton house is probably owned by a private landlord. It was in mid-century council houses that you were most likely to find automated waste-disposal units, under-floor heating and endless electricity sockets. The trickle-down effect also doesn't account for why some devices took much longer to get taken up than others. The vacuum cleaner took roughly forty years (from 1915 to 1955) to move from having a 1 per cent presence in English and Welsh households to achieving the 50 per cent threshold: the radio took only ten years (from 1923 to 1933) to reach the same level of diffusion.[4] If women were in charge of buying consumer durables and not just perishables, would it have been a different story? Probably.

For most people, buying a vacuum cleaner or a wireless set was a large financial commitment. But it was nothing compared to forking out for a fitted kitchen or for getting central heating installed. For most of the twentieth century the majority of householders rented the properties they lived in. At the beginning of the First World War only 10 per cent of houses were occupied by their owners. It is only by the early 1970s that half the housing stock becomes owner-occupied, and by the end of the twentieth century it reached a plateau of around six houses out of ten.[5] It is, of course, no coincidence that it isn't until the 1970s that central heating becomes a feature of over half of British households – how many private landlords would make that sort of investment if they didn't have to? This shift from 90 per cent of householders renting to a majority of households owning their properties is a social revolution on a massive scale.

In many ways it explains a good deal of what happens to the home in the twentieth century and the practices that characterise it: for instance, the rise of DIY is clearly dependent on ownership. (Who would invest so much time and money into a building that was owned by someone else?) To bring such a revolution about required a change in the way that a society thought and acted. Mortgages, rather than being seen as morally dubious forms of debt, or as millstones inhibiting the enjoyment of life, had to become seen as a form of investment and as a way of getting on in life. Building societies, estate agents and banks eventually convinced us that owning, and the debt that went with it, were the way forward, the way to 'get on'. Clearly for the vast majority of people in the early decades of the twentieth century not being on 'the property ladder' was not the problem that it is now perceived to be.

In the chapters that follow I want to give a sense of lived-in-ness to the rooms that I explore. Perhaps one of the most significant changes in our day-to-day domestic living has to do with the manner in which we occupy space. Whether you call it a lounge or a sitting room, or opt for the anachronistic name 'parlour', something has changed in the living rooms of British houses: a sense of informality has invaded the home. Stuart Hall (the Stuart Hall who was responsible for establishing the discipline of cultural studies in Britain rather than the one who compèred *It's a Knockout*) came to Britain in the 1950s from Jamaica. He remembers how families created formal rooms under restricted conditions:

> as you can imagine, the houses that West Indian families could afford at this stage were very small and the front room was a more confined space: but people still found a way to designate a space which is not packed out with people, where the family don't slouch about and relax and where there are

distinct rules as to when the whole family went in there and
when they did not.[6]

Such rooms were for very formal socialising, but they were also a
place where sacred objects were kept: souvenirs from travels, certificates of achievements, pictures of loved ones living far away.
These parlours – especially for those who had newly migrated
– spoke of values tenaciously held on to, of complex and contradictory desires, and, importantly, of memory.

In the period I'm looking at, domestic interiors became places
for self-expression – for everyone. But before this, throughout
the first half of the century and into the post-war period they
are places requiring instruction, advice and concern. Concerns
about hygiene, about how best to bring up an infant, about what
kind of manners to display in the home, about how to use the
rooms of the house (how to clean them, heat them, use them) are
offered by magazines, books and government policies – endlessly.
The move towards the expressive interior also seemed to require
lots of advice, but this time it was aimed at getting the interior to
reflect your personality.

The home is a place where you are meant to express your
taste, your cultural loyalties and your aspirations. These might
be expressions of a common culture – of religious commitments
and national pride – or they might be about the idiosyncrasies
and modishness of taste (which is a different sort of commonal-
ity). If you could afford it – and more and more people could –
your house could reflect your sense of being modern or your love
of the past. Your house, in other words, could be your lifestyle.
But the home is always and primarily a practical environment
determined by money and by the day-to-day business of living.
How we negotiate between the practical and the expressive is a
consistent theme in this book.

To want to be up to date isn't a desire limited to the twentieth and twenty-first centuries. But during the last hundred years it has become something of an insistent preoccupation – especially for the industries devoted to making and promoting new domestic furnishings, as well as for the myriad of voices telling us how we should live. From about the 1920s being ultra-modern and up to date has resulted in a general de-cluttering of the home – ridding it of endless shelves and display cabinets filled with crockery, ornaments, sentimental knick-knacks and so on. Of course, being ultra-modern has not been the preoccupation of all: during the twentieth century it has been taken up most enthusiastically by the young and aspirational. Implementing the modern could be seen as a form of self-expression: embracing the clean simplicity of geometric space left un-fussed by the ornamentalism of over-stuffed interiors. Or it could be seen as practical: a menagerie of knick-knacks requires a serious amount of dusting. The twentieth century witnesses a general shift in middle-class life, as domestic servants become something only the properly wealthy could afford. The moderate white-collar earners would have to manage their own household chores. The de-cluttering of the house is neither just an issue of taste nor an issue of pragmatism – it is both simultaneously, and it is this tangled relationship that we continuously find in our tour of the house. It has a credo much loved by advertisers – not only does it look great, it is super-efficient too.

Compared to today's ideal domestic interior, the Victorian and Edwardian home looks so much darker, so much heavier and so much fuller. But images tell us only part of the story. When it comes to what these rooms mean and how that meaning has changed, we also need to look at how they are used. A house, we say, is our private space. But within that space is a subtle range of more private and more public spaces. A downstairs toilet might have a sense of public-ness in a way that an *en suite* bathroom could never have; a kitchen will always, I would think, seem less private than a spare room. And then there are rooms that seem to have a range of public and private functions. A teenager's bedroom often functions as a relatively public space for hanging out with friends but is also a deeply private space within the circulation of the house (entrance is by invitation only). Before central heating these were rooms that were rarely heated and wouldn't have been used at all during the daytime (unless the child was ill). Once upon a time, to be sent to your room really was some sort of punishment: now it is often the place where children and young adults would ideally want to be. And now, since the internet, these places are no longer the private cocoons for morose self-reflection (though they can be this too). Instead they are portals to all manner of opportunities, adventures and dangers. For many parents the bogeyman that haunts their nightmares isn't the stranger in the park offering sweets to young innocents but the internet groomer passing as a teenager in a chatroom in cyberspace seducing your young ones in the security of their own home.

In *The Great Indoors* I'm interested in two sorts of houses. One is the idealised house as it is imagined by exhibition designers such as those involved in the annual *Daily Mail* Ideal Home Exhibition. It is the house imagined in the pages of magazines and newspapers by lifestyle columnists and tailored to a variety of pockets and aspirations (from aristocratic to 'shabby chic'). It is there in aspirational DIY television programmes such as *Changing Rooms* (BBC, 1996–2004) and *Grand Designs* (Channel 4, 1999– ongoing). And it is pictured by retailers dealing in the accoutrements to domestic life.

The other house is the actual sort that people live in. According to the first type, it might seem that the average house is lived in by what is still sometimes called the nuclear family (in the sense of a nucleus of a pair of adults and their offspring rather than a family living off atomic energy). This imaginary house is people by effortlessly beautiful people at ease with their lovely interiors: here Aran-sweatered dads relax on white leather sofas watching football while tousling the hair of young sons; trendy mums in skinny jeans rustle up rustic food while curly-haired daughters cut cookies. The second, 'realist', type of house shows that this nuclear family household is now in the minority. According to the Office of National Statistics, about half the population lived in family homes in 1961; by 2009 this had fallen to about a third. The big growth areas are households of childless couples and single-person households. Families are also much more varied today than they were in the middle of the last century, with many more single-parent families, with blended families that mix biological and 'stepped' relations and with the new visibility of same-sex couples and their children.

It might seem that the idealised house is simply a fiction and that it is only the actual house that is real. But the idealised house not only shapes our imagination; it also shapes our real homes. In the chapters that follow I often refer to interior design advice provided by Terence Conran. In the 1950s Conran was a furniture and textile designer. In the 1960s he became a retailer, launching the Habitat chain of shops selling upmarket furnishings at relatively affordable prices. In the 1970s he launched a series of books advising people how to make the best of their homes. When I first started researching this book, I came across a reference to Habitat in the Mass-Observation archive. It is in a response to a directive asking Mass-Observers (in 1982) to describe their homes for the benefit of the historians of the future: 'I am interested in this project but do not see how any house is "typical" of the period. Well some are I suppose. Perhaps the '70s and '80s when reconstructed in museums will be pure Habitat? But isn't that a class thing?' This diarist is right, of course, Habitat was a 'class thing' – it was aimed squarely at the middle classes and those that wanted to be part of that group. But Conran and Habitat also stand for something more general: for an informality and eclecticism that can be found in the mass adoption of the duvet instead of traditional bedding, or the way that a second-hand pine kitchen table might simultaneously refer to traditional working-class domesticity and a more bohemian middle-class lifestyle.

Navigating between the mythic ideals of 'home' and the actuality of British houses is the challenge I've set myself. When, in 1964, the writer Richard Hoggart was looking for a middle-class family house to buy in the Greater Birmingham area, he was moving away from his working-class roots in the back-to-back neighbourhoods of Leeds where he had grown up. Ever sensitive to class differences, Hoggart notes how, when being shown around someone's home, he would often be surprised by the general eccentricity that was evident: 'the owner would swing open a door to exhibit the great size of a built-in wardrobe, and out would fall a profusion of operatic gear, amateur dramatic costumes, voluntary association uniforms, Country and Western, Civil War and pantomime outfits.'[7] This, for Hoggart, felt very different from the houses that belonged to those aspiring to middle-class values: 'by contrast, prick-neat kitchens, shining like colour supplement ads, more often appeared lower down that middle-class scale. There, the homes were prosperous but still striving; the casual, careless style, which did not bother about what the neighbours might think, had not been acquired and almost certainly would never be.'[8]

For Hoggart you were much more likely to find signs of the ideal-type house in those who aspire to be in a class that they weren't born into. Eccentricity, it would seem, is the privilege of those comfortable in their class-skin. I'm not sure about this. As a rule of thumb, I'm going to grant everyone eccentricity until proven otherwise. Similarly I'm going to assume that no one remains untouched by the vast welter of forces telling us how we should live our lives and showing us what this should look like in our homes. We may like to think we are invulnerable to the influence of the promotional culture around us, but the truth is that our taste is shaped in ways that are practically impossible fully to see. Taste is also determined by availability: in this we are historical creatures, and this is much easier to see. When I was growing up, it was fashionable to have bathroom suites in colours such as peach, pink and pale green (colours that are still used for toilet paper). Today your best chance of getting hold of such a suite is via eBay. However much you might like to think that your taste in white and chrome bathroom fittings is unforced, you might find you have less choice in the matter than you thought. And who knows? Perhaps if I teleported you back to the 1970s, you'd start hankering after an avocado-coloured toilet too.

In what follows I want to take you on a tour of the lived-in house. In each chapter we will stop off in a different room or a different area of the house (hallways, staircase, garden and so on). I will be scouring kitchen manuals, lifestyle magazines and advice literature for nuggets of domestic sense. Novels, films and TV programmes will be my witnesses. Television, in particular, is the mass medium that has focused most insistently on domesticity. It has catered for our domestic desires through endless cookery programmes, through programmes telling us how to buy our homes, do them up and then sell them on. It has dramatised our homes through the genre of the situation comedy, which, apart from a few notable exceptions, often seems to be almost housebound. Shops, exhibitions and catalogues will cause us to stop and nose around a while. The voices of Mass-Observers, and of memoirists, will remind us that houses are always lived in specific ways that aren't reducible to the dream worlds of magazines. So make a cup of cocoa, switch off the TV, pull up a comfy chair and read on ...

The decompression chamber ...

PLEASE COME IN

(Halls and Hallways)

Nestling in the gentle contours of the South Downs, not far from Chichester, is the Weald and Downland Open Air Museum. It's a living museum that combines the restoration of rural houses (cottages, farmhouses and the like) with a commitment to maintaining traditional crafts such as charcoal preparation. Set out as a small hamlet, the museum has a mill, a school, a group of buildings clustering around a market hall and a scattering of farm buildings (barns, cottages and farmhouses). The houses and barns have all been moved to their present location from across Sussex, Kent, Hampshire and elsewhere, and have been lovingly restored to their original state. At the museum the houses are as lively as possible: with beds made, food and drink being prepared and fires lit.

Visiting the museum on a bright and bitterly cold winter's day, you can get a sense of how much houses have changed over the centuries. Entering the 'Bayleaf Farmstead', a timber-framed hall-house which was built in the first decades of the fifteenth century, the first thing that hits you is the smoke. Shards of sunlight stream in through the rudimentary shutters and pick out regular, almost solid, angular columns of dense smog. The central hall constitutes the vast majority of the building, with two storeys of tiny side-rooms (pantry, buttery and bedroom) at either end. The smoke is wafting up from a central fire built on the floor and hangs in the air before finding freedom through gaps in the roof or out through the unglazed windows. Anyone visiting here will take the smell of the fumes with them when they leave.

A hundred years after this house was built, the arrival of chimneys will drastically alter buildings like this one; wait another hundred and fifty years and the availability of glass will mean a house can have fitted windows rather than shuttered holes in the wall. Standing in this smoke-filled room, you feel that it must have been a constant toss-up between wanting to let the light in and the smoke out, and needing to keep warm. It puts a good deal of must-have necessities into perspective. TV and the internet seem to diminish in importance as the more basic technologies of the house become newly visible and important. Other basic changes in the house must have been equally radical: Bayleaf Farmstead's toilet consists of a *garderobe* – a small cubicle with a hole in the floor that juts out of the wall of the upper bedroom, projecting into thin air. It's a big hit with the kids, as you can imagine, as they pretend to do their business on the top of the heads of people passing below.

Standing in the large smoky and draughty hall of the Bayleaf Farmstead, you are vividly presented with the fact that one of the biggest changes to have taken place over the centuries has been the shrinking of the space of the hall, from this central, expansive communal space of the Farmstead down into that measly, cramped little corridor called the hallway, whose task is only to shepherd you off into other rooms. Architecturally, the modern hallway functions as a service corridor, allowing for a linear placing of rooms without having to move through one room to get to another. Here in the South Downs the house is all hall: it is the gathering place, the kitchen, dining room and sitting room combined. To walk into the hall here is not to enter a vestibule or an antechamber but to enter immediately into the throbbing heart of the house. It is the house as one big, open, sociable space.

The dream of total open-plan living is really only a return to the hall-house. The transformation of the hall into the hallway has had a huge impact on the way houses are used and experienced. It is harder, for instance, to welcome a guest effusively when you either have to turn your back on them and walk away to let them in or back down the corridor while they follow. In larger houses this is less of a problem, but for most of the twentieth century, and still today, the hallways of many houses have been unwelcoming places. The modern hallway is an in-between space: it is not quite in the house but not outside it either. The majority of Britain's housing stock is made up of terraced housing and streets of semi-detached houses. From the 1870s various by-laws were introduced that required new houses to be built with adequate light, water and drainage. Builders responded to this by building houses (the by-law terraced house) that were narrow – and became narrower as you headed towards the back of the house – but were also surprisingly deep. These were the 'tunnel-back' terraced houses that tapered as you moved to the back so as to provide light for the rooms in the middle of the house. In these terraced houses and their posher semi-detached neighbours the hallway is often simply a thin straight line leading from the front door to the back of the house, containing the stairs to the first floor, as well as a precarious avalanche of coats, racks of shoes and boots, nests of umbrellas and sometimes, just to add to feeling that the hallway is really an assault course, a couple of bicycles.

Coming to London in 1932, the Trinidadian writer C. L. R. James described his terraced lodging house: 'I lived at No. 14. But from No. 1 to the next corner, all the houses were joined together. You could only look out of the window to the front if you had a front room, or to the back if you had a back room. You could not look out at the side anywhere, because the side of one house was the side of the other. I now have quite a tolerable idea of what it must feel like to be in gaol.'[1] In this house the hallway was two feet in width, and the only natural light would come from a glass pane above the front door and any light from the kitchen or back door. Compared to the airiness of most domestic housing in Trinidad, James must have felt that the housing of the Imperial metropole was pokey and austere in the extreme.

In these terraced houses the architectural function of the hallway seems to militate against its job as a welcoming entrance to the house, and encourages ambivalent feelings towards it: should the hallway be seen purely as a practical space or as one that should be treated with as much love and care as any other room? The magazine *Good Housekeeping* is, in 1968, adamant – it wants you to lavish all your flair on this unprepossessing space:

> Flair is: establishing a mood as soon as the front door opens and setting the scene for the rest of the house; painting hall walls a warm topaz yellow to lead the way for hot colours to come; running sisal carpet through into the kitchen-dining room for common sense and continuity; furnishing cheaply and sturdily, so the children of the house can feel at home too.[2]

For *Good Housekeeping* the entrance into the house needs to embody the look and feel of the rest of the house. It is an entrée, a taster for the delights that the rest of the house will deliver.

Yet it isn't at all clear that this is what householders would really want. In a government report aimed at establishing minimum standards for future housing (and published a few years earlier than the *Good Housekeeping* article) it was clear that making a hallway cosy might be the opposite of what is wanted:

The general preference is for a hall, as providing a neutral space in which to deal with visitors whom one wishes neither to leave on the step nor to invite to meet the family, and as a place to store outdoor clothes and a pram. If a home is large enough it can have a fair-sized hall without the detriment to other requirements, though in homes for small families a solution using a porch or lobby with outer and inner doors may be more satisfactory, taken as a whole.[3]

Here the hall or porch acts as a decompression or decontamination chamber: somewhere that will act as a holding bay for those you might not want to keep in the cold, but who you definitely don't want getting too comfortable. Any number of people could fall into this category: rent collectors, annoying neighbours, door-to-door salesmen, charity collectors, religious zealots. The hallway or porch is a necessary barrier that will protect the rest of your household from such intrusions.

Not all houses had halls and hallways. Cottages, for instance, will often have a front door that leads directly into the main room. The cheapest types of urban housing used a similar arrangement and were often only one room deep. Built before the advent of by-law housing, the notorious back-to-backs of the urban poor were three storeys of single rooms with a mirror-image house built directly behind and onto the sides of the house – so that you were entirely surrounded by other houses except for your entrance at the front. The smallest sorts of terraced house also had no hallway and often no front garden. Those interviewed for the *Homes for Today & Tomorrow* report – who might currently be living in hallway-less conditions – may well have felt that the luxury of the hallway (narrow or not) was to afford a household some privacy when the world came knocking. A front door that opens onto the main living area – which is common to the ancient hall-house, the modernist open-plan house, the cottage and the back-to-back – is not necessarily good or bad. It depends who it is that's calling. My guess is that if you are poor and living in terrible conditions you are much more likely to get unwelcome callers – health visitors, welfare officers, landlords, police and so on – and much more in need of the bare protection of a porch and a hallway.

Papering over the cracks
The message repeated in countless magazines, books and TV programmes is that domestic decoration needs to be practical but, importantly, should also reflect your personality in some way. This is going to be advice that will be trotted out for every room in the house. Domestic advisers, though, as was clear from *Good Housekeeping*, insisted that the hallway should be welcoming, cheerful and positive, to the point of telling those who are redecorating them that they should make sure 'never [to] direct light into the faces of visitors as they come through the front door' (which might be one way of dealing with some of your unwelcome visitors).[4] Of course, the way to reflect your personality in the twentieth century, especially if your income was limited, was to buy relatively cheap, mass-produced decoration.

Throughout most of the nineteenth and twentieth centuries wallpaper manufacturing was an industry that was consistently expanding. Its huge achievement was its transformation from an expensively crafted item into a form of decoration that was comparatively inexpensive and pretty much available to all. Today the industry is in decline; the wallpaper is fading. At the start of the twentieth century – in some ways the heyday of wallpaper – decorators would present their clients with pattern books from single manufacturers (often renewed twice in a season) that might have up to 800 predominantly new patterns from which to choose. Changes in printing and dyeing technologies meant that by the twentieth century not only was wallpaper

more widely affordable, but it was also a practical decorative
solution in houses where dirt (from fires and from urban pol-
lution) was always an issue. In the first half of the nineteenth
century wallpaper inks were still soluble, so any attempt to wash
the paper ended up ruining the pattern. Domestic advice was
filled with suggestions for waterproofing the paper, but this was
often a perilous business. In the 1870s the wallpaper industry in
Britain and elsewhere developed patterned wallpapers that could
be washed and had the delightful name of 'sanitary paper' (which
presumably meant that all other paper was now unsanitary).[5] In
the era of open fires, which burned coal and wood, cleanable
paper was crucial. Dirt, of course, is also passed to walls through
grubby hands and through the paws and coats of pets. So the
animated household really needed walls that could be mopped
down as muddy kids and animals slalomed through the hallway.
The washable papered wall reaches its zenith in the 1970s with
vinyl wallpapers such as Vymura, with characteristic swirls and
large flowers.

New processes in wallpaper manufacturing altered the class
connotations of wallpaper: the mass-produced, and in many
ways technically superior, paper was associated with lower-mid-
dle-class and working-class houses. Expensive handmade wallpaper, which was almost impossible to clean, became a way of
maintaining the patina of wealth: grubbiness as a badge of class
distinction.

Throughout the nineteenth and twentieth centuries wallpaper design is characterised not just by elaborate patterns but
also by extremes of texture. Embossed and flocked papers seem
almost smooth compared with the rugged landscapes of Ana-
glypta and Lincrusta, with surface patterns that protrude to the
point of becoming hazardous to small children who are still in
need of stabilisers. A quick history of the modern interior could
do worse than point to the changing patterns and textures of

wallpaper to give a quick feel of different decades: the subdued patterns of Arts and Crafts design at the turn of the nineteenth and twentieth century; embossed Nouveau and Deco designs in the 1920s and '30s; the biomorphic and nuclear patterns of 'contemporary style' of the 1950s; the hessian textures of the 1960s; the orange and pink cartoon blooms of the 1970s; and on into a return of Regency stripes for those that identified with Sloane Rangers and Margaret Thatcher. Today's wallpaper industry, while considerably smaller than a hundred years ago, offers the householder assorted retro designs (1950s' dandelion clock patterns being particularly hot today) as well as new designs. For hallways, though, the most practical solution is often paint.

Elite taste has sometimes denigrated wallpaper as too loud in its effects, too demonstrative and not in keeping with a desire for pre-industrial life which can be witnessed in many areas of domestic design. But those who have championed wallpaper have in the twentieth century seen it as an emphatic example of the democracy of taste that modern mass production can bring about. You might think that the key to democracy is fair and free elections: the editor of *The Crown Wallpaper Magazine* is there, in 1938, to put you right:

> *'An Englishman's home is his castle.'* No other country in the world can boast such a democratic phrase, and, again, what subject is more akin to democracy than wallpaper? On a visit to one of our wallpaper mills I once saw a production being printed which was intended to grace the walls of one of the palaces of his late Majesty King George V, and not very far away I watched another wallpaper being produced which would probably reach the home of one of his late Majesty's most humble subjects, and incidentally, those two products, from an artistic point of view, were not a great deal different from each other.[6]

Householders are doing it for themselves

If twentieth-century printing technology made wallpaper much more affordable, there was still the problem of paying for the professional wallpaper hanger. Wallpapering in the first half of the last century required skilled decorators; the investment in the paper was only part of what it cost to decorate. The true democratising of wallpaper occurs in the 1950s, when a new attitude dawns on promoters of domestic lifestyles: perhaps you don't need a two-year apprenticeship to be able to hang wallpaper; perhaps, given the right tools, any Joe or Josephine could do it too. The great surge of interest in learning such skills as an amateur and as a hobby took off in the mid-century and made wallpapering more affordable and more accommodating to fashion's whims. In 1955 the magazine *The Practical Householder* was launched, and in 1957 the magazine *Do It Yourself* appeared. The 1957 *Daily Mail* Ideal Home Exhibition displayed the practices and tools necessary for successful DIY:

> Here is a feature especially designed to instruct in an entertaining way. For the uninitiated this is a show that will demonstrate the money to be saved and the pleasure to be gained from 'doing it yourself' in the home. For the confirmed DO-IT-YOURSELF addict this is an opportunity to pick up some new ideas for here is a selection of the very latest materials provided and techniques suggested by manufacturers alert to the fact that DO-IT-YOURSELF is a home hobby that is here to stay.[7]

F. J. Camm, the editor of *The Practical Householder*, in the first issue of the magazine characterises DIY as a pleasurable hobby that can save you money: 'apart from the thousands of people who enjoy making and repairing things and doing jobs around the home, rising labour costs have compelled many more to undertake work themselves.'[8] The magazine promises that it will enlighten the reader about the arts of wallpaper-hanging and linoleum-laying. But the ambition of the magazine didn't stop there. You would also be told how to fix fridges and vacuum cleaners, lay crazy paving and reupholster furniture, as well as install hot water systems and, if all that wasn't enough, build your own house.

At the same time that *The Practical Householder* was being launched, British television was starting its long love affair with showing us all the things that we could do with our houses. In the 1950s it was Barry Bucknell, in shirt and tie, with Brylcreemed hair, that introduced TV audiences to DIY. In programmes such as *About the Home* (BBC, 1951–58) and *Barry Bucknell's Do it Yourself* (BBC, 1957) Bucknell showed us how to cover up all those unsightly aspects of Victorian and Edwardian houses: how to get rid of ceiling roses and cornices by fitting a false lowered ceiling; how to cover up panel doors with sheets of plywood so that they looked modern and new. Of course, it will only take a few years for DIY experts to be telling us how to remove such ugly forms of modernisation to reveal the 'original features' of our houses.

Barry Bucknell's message was about offering practical solutions for the modern home. By the time of the housing booms of the 1980s and 1990s something more flamboyant seemed to be demanded. BBC's *Changing Rooms* put home design on TV in an extravagant fashion. Set up as a design joust, the programme coupled two households with a designer and got them to redecorate each other's houses. Sometimes it resulted in modest and practical changes, but more often than not one of the designers – such as Laurence Llewelyn-Bowen, with flowing locks, dandyish shirt cuffs and purple crushed-velvet suits – persuaded neighbours to inflict mock-Baroque flourishes on the lounges or bedrooms of their neighbours. Each episode of *Changing Rooms* enacted a little class-war skirmish as ostentatious designers inveigled

'Handy Andy' – the show's cockney carpenter and handyman –
as well as the Glaswegian compère Carol Smillie into believing
that what they were doing would be liked by the homeowners.
The ante had been upped, and the natural direction for television
DIY seemed to result in two diametrically opposed but symbiotic programmes. On the one hand, there was *Grand Designs*, for
whom merely doing up an existing house wasn't enough. *Grand
Designs* showed the tenacity and the deep pockets that would
be needed if you wanted to build an underground eco house, or
convert a water tower into a family house. For those for whom a
grand design was a recipe for disaster there was *DIY SOS* (BBC,
1999– ongoing). *DIY SOS* shows the results of DIY-ers whose
ambitions have significantly outstripped their abilities, and offers
you the larger-than-life Nick Knowles to mop up after your cata-
strophic attempts to knock-up an extension.

The take-off of DIY wasn't simply about sharing skills and
techniques that had been the insider knowledge of professional
decorators: the decorative materials themselves changed. In the
early years of DIY you need to be a pretty dedicated enthusiast
to learn the decorators' arts, let alone the skills of the plumber
and electrician. But as DIY took off, manufacturers developed
products that were precisely fashioned for the ease of use of
amateurs. In the 1970s, for instance, the wallpaper manufacturers
Crown developed a line of 'ready-pasted' wallpapers that simply
required a small water bath rather than the cumbersome fold-
ing-table, paste and brushes. This wallpaper was also 'strippable'
without the use of hazardous chemicals – which added to the
ease of redecorating. But it was paint that underwent the greatest change.

Decorating was considered a skilled profession mainly because
house paints were fiendishly hard to apply. Unless they had the
brushes and the know-how, amateurs were in danger of producing newly painted doors that looked like Jackson Pollock had had

a hand in it. The development of new forms of paint – water-based emulsions, non-drip gloss paints, one-coat colour paints – really opened up domestic painting to even the most ungifted decorators. But paint was still a challenge if you followed the new paint advice that was coming out from the 1960s and '70s. Aside from simply painting the walls with flat whitewash or coloured paints, painting could involve such exotic practices as colour washing, sponging, ragging, dragging, combing, spattering, cissing, marbling or stencilling. So plenty of opportunities to mess up your walls and ruin your clothes.

Paint was often the covering of choice for those decorating hallways in the age of DIY, and this is partly because even the narrowest hallways – as anyone knows who has decorated one – seem to go on and on, making wallpapering an extravagant challenge. The hallway walls take you upstairs, they take you to the back of the house – they present you with corners that are almost impossible to reach without some form of hoist or platform. Those without platforms and hoists have to resort to the most makeshift of items: the paintbrush tied to the broom-handle.

By being tuned in to the passage function of the hallway, designers sometimes came up with what could seem like counter-intuitive ideas. Writing in 1974, in what was for many the domestic design Bible of the 1970s and '80s (and will be a fairly constant reference in this book), Terence Conran tells his readers that hallways, stairs and landings are 'first and foremost [...] by their very nature, traffic routes, designed to get you from one part of the house to another as simply and easily as possible', but that today 'they may combine the function of telephone booth, art gallery, laundry, library, storage area or home office'.[9] But function alone can't satisfy a modern need to express yourself:

> The hall is the first place your guests (and you) will see on entering your house, so it should be as friendly and welcoming

as you can make it. It will colour everyone's reaction to the rest of your establishment, and since it is the one place where visitors will spend comparatively short stretches of time, the decoration can afford to be on the dramatic side.[10]

Precisely because it is both functional and fleeting, you can afford to be flamboyant with decoration in a way that would be hard to stomach in a room designed for spending considerable amounts of time in.

Until the start of mass central heating in the early 1970s, the hallway in winter (which in Britain seems to be most of the year) was hardly going to be a cosy and inviting space. Even in larger homes the hall was not a forgiving place. For the art critic David Sylvester, whose parents moved into a prosperous and roomy house in north-west London in 1928, the hall was an imposing and slightly frightening place:

> The entrance hall, which was big enough to contain a large fireplace, had probably been designed to be used as a break-fast-room. The first thing seen on coming in was a statue two-thirds life-size, a wood carving of a helmeted guardsman with a shield and spear standing on a pediment carved with animal heads. It was one of a number of pieces of furniture and pictures and other art objects which must have been acquired along with the house.[11]

Surely this was enough to see off the annoying neighbour? But the majority of houses wouldn't have had such imposing halls – and it is the vast terrain of the more modest house that is my concern and my muse.

It's for you

David Sylvester's memoir notes how his mother 'commandeered

the telephone, which sat in the hall, so that her voice echoed through the house'.[12] For decades the hall and the hallway were the place where the telephone lived. It is a sign of the ambiguous nature of the hall as well as people's suspicion of the new technology of private telephony that initially – before it found its way into everyone's pocket – the phone was banished to cold and busy hallways. Many new technologies find it hard to feel immediately at home in the house: the house, it seems, isn't always welcoming to machines. The story of the freezer is a story of a technology gradually coming in from the cold, as it is at last given permission to come indoors after decades languishing in the chilly garage. Computers take a good while to set up home in people's living rooms, and have to do their time sitting underused in box rooms and guest bedrooms. Partly this has to do with the connotations that are initially associated with them: the computer smells of work – it takes a while for it to become an entertainment device too; the freezer is just too industrial. The phone is part of a public world, connected to the sort of messages that might be communicated by telegraph ('come quickly, jeopardy is afoot') rather than forms of intimate communication that are for most of the twentieth century still the province of the letter.

Situating the phone in the hallway was a way of letting the machine into the house but not quite into the home. The hallway is then seen as partly connected to the world outdoors, not part of the intimate spaces of the house. As I've been keen to point out, the hallway is an intermediate space protecting the privacy of the house from unwanted interruptions from the outside world – and this might work for 'virtual callers' as well as those physically present. For the well heeled (who were the first to adopt the domestic telephone), placing the telephone in the hallway was a way of acknowledging the social uncertainty of the telephone. How would you use it? Who would you telephone, and who would telephone you? Would servants use it for ordering fuel and food? Or would friends want to ring you to invite you for a meal? Class distinction in Britain was often marked in the geography of the home, for instance, through having a side or back door that was also called the tradesmen's entrance to distinguish it from the door where the 'heads of the house' might receive guests of equal social standing. The telephone confused such distinctions by allowing anyone access to the house through the same channel. The hallway (rather than the kitchen or the living room) was a way of leaving it in a fairly neutral social space in houses where servants worked: when it was more generally taken up in households living in servantless terraced houses, the convention of placing the telephone in the hallway continued. This was partly just continuing a convention, but also a way of keeping the phone and its random intimacies at a distance.

Initially the phone was simply an instrument for communicating instructions and news (more like the telegram than a letter). Indeed it was only after a number of years that the tariff was connected to how long you spent talking on it (initially it was a flat-rate rent, the same cost for heavy use as for light).[13] The conventions of telephone use had to be learned. On the one hand, there was the practical and technical business of using directories and getting through to the operator; on the other, there were forms of social etiquette that had to be taught. If you had never used a telephone before and it rang, what did you do? What did you say? The General Post Office film *The Fairy on the Phone* from 1936 told you. The film imagined a ghostly telephonist going around the country showing people telephone etiquette. The fairy told you things that today are only an issue for very small children. If you phone someone and only hear breathing, it normally means that you have dialled a pervert by mistake or a very small child. In the 1930s it seems that this might have been a more general response. The fairy taught you that you had to speak. The convention of the time, and it still persists among a small fraternity of 'seniors', is to answer the phone by parroting your own telephone number: 'Hello White-hall 902'. Of course, if your telephone number has thirteen digits, rattling off the number is no help at all in ascertaining whether you are talking to the right person. And while some older tele-phone users might still answer the phone by recounting their own number, it is hard to imagine that anyone with a mobile phone would do so. The crucial difference between a landline and a mobile phone is that when you phone a landline you are telephoning a home often with multiple occupants; when you phone a mobile you are phoning an individual person. Perhaps in the era when landlines were dominant the telephone number suggested the same anonymity as a house number.

By the 1930s the domestic telephone was becoming part of the house and was sold (like many commodities) with a promise and a threat. Aimed predominantly at women, it was seen as emancipating and as a convenience. One advert ran:

> I am the telephone ... I help make the ideal home ... I bring the voice of your husband, your brother, your friend. I summon the Doctor when illness comes suddenly upon you and yours ... I do your shopping – I catch the shops before they close – all your up-to-date Tradesman use me ... And yet how little I cost![14]

The same year as this advert the *Daily Mail* Ideal Home Exhi-bition set up a display to promote telephones and offered the following commentary: 'Nowadays the housewife refuses to be a drudge; she is constantly on the look-out for devices which enable her to save time on her household duties and leave her more leisure for her social activities. Of such devices the tele-phone is pre-eminent.'[15] But while liberation from drudgery is promised, another delight is imagined that brings with it a form of social anxiety that is still very much a part of our lives. The original telephone, like today's mobile phone, is as a must-have necessity with its own social stresses. Today's mobile allows us to contact people wherever we are, but consequently we are never away from bosses or guardians: yesterday's phone offered a whole new realm of communication and a whole new arena for worry. Technological communication, whether it is landline, mobile or today's social media, allows us instant connections to others but also the ego-deflating effects of people not returning our calls, our attentions.

The instant communication and convenience of the telephone meant that it became the dominant vehicle for arranging social life. In the early decades of the century it would have been considered bad manners to invite someone to dinner via the telephone; indeed at the end of nineteenth century it was suggested that only servants should answer the phone and relay any message through an internal system of communication.[16] But now, in the 1930s, 'the modern woman has come so to rely on the telephone as the means of communication between herself and her friends that gradually – perhaps unconsciously, but nevertheless surely – she loses touch with those of her former friends who are not on the telephone.' And this is the threat of the telephone: what if you don't have one? How will you be wanted and loved without a phone? Who is going to invite you to the cinema or out to dinner if you can't be reached, immediately? How will anyone know you exist if you aren't listed in a telephone directory? Having a telephone is not only a prerequisite for being modern and sociable, it is now a duty: 'For those women who are unfortunate enough to be thus overlooked by old friends, the remedy is simple – to have the telephone installed themselves. It is a duty every woman owes herself and her friends.'[17] Friendless and alone, it is your fault.

By the 1950s the telephone was part of the furniture. But

while there were clear benefits of having a phone, there were voices worrying about its effects: perhaps there was a cuckoo in the nest. Like many other technologies, what seemed like a beneficial instrument starts making its own demands. It becomes less a friend and more a high-maintenance and slightly unstable presence:

> Yes, the telephone, enlisted as our slave, is now frankly our master. We have no more control over it than over the rain. Sometimes it is amiable, and allows us to profit by its brilliant power, but it can equally cut us off with its relentless caprice; often we never get on at all. Contrarily, it sizzles in our ears when we are asleep, usually to convey some unwelcome intelligence. It distorts our voices, mocks our lonely hours and interrupts our busy ones.[18]

Although this was written in the 1950s, it could have been written today. How many complaints are there about the demands made on you by email or by telephone texts? But we have established these co-dependent relationships: it is us who constantly check emails and mobile phones, as if we are in constant need of some affirmation that we exist. The success of Twitter and Facebook is partly due to the constancy of them: there is always someone chatting. Even if no one is asking me out, people are talking to me (sort of) or talking near me (sort of).

Heating the hallway

Today's mobile telephones are, of course, not relegated to any specific room (unless it is due to the limited signal coverage in the house). Today, when it is quite usual for all the occupants of the house to have their own phone, it is not unusual for people who share a home to text one another or email while in the same building. The TV comedy *Outnumbered* (BBC, 2007– ongoing) gives us a contemporary middle-class family (liberal, profession-als with three children) in an end-of-terrace family house in the endless sprawl of London housing. The family is preparing for Christmas, and the younger boy is wondering why his sister isn't helping. When the mother says that she will text her daughter to get her down, the father sardonically remarks, 'That's what I hate about texting – it's destroying the ancient craft of shout-ing up the stairs'. Changes in technology alter the social forms of housing: stair bellowing can now be replaced by family 'text' arguments.

Changes in where telephones resided and how they were used were due to a number of factors: cost (particularly the declining cost of having multiple extension phones); changes in manners and in our sense of what is private and public life; and changes in technology. Sometimes technological developments are fairly rudimentary: for instance, the twenty- or thirty-metre telephone extender (popular in the 1980s), which allowed you to walk around some of the house being followed by a springy cable, knocking over anything not screwed down. This was an intermediate stage between the cordless phone and the traditional fixed phone. The phone extender was an extraordinary coil of plastic wire that attached the handset to the phone and was characterised by the amazing knots that it would form when you tried to walk off with the handset.

Placing the telephone in halls and hallways before the advent of central heating was to exile the machine in a space with an inhospitable climate. Certain types of telephone conversation became difficult not because of the cold and the general dis-comfort but because talking on the telephone in the hallway was a quasi-public act. How, for instance, to use such a device as a teenager so as to kindle the flames of a new love when broth-ers, sisters, parents, aunties and others are all, potentially, within earshot? The singer Boy George, who grew up in the 1960s and

'70s (he was born in 1961), remembered how difficult it was for someone growing up gay to use the hallway telephone for anything approaching a private life: either you used it in an impersonal way or you invented some form of code that allowed private communication to take place in such a semi-public space.[19] Is it my imagination, or do teenagers speak more clearly today, more loudly? Perhaps this is because previous generations got used to whispering into telephones in hallways.

Telephone desks, telephone benches and seats were part of domestic furniture by the 1930s and often included natty conveniences such as flip-out ashtrays and bookcases to hold the increasing large directories, diaries and address books, and novels – for those long times when the operator is too busy to connect you. Exiling the phone in the hallway required some paraphernalia – especially if you wanted to defeat the potentially freezing climate there. The magazine *Good Housekeeping* offered in 1967, an 'attractive telephone seat [that] is also an off-peak storage radiator – an inspired choice for a hall where phone calls are both chilly and uncomfortable'.[20]

By the end of the 1960s, at just the point when manufacturers are producing telephone seats with built-in heating, mass central heating was becoming a reality. And it is central heating more than anything else that will bring the hallway into the rest of the house, make it a room among rooms. As one advert suggests, the time for central heating is now: 'To head of family (YOU know who we are getting at don't you? So make sure HE sees this advertisement): Just a note to remind you that this is 1967 and that your family all hope that you will not ask them to face yet another British winter of hearth-huddling, water bottle cuddling, bathroom shivering misery.'[21] Central heating means you can leave doors open, means that shivering hallways and cold, clammy bathrooms could be things of the past. Nothing has done so much to alter the geography of the British house.

Not everyone was going to be happy about it, and not everyone embraced it as something for the entire house (it was quite usual to fit central heating but not to include the bedrooms or the hallway in the system). Asked to name domestic objects that had turned out to be follies, one Mass-Observer has no hesitation: 'The central heating which I can't afford to run and the great big radiators everywhere limit where you can put the furniture. I'd rather have a gas fire in every room any day.'[22]

For nearly everyone else there was no desire to turn back the clock. Central heating, like telephones and DIY, was here to stay (for now at least). It altered the geography of the house because now everywhere was a temperate zone. Central heating decentralised the house, and this would have major repercussions for a room that often staked a claim to be the heart of the house: the living room. Technology not only moves about the house; it alters the shape of the house as it moves. We will – I predict – need to return to the question of radiators.

The armed mantelpiece – just in case.

TAKE A SEAT

(Sitting Rooms, Living Rooms, Lounges etc.)

Grown-ups call it the living room, but that's silly. It's our playroom! Sometimes they do their work in it, or we do our drawing – and we eat here, as well. We make it a cinema, and other people come and stay the night, too, like friends or grannies.[1]

In certain streets in Britain you can hear the sound of young, style-conscious, neophyte home-owners going about the business of updating older interiors. The piercing yell of the industrial sander tells you that fitted carpets are being replaced by waxed or varnished floorboards. The serpentine hiss of wallpaper strippers suggests that patterned wallpaper or magnolia-tinted woodchip is going to be swapped for off-white emulsion or something equally minimal. The gentle aroma of silicone sealants accompanies the installation of clawfoot white baths and chrome shower units. Outside on the street, a skip is piled high with plywood doors, polystyrene ceiling tiles and what looks suspiciously like the avocado-coloured bathroom fittings that I mentioned in Chapter 1. Sometimes entire streets are dotted with such skips, and the sounds combine into a wail of upward mobility. Soon you will be able to buy a latte from the organic delicatessen that will open in a nearby street, selling ludicrously expensive olives and goat's cheese that requires an additional mortgage to buy.

A time-travelling visitor from the Victorian or Edwardian era (the favoured architectural periods for young gentrifiers since Georgian housing is now well out of their pocket) might think that these houses had now fallen on hard times. Should they enter the front room, they would see that the parlour has been turned into a modern living room: instead of high-backed armchairs replete with antimacassars, they would see low-lying, plain-coloured settees; instead of huddled groups of paintings, ornaments and knick-knacks, they would see white walls and a large black-and-white photograph of pebbles; instead of luscious rugs and tasselled lampshades, they would see bare floorboards and large, spherical paper light shades. Stripped back to a minimalist decorative style, we can see the triumph of a generalised and watered-down Scandinavian modernism mixed with a nostalgia signalled by the insistence on including a few 'original features' – ornamental ceiling roses, open-grate fireplaces and wooden-panel doors.

But perhaps even more surprising to the Victorian and Edwardian time-traveller would be to see what was happening in these rooms. Used to seeing front rooms as 'kept for best', our time-traveller would be shocked and horrified to see the informality that animates them and, perhaps most outrageously, to see toddlers scatter their wood or plastic bricks while a television twitters away in the background. It wouldn't be the technology so much as the presence of children in a space that had been defined by its commitment to propriety and formal talk. Rather than being reserved for important visitors or for Sunday family gatherings, the parlours seem to have been colonised by informality, mess and lounging.

Of course, this is all an exaggeration, a cliché of modern mores and upward mobility (of the house as much as the household). Even so, it does catch something of the actuality. This chapter tells the story of how the Victorian parlour was transformed into the lounge and living room. But just as a whole nation doesn't suddenly swap swirly patterned carpets for sanded floorboards, so the story told here is not one of unified ascent (or descent). In fact, it would be hard to find a room in the house more riven with disunity and contradictions. I mean, if we can't even agree on the name of this room, what hope would we have of telling a single story?

So what's it to be: lounge, sitting room, day room, den, drawing room, parlour, front room or living room? Is it simply a matter of class whether you call it a drawing room or lounge? Estate agents get round the problem by naming ground-floor rooms that don't have a built-in function simply as 'reception rooms'. 'Living room' sounds like a practical solution to the posh-ness associated with a term like 'drawing room'. To call a room a 'drawing room' is often anachronistic unless people still continue the practice of having female householders and guests withdrawing to this room while men drink and smoke on their own in the dining room. But the problem of naming a room a 'living room' is that it means deciding which room is the one where the living gets done. In the first half of the twentieth century, in working-class housing, the 'living room' usually referred to the room at the back of the house where the cooking and eating were done (though, confusingly, this was also called the kitchen). Sometimes there was a small scullery with a sink that was named the 'back kitchen'. If you were lucky enough to have a reception room as well, then this would be the parlour or sitting room. One person's living room is another person's dining room, parlour or kitchen. As one Mass-Observer commented in 1983, 'When I was little, my mum, dad and I lived in a house in which we had a living room (for general use) and a sitting room (for "best"). When we moved to a bigger house the words became changed to "lounge" and "dining room"! Now I call my main room either a lounge or a living room.'[2]

The sheer number of names for a main reception room is partly a hangover from large aristocratic houses that had to come up with names for the mass of rooms dedicated to sitting. But the class connotations won't go away, and whether you call your room a lounge or a sitting room, for example, says something about you, your background and your sense of the house. Even couples can disagree on what name to give this room: 'I tend to call it the living room; Jean uses the term sitting room. Just to get up her nose, I think I'll start calling it the parlour.'[3] While 'sitting room' might seem more resolutely middle-class than the more neutral 'living room', it was not quite as posh as 'drawing room' (and 'living room' never managed to get the full popular appeal of the 'lounge' – with its sense of unselfconscious hedonism). The one name that signals a decisive change is the term 'parlour'.

By the 1980s (at the very latest) it would be impossible for anyone to imagine their front room as a 'parlour' without seeming deeply old-fashioned or ironic. The word 'parlour' designates a room for grown-up conversation ('parlour' derives from the French verb *parler* – 'to speak, to talk'). It was a room that existed in modest terrace 'by-law' houses of the relatively prosperous working classes and in the more prestigious semi-detached houses of the lower and middle middle classes (so to say) from the nineteenth century into the first half of the twentieth. It was a room where you kept your best furniture, your pictures and your ornaments: it was a statement of where you were in the social world, or at least where you thought you were. But you rarely used the room. You certainly wouldn't let children in there, unsupervised. Some households locked their parlours, precisely so that children couldn't get in. The parlour was where you entertained visiting relatives, or offered tea to the vicar. So what caused the death of the parlour? It probably wasn't any *one* thing, of course. Fashions changed both in terms of interior decoration and in terms of social etiquette. What is clear is that a social ethos that could maintain the parlour as an almost sacred room dedicated to propriety and social standing was not one that could also embrace TV and changing social attitudes towards children (where they might be heard as well as seen), let alone a world where practical considerations might have the edge on tradition.

Whatever we call it, this room can be seen as a barometer for the changing climate of the domestic interior. When the parlour opens its door to unsupervised children, we know that a new informality has entered the home. If childhood, through most of the twentieth century, was lived outdoors, in the twenty-first century it is much more likely to be lived indoors, in front of TVs and computers and in the room where these monitors are found. When the front room swaps high-backed chairs for scatter cushions, we know that the idea of relaxation has changed. The changes that occur in this room are vivid versions of changes that take place more subtly across the entire ecosphere of the house.

But change isn't always easy. One Mass-Observer notes how, in 1941, the desire to keep a parlour clashes with a fashion for using such rooms for everyday living. His wife

> is trying to keep the front room in the traditional 'parlour' style – i.e. not used except on special occasions, and all the best furniture kept there. She really feels bitterly the necessity of having to use it every day as a living room, and being unable to show it off to visitors as something special. This contradiction between her wishes and the facts gives her a

lot of extra work, because she has the room crammed with her best furniture and all sorts of ornaments and oddments and has to keep it going as a living room – dusting all these multifarious objects everyday and sweeping the overcrowded floor.[4]

The parlour was a display cabinet; the front room was less cluttered. Why the former turned into the latter was due to a host of social and cultural changes.

Keeping up appearances in the house of convenience

The Victorian parlour, crowded with ornaments and bloated with furniture, either required ultra-diligent housework from the householders (well, from the wife) or from an employee – a servant of some kind. By the end of the First World War the numbers of servants within the range of middle-class houses were dwindling, and this gave rise to an array of issues and solutions. Indeed the term 'the servantless house' was coined explicitly to name those houses that in the nineteenth century would have had a servant (a maid-of-all-work, for instance) but which no longer did so. In the 1920s the push for middle-class householders in servantless houses was towards 'convenience' and 'labour-saving', and the struggle was to negotiate between the values and associations of a previous time and the necessities of modern, servantless life.

The result of such negotiations often led householders to embrace a world of labour-saving devices, modern decorative ideas and a future that could be easily wiped clean, and gradually to let go of some of the traditions of the past. If knick-knacks need constant dusting, and such dusting is a problem, then lose the knick-knacks. By the end of the Second World War a future of 'utility furniture', gas fires and easy-clean surfaces was being devised. Yet persuading people that their ornaments should go was no easy matter. The cartoonist for the *Daily Express* thought that in the face of a sleekly modern future people would rather dust (but, of course, as a man, the burden of dusting might not have fallen on his shoulders):

> The open plan, the mass-produced steel and plywood furniture, the uncompromising display of the structural elements, are all in theory perfectly logical, but in the home logic has always been at a discount. The vast majority, even including many readers of the *New Statesman*, crave their knick-knacks, though not in Victorian abundance, and are perfectly willing to pay the price in prolonged activities with broom and duster.[5]

Even left-leaning householders (who might read the *New Statesman*) might want to indulge their penchant for keeping ornaments.

Like any other room, the sitting room requires upkeep. But whereas the kitchen–living room is very visibly a place of work, the parlour–sitting room needs to stay clean miraculously. Keeping your sitting room spick and span in an age of solid-fuel fires was a Sisyphean task, but in the twentieth century help was at hand. The shine and sparkle of the sitting room were going to be enhanced by a range of domestic cleaning products aimed at beautifying the home. In the inside front page of the May 1946 issue of *Housewife* sits a colour picture of a living room. The main light source is a glowing fireside. The room is cosy, with armchairs and a table with a chintz cover and a vase of flowers. The writing below the picture conjures up a feeling of safety and comfort, even though it recognises that many people had not yet returned from the war: 'in the silence and safety of this fire-lit room there's a memory and a promise for those thousands far away. This friendly hearth, this shining room reminds us that while men make houses women make homes. In the quiet welcome of this peaceful room how easy to forget you're in a house and only know that you're at home.' But how are the women going to make this home? *Housewife*, knowing that its main source of revenue is advertising, points the way: 'And how much this happy room owes to little things: to a little care with gentle Silvo; to linens made lustrous white by that last rinse in Reckitt's Blue; to Zebo's winning way with gloomy grates; and to copper and brass all laughing and gay because of Brasso.'[6]

The servantless house of the first half of the twentieth century, seemingly brim-full of home comforts and domestic ease at evenings and weekends, is driven by a working day that would make contemporary factory shift work look like a stroll in the park. The *Daily Express*'s 1937 guide to housework (in its inventively titled *The Housewife's Book*) lays out the daily and weekly tasks in a handy grid titled 'Plan of Work for a Small Servantless House (3 or 4 in family)'. Starting at 7 a.m., when she gets up, the first set of tasks for the housewife lasts until 11.30 a.m. and includes having to

strip the bed and air the rooms, stoke the boiler, light living room fire if necessary, prepare breakfast, clear away and wash up breakfast, sweep porch and steps, lay sitting room fire, do dining room and sitting room carpets with vacuum cleaner, mop the surrounds and dust, make beds, mop and dust upstairs rooms and W.C., attend to bathroom, wash out bath and lavatory basin, sweep and mop bathroom floor and landing, sweep stairs, look over larder, prepare vegetables or pastry for midday or evening meal.[7]

It's just gone 11.30 a.m. Between 11.30 and 12.30 it was time for shopping and the 'Housewife's Weekly Duties', which on a

Thursday included the 'special turning out of the sitting room'. In the afternoon between 3 p.m. and 4.30 p.m. there could be time for recreation and visiting but also the 'minding of young children' (so, more work then). At 8.00 p.m. (thirteen hours after commencing the working day) the housewife had to clear away the meal, but the washing up 'can be deferred until the morning', which gave her time for 'reading, recreation, letter writing, accounts' before bed.

In working-class houses the amount of labour is, as you might expect, equally high for women, but with the added pressure of consistently having to scrimp enough money so as to put food on the table each day.[8] Working-class housing was split between those who lived in homes where there was a small parlour-type room (the by-law terrace house, for instance) and housing where the only room that wasn't a bedroom was a combined kitchen–living room (for example, in back-to-back housing). In Mass-Observation's exhaustive wartime housing enquiry, specifically designed to find out what working-class people wanted from post-war reconstruction, the most insistent desire is for more rooms, and specifically for a parlour–sitting room:

> If people's wishes are listened to, it will in effect mean a minor revolution in working-class housing. People are no longer content to eat and live in the same room; what they want today is two living rooms, one for every day in which to eat and relax, another where visitors may be entertained and which they like to keep for best.[9]

By the mid-1970s, when most of the worst housing had been cleared, the idea of a room that would be kept solely for best was fading: much more likely for aspiring householders to favour a lounge–diner with a separate kitchen.

But a room kept 'for best' might not necessarily mean a distinct space that can only be used on Sundays or when Aunt Agnes comes round; it might mean a room where you keep your best things and where you are at your best. Both these senses have led to a long-held conception of the living room as the place emphatically to express your taste. In his *The House Book*, from 1974 (the book started out as a training manual for Habitat staff), Terence Conran describes the living room as both private and public, a place to express yourself for yourself and for others:

> The living-room has to be both private place for being peaceful in, and public platform where you can sparkle when you are, as it were, at home to the world. It must be a place where you can relax, and it must, moreover, enable you to recharge your energies. You will want the room to reflect your tastes and your personality (or at least the facets that you choose to put on display).[10]

The balance of creating a space that is comfortable for the householders while also inviting and hospitable for others is, for Conran, a key for successful sitting-room design. So the road from parlour to lounge isn't just a pragmatic adjustment to changes in housework; fashions and tastes are changing too.

By the twentieth century there was a barrage of publications to advise you on how to create the right effects and ambience for your sitting room, and instructing you how to part with your money in order to achieve this. While it wasn't the first British magazine to campaign for modernising the home, the publication *Our Homes and Gardens* can serve as a useful example. Established in 1919 in the aftershock of the First World War, it billed itself as a 'practical magazine dealing with houses, furniture, equipment and gardens'. It promoted a sort of mild modernism that at times came close (but not intimately so) to continental modernism. In its first editorial it set out its store: 'Always we shall strive to avoid the extreme, devoting ourselves instead to what is within the compass of those who think that good taste, expressed in a moderate way, is far more to be desired than what is bizarre and extravagant.'[11] The magazine had a modern feel, with centred, symmetrical images and large white margins. It promoted a less provincial sense of the British home and looked encouragingly to Scandinavian countries for decorative ideas, as well as to North America for ideas about more efficient uses of space.

The magazine was geared towards the servantless middle classes and ran competitions for readers to supply the best solutions for the labour-intensive houses that as a class they had inherited. A favoured method was to combine kitchen and dining room in a way that aped the working-class house. In the editorial for the second edition it stated: 'We live in times when special thought is being given to overcome the inconveniences that are so common in the ordinary home, and more than ever today it is necessary to scheme our homes and to equip them in such a way that all unnecessary labour is eliminated, while a maximum of comfort is secured.'[12] The magazine was insistent in its attempt to distance the contemporary British home from its Victorian past. In an article tellingly titled 'The Charm of White Interiors' the magazine can promote what, in 1919, was a fairly radical style choice: 'No longer is the respectable dinginess of Victorian days an approved method. [...] It is not long ago that, whatever colour had to be applied it was always in the same drab tone. Sage green was an especially favoured tint, supposed to be expressive of an artistic taste.'[13]

Of course, just because a magazine like *Our Homes and Gardens* champions a particular aesthetic preference doesn't mean that this was widely accepted. Thirty years after this article was published, Mass-Observation ran a large survey about household paint colour choices and found that there was little to distinguish between classes on this count. More crucially they found that, while roughly half of the women interviewed had no discernible preference for a particular colour scheme, the other half, the ones that did have a preference, overwhelmingly chose green. Green paint lovers were emphatic; one respondent seems almost obsessive in her devotion to green and wanted 'as much green as I can get'. She remembered that 'when I was first married we had everything green. It's meant to be unlucky, but I like it.' Another respondent from Durham tells Mass-Observation that 'all the rooms are green', and another that, 'I'm all green in the kitchen, and the bedroom is green. I have it green for the kiddies. It seems to suit their eyes a bit.'[14]

Green – particularly dark green – faded out as the dominant colour during the Second World War – though it is still a popular colour, especially for those wanting to get an aristocratic, old-world look. Today colours are determined by much faster trends, and it is hard to imagine any colour (apart from the non-colours of neutral creams and magnolias) being as dominant as sage-green was and for so long. Fashion today might favour taupe and red; by this afternoon it might be aqua-chiffon and yellow.

The literature on the gap between popular tastes and what is considered to be 'good taste' rarely comes down in favour of the popular (unless it is the ironic love that goes by the name of kitsch). For most of the twentieth century British popular taste is something to deplore. In 1912 the aesthete Roger Fry mockingly described the decoration of a railway refreshment room as consisting of: wallpaper 'in which an effect of eighteenth-century satin brocade is imitated by shaded staining'; lace curtains 'with patterns taken from at least four centuries and as many countries'; tables carrying at their centre large pots 'in which every beautiful quality in the material and making of pots has been carefully obliterated'; and so on.[15] He chose this room not because he had a grudge against the railways, but because such public places 'merely reflect the average citizen's soul, as expressed in his home'. The hotch-potch of styles results in a room that is essentially comfortable but profoundly ugly (according to Fry). For Fry the contemplation of the furnishings and decorations 'can give no one pleasure; they are there because their absence would be resented by the average man who regards a large amount of futile display as in some way inseparable from the conditions of that well-to-do life to which he belongs or aspires to belong'.[16]

It is a common complaint, and one aimed at the well-to-do (especially the *newly* wealthy) as much as at the poor (at least they have the excuse of not being able to afford 'good taste'). Aesthetes and some sociologists might fundamentally disagree about the possibility of 'true' good taste, yet they are surprisingly consistent in assuming that our choices about furnishing and decorations are driven by something other than by an actual liking of the stuff we acquire. For some, perhaps for most sociologists, taste reflects aspirations and class affiliations – it is a way of making and marking social distinctions (keeping up with, or overtaking, 'the Joneses').[17] In a more cavalier move the aesthete accuses everyone, apart from the brave pioneers of real beauty (i.e., their crowd), of having mendacious preferences: 'nearly all our "art"', and Fry is including decorative arts and furnishing in this, 'is made, bought, and sold merely for its value as an indication of social status.'[18]

Imagine these aesthetes and sociologists coming into your home (if they could stop bickering for a while); both would be highly sceptical about why you decorated your sitting room in the way you did, why you chose those particular pictures, what you decided would go on your mantelpiece. They might ask you about a particular ornament. You might have various reasons for choosing it: you might be moved by it, attracted by its form; it might bring back memories or have deep associations of a specific place; you might just love it for that complex set of reasons that makes us fill our houses with what seems like random stuff. For these aesthetes and sociologists this won't do: your reasons for buying it, even if they aren't visible to you, are to do with status. For them your choice is in some ways always pretentious, inauthentic and determined by social positioning.

At times people probably do hanker after things that will send out signals to others that they are people of discernment and like the finer things in life. But this isn't incompatible with actually liking those things and appreciating them. At times people do acquire objects that they don't really like, enjoying the statement that they make: 'Above the fireplace is a large, block-mounted print of Bruegel's village wedding. It was put there as a conversation piece for visitors as my taste in art is not pleasing to other people. This is the version in which the bag-piper is indulging in a sexual fantasy though none of the wedding guests have noticed his predicament.'[19] In a previous century (the eighteenth) the conversation piece was very much a part of the furnishings of an enjoyable living room and showed that you were a generous and prepared host: should there be a lull in the conversation, just ask your guests what they think the bagpiper is up to and why none of the wedding guests is paying him any attention.

In 1988 Mass-Observation asked its diarists to describe objects about the house that meant something to them, or that they had a particular affinity with. The results showed how much our important household objects are tied to our sentiments and our sense of our own histories. Take this example of a secretary born in 1929:

We have a large elephant ornament about 20 inches high. I have known him all my life. He is life-like and benign although not valuable. I need to know he is there. In the Second World War when I was a child we lived in Cardiff – the bombing was very bad and my father got a transfer to Hereford. We let our house furnished to some munitions workers who had to be in Cardiff. During one blitz when windows were blown out the elephant crashed to the floor in pieces. The tenants lovingly stuck him together again and when they left and our furniture came to our new home in Hereford after the war – there he was, bless him – not as good as new but at least in one piece. My mother brought him to this house when she moved in with us at the age of 84. He was in her room when she died four years later. The elephant consoled me.[20]

What matters here is neither taste (as a form of distinction or discrimination) nor monetary value but a sense of condensed history, of this elephant being a witness to events that are both collective and deeply personal.

Of course, sometimes stuff is just stuff and doesn't have an emotional charge to accompany it. 'I must be peculiar, unusual, odd, weird or something', writes another Mass-Observer, 'but there's nothing in the house, apart from all my several thousand books, which means a single thing to me.'[21] 'Several thousand books' might answer a need to surround yourself with things that matter: in many houses having this number of books wouldn't leave much room for knick-knacks.

Learning to be modern

Learning to live without knick-knacks and learning to embrace the 'contemporary' style was something that was being taught to the British in the late 1940s and early 1950s. Being modern in your choice of interior design was a way of showing national pride in a post-war reconstruction that would promote efficiency and rationalism. While cartoonists and social critics such as Osbert Lancaster were proclaiming the continued joys of knick-knacks, designers, architects and even government agencies were championing the de-cluttering of the home. Certainly in the post-Second World War period it was as if there was a consensual effort to promote the idea that a 'tidy room is a tidy mind'. In the 1950s and throughout the second half of the twentieth century the architects Alison and Peter Smithson designed houses that incorporated what they termed the 'put-away aesthetic'.[22] This meant that the actual design of the house had to be based around storage as an important structural ingredient: de-cluttering was its *raison d'être*.

Yet a contemporary look could also be achieved by using the services of the dustbin and the jumble sale:

> I was married in the 1950s and our first home was completely devoid of ornaments. Vases and knick-knacks given to us as wedding presents were soon hidden away and disposed of as quickly as possible. Our flat was decorated in what we considered to be the 'contemporary' style, which as far as we were concerned meant two walls papered in stripes and the rest with spots!![23]

A range of exhibitions promoting British domestic design were staged directly after the war, showcasing furniture makers, textile manufacturers, craft makers and a host of new gadgets and appliances. In exhibitions such as the *Daily Herald*'s 'Modern Homes', the Victoria and Albert Museum's 'Britain Can Make It' (both from 1946), and in later exhibitions associated with the Festival of Britain (1951), visitors were shown how to decorate their homes and to furnish them with modern quality items, in a way that was decidedly knick-knack-free (or at least knick-knack-reduced, and knick-knack-managed).

'Britain Can Make It' was an enormously popular exhibition in London's V&A and showcased modern British domestic and industrial design. The main rooms of the exhibition consisted of large displays of clothing as well as fitted-out domestic interiors as exhibition displays. The most popular exhibition space was dedicated to the living room and dining room. It seemed, from the surveys conducted, that furniture was the one thing that men and women shared an interest in. Under the auspices of the newly founded Council of Industrial Design (which was established in 1944, and changed its name to the Design Council in the 1970s), 'Britain Can Make It' sought to instil post-war optimism in the domestic arena. It combined the wartime design initiative of 'utility furniture' (modern 'basic' designs that promoted the war effort by combining good design with the frugal consumption of materials – a sort of minimalism born of necessity rather than desire) with the futuristic: a temperature-controlled bed that looked like a cross between a bobsleigh and a space rocket, for instance.

'Britain Can Make It' combined national pride with a post-war social democratic ethos alongside an attempt to convince a style-allergic nation that they too could live in well-designed houses. Gordon Russell, the man in charge of furniture displays at the exhibition (and who would soon become the director of CoID), promoted modern design as a national attitude: furniture, for Russell, 'will be "period stuff"! Our period, the period that won the Battle of Britain, the period that showed the world what we can do when we put our minds to it. Why should I have to apologise for it? Surely I'm entitled to believe that we can build furniture as well as we can build aircraft.'[24] But if 'Britain Can Make It' sought to instil national optimism with good design, it had to cast off the association of 'good design' with prohibitive cost and snobbery. Stafford Cripps, the president of the Board of Trade, insisted that the exhibition was an attempt to democratise design, and that this in turn would benefit national life:

> Industrial design has, in fact, the most intimate connection with the comfort and happiness of our daily life. Good design can provide our homes and working-places with pleasant articles which combine good construction and fitness for purpose with convenience in use and attractiveness in shape and colour. There was a time when the satisfaction of living amongst beautiful and useful objects was regarded as the monopoly of a favoured few. That time is passing, and it is now becoming recognised that low-priced goods need not be ugly, nor mass-produced articles ill designed.[25]

Raymond Mortimer, writing in *New Statesman and Nation*, was exceptionally enthusiastic about the exhibition: 'On Monday I emerged from the Victoria and Albert Museum exhilarated, astounded, almost incredulous [...] "Britain Can Make It" is, within the limits of its size, decidedly the best exhibition I have seen.'[26] But he also noted the general assumption that Britain, or at least England, might not necessarily embrace good design: well-designed objects, he mused, 'may be good enough for foreigners; they are certainly not bad enough for the English'. The exhibition confused some people as to whom the designs were actually for: one visitor remarked, 'I want to see what it is we're sending abroad and can't have ourselves. Anything that's good gets sent for export, only the rotten things remain for us to use. It's a downright shame the way we're treated after sticking six years of war.'[27]

It was assumed that bad design and people's willingness to accept it were a constitutional part of being British. The

problem, it seems, is not just status-seeking but the fundamental deceit in the look of things. Things, it appears, are not
what they seem. Writing some time after the V&A exhibition,
Osbert Lancaster jokingly treats 1930s' design as a premonition
of war:

> It is significant that the old English fondness for disguising
> everything as something else now attained the dimensions
> of a serious pathological affliction. Gramophones masquer-
> ade as cocktail cabinets; cocktail cabinets as book-cases;
> radios lurk in tea-caddies and bronze nudes burst asunder
> at the waist-line to reveal cigarette lighters; and nothing is
> what it seems. On reflection it is not perhaps surprising that
> disaster should have overtaken a generation which refused
> so consistently to look even the most ordinary facts in the
> face.[28]

Being modern in 'Britain Can Make It' meant equating good
design with clarity of purpose: a gramophone should look like
one. To promote this message the exhibition sold little booklet
quizzes asking visitors to judge whether a design was good or
not. Alongside a photograph of a lamp it offered prompts for
readers so that they could judge whether it was good or not: 'Is
it designed first and foremost to give light?' Alongside a photograph of a radio it asked, 'Does it look like a wireless or an imitation of something else?' Design that wasn't disguised could
claim a moral purpose: it was honest. While it might be hard
to accept Lancaster's sense that a nation that disguised radios as
tea-caddies might misrecognise Nazism as unthreatening, it does
seem clear that embracing a more straightforward and honest
design aesthetic was part of a post-war mood that wanted to
promote rationalism against the irrationalism that culminated
in a world war.

But the furniture that we choose to sit on isn't simply to do with rationalism – after all, it isn't any more rational to sit upright than in a more reclined manner (though we might associate rationalism with an upright demeanour). Clearly frills and embellishments will seem unnecessary and perhaps irrational, but furniture offers a more extensive sense of the social world of the sitting room. The design of furniture determines, to some extent, how we sit and how we position ourselves. For instance, the high-back winged chairs that we associate with the Victorian and Edwardian eras seem to be designed for upright relaxation. You can imagine (actually you don't need to imagine, you can watch it on most 'period drama' TV programmes) an older gentleman, with a whisky or three inside him, gently snoozing in such a chair. The chair seems designed to catch inebriates: the wings stop the head from lolling too much; the uprightness means that a snoozer can be in an alert position almost instantaneously.

It was unlikely that such winged-back chairs and settees, in the parlours of modest houses, were used like this. Here the posture that the chairs and sofas seem to encourage is not one of slightly sloshed relaxation but the opposite: sober concentration. Given that the parlour in many houses was reserved for formal visiting from 'official' visitors and from other members of the family, the uprightness of the chair's back was meant to signal and instil a moral rectitude in the sitter.

Modernism only very slowly found any purchase in British houses. While some wealthy bohemians may, in the 1930s and '40s, have bought the chairs designed by the likes of Charlotte Perriand or Marcel Breuer, most stuck with the sort of furniture their parents had and perhaps a generation before that too: over-stuffed, high-backed and with the addition of anti-macassars to stop the sitter's hair oil from staining the fabric. In some ways the war was a help to getting a less fussy, more modernist type of seating for the living room. Utility furniture might not be an example of modernist design, but the lack of frills and the back-to-basics ethos brought about by the need to use limited resources as sparingly as possible made for a style where structure was much more evident than decorative detail. The 1950s, perhaps, was the period that found British homes (those that housed fashionable furniture, at least) getting as close as they ever would to European modernism. The contemporary style – seen in wallpaper designs, seating, tables, magazine racks and gadgets – favoured spindly supports and minimalist forms.

One of the most general changes in domestic life in the twentieth century is towards more informal ways of living and socialising. One material sign of this is the way that furniture gradually gets nearer the floor. The lower the chair is to the floor, the easier it is for the sitter to sprawl and to flop. Perhaps the apotheosis of this is the beanbag and the floor cushions that were popular in the late 1960s and early 1970s: if this was your seating, you had no choice except sprawl and flop. But since then an optimum height of armchair and settee seating seems to have been found: low enough to flop into but not so low that you're likely to spill out onto the floor at any moment. Certainly – outside of shops specialising in furniture for the infirm – it is hard to find much comfy furniture that has the sorts of higher seating favoured in the early part of the twentieth century.

While de-cluttering and clarity of purpose were part of what it meant to have a modern sitting room in the post-war period, there was also a recognition that the feelings associated with the pre-war parlour needed some form of outlet. In some of the 1930s' local authority housing, where the downstairs rooms comprised a large living–dining room with adjoining kitchen, tenants erected interior walls to produce a small parlour. In the 1951 Festival of Britain exhibitions the parlour and its knick-knack aesthetic

were seen as a 'design problem' facing the modern living room:
the parlour, as we have already seen,

> has long lost its original meaning as a place where people
> could sit and converse. To-day the very word has a frowsty
> sound. Yet, quite often, when architects have provided a
> family with a larger living room instead of a parlour, one
> corner has been turned nostalgically into a token parlour-
> substitute. It is evident, then, that many people still feel the
> need for a room apart, where photographs and souvenirs can
> contribute memories, and where fireplaces can be treated as
> an altar to household gods. So the designers have shown how
> such a need can be met, in twentieth-century style without
> any trace of frowstiness. And they have done so in several
> different ways, in presenting corners of seven rooms, all with
> a special character.[29]

One way of solving the 'parlour problem' was to create parlour
spaces within living rooms. In some ways the mantelpiece (a
feature of any room with a fireplace) had always held this role,
but in the post-war period, as central heating took off in the
1960s and '70s, mantelpieces were becoming endangered as DIY
experts like Barry Bucknell suggested we rip out hearths and
plaster over fireplaces. But often what was wanted to create
parlour space was a form that could simultaneously partition off
a space within the room while also allowing for the display of
treasures.

System shelving, such as Ladderex, designed in the mid-1960s
by Robert Heal, offered cheap ways of marking off spaces within
modern homes that were built with an inclination towards more
open-plan living; systems shelving had the added advantage of
being purposefully designed to hold vases, photographs, hi-fi,
TV, radio and so on – if, that is, you weren't the owner of 'several

thousand books'. System shelving like Ladderex could fit everywhere and anywhere and combined ordinary shelves (clipped on to the vertical ladders) with units such as cupboards, pull-out desks, glass cabinets, drink holders and so on. Your shelf could simultaneously be an office, an entertainment centre and a cabinet of curiosities. With system shelving you could simultaneously indulge in a passion for knick-knacks and look de-cluttered and modern. You could have a 'put-away aesthetic' while having your treasure on display.

System furniture was a canny marketing ploy as well as a solution to the parlour problem: it encouraged brand loyalty in a significantly material way. The kit form that systems furniture was based around meant that it was easy to extend and to add units to. Ladderex was one example of a form of furniture that had been pioneered during the war through 'utility furniture'. The idea of everything following the same design principle meant that you could attain a single look without having to search around for compatible designs: it was all meant to go together. But utility furniture resonated with a wartime feeling of 'make-do-and-mend' and lack of resources.

The real breakthrough with system furniture and a consolidated style came with G-Plan in 1953. The idea behind G-Plan was that it supplied furnishing for every part of the house and that, if you bought any one item, all the other items would suit 'the look'. This, though Roger Fry most certainly wouldn't have approved, was the popular solution (for those that could afford it) to the hotch-potch look of many homes.

G-Plan promoted itself as quality furniture at a low price that, unlike other furniture stores, offered a coherent style across all their ranges:

> Spaciousness … a new subtle elegance … supreme comfort
> … these make a lovely background to life. And they're easily

achieved with G-Plan upholstered chairs and sofas, all of which combine heavenly comfort with unfussy, uncluttered design. Choose them as you please, group them as you please. Because of the underlying unity of their design, they can be rearranged whenever you feel like a change.

And once you had one item, why go looking around other furniture shops for something compatible when clearly what you really needed was just more G-Plan goods? 'You can add a piece at a time. You can replace old furniture gradually. Or you can furnish whole rooms, sure that you've chosen well because all G-Plan furniture shares the timeless elegance that comes with good design and superb quality.'[30]

G-Plan is perhaps the first example of what will become a standard way of furnishing your house with mass-produced furniture. With G-Plan, or later with Habitat or IKEA, you are encouraged not just to buy a product but to buy into a lifestyle. The success of retailers such as Habitat and IKEA, unlike previous department stores or furniture stores, is that not only do they have all your furnishing needs in one place, but they also provide a unified style for decorating: nothing goes with a Habitat sofa like a Habitat rug or a Habitat poster.

Radiators and televisions

Systems shelving and systems furniture were a design style of furnishing appropriate to the centrally heated house. Without a fireplace there was no reason for huddling furniture in any one particular place. If central heating meant the house became spread out as a more diffuse space, the same was also true of individual rooms, particularly the sitting room: without the pulling power of a fireplace there was no need to centre the room on warmth (sitting around a radiator was never going to be an attractive proposition). But, of course, one piece of furniture came to dominate the sitting room in a concerted and concentrated way: the television. The television wasn't just the dominant medium of the second half of the twentieth century; it was the object that determined the shape of your room and the direction of your furniture. In the US sitcom *Friends* the character Joey dates a woman who doesn't own a TV: 'But what does your furniture point at?' asks Joey, and we might ask the same thing.

Lawrence Wright, the great historian of domestic infrastructures, connects the birth of central heating with the rise of the TV as the modern hearth:

> Where full central heating releases the family from a huddle round the open living-room fire, many will dispense with this obsolete ornament. The juniors can now do their homework, play their discs and entertain their friends in the privacy of warm bedroom-dens. The Romans called the hearth the *focus* – if modern family life has a focus, it is to be found in the television screen. Children no longer see pictures in the fire, and the cricket may be watched, but not on the hearth. Santa Claus and roast chestnuts are necessarily out. The poet seeking an image of love growing cold must think in terms of faulty thermostats. Soldiers may still be homesick, but they will never sing 'Keep the home pipes warming'.[31]

The idea that central heating would ruin the arrangement of rooms was something that was associated with it from the start. In 1936 the poet W. H. Auden could send out his warning about this pernicious form of heating:

> Preserve me, above all, from central heating.
> It may be D. H. Lawrence hocus-pocus,
> But I prefer a room that's got a focus.[32]

Auden knows that to rally against central heating may seem old-fashioned (the hocus-pocus of Lawrence), but how could you give shape to a room that didn't have a fireplace? Luckily TV was there to reinstall the idea of a focus to the British sitting room.

The first experimental television broadcasts in Britain were in 1936, and in 1937 at that year's *Daily Mail* Ideal Home Exhibition it was announced, perhaps a bit presumptuously, that 'High-definition Television has now arrived in the form of a regular public service.'[33] While the war delayed the development of broadcast television, the post-war period quickly picked up the pace for installing the television as a constituent element in the modern living room. Indeed it was another of the Festival of Britain's design problems for the modern home. The Festival designers recognised the importance of entertainment being piped from outside into the sitting room. Such entertainments (which they describe as 'passive') were competing with home-grown ones, altering the space of the front room, and would require particular consideration:

> television, wireless, gramophone [...] all call for special methods of restricting the spread of light or sound, so that people in the home who would rather not be entertained just at the moment can get on with what they are doing without being distracted. This is a designer's problem, as is the question of furniture that can house all the apparatus needed for this entertainment in the smallest space with the maximum convenience.[34]

This sense of the TV spreading throughout the room, beyond its immediate environment, was of course what happened: it is hard not to be distracted by TV if you are in the same room as it. The question of making purpose-built furniture was also a central question: how could you have such a modern technology without it clashing with your other furniture? As with radio, enormous effort went into making cabinets and cupboards that could house these sets or to disguise them. For the furniture manufacturer Gordon Russell such media furniture was a real boost to cabinetmakers:

> It is worth noting that just as clockmakers in the 18th century insisted on high standards of cabinetwork to house their movements, so radio manufacturers stepped in now. I think it is true to say that the best radio cabinets produced in England between the two wars can not only hold their own with those produced anywhere, but they can hold their own for quality, especially quality of design, with any other items of mass-produced cabinetwork.[35]

Throughout the second half of the twentieth century the presence of TV in sitting rooms was both a problem and an opportunity. For Terence Conran the fireplace was still the most convivial presence for the sitting room: 'Traditionally the fireplace is the chief focus in the living-room. Firelight in itself induces a feeling of well-being, and when seating is grouped around it, the whole area becomes an expression of hospitality at its warmest. However, since the general use of central heating has sadly made so many fire-places obsolete, alternatives have to be considered.' Such alternatives could include TV: 'Television and hi-fi, provided that they play a large enough part in your life, can be used as focal points.'[36]

Cabinetmakers would benefit from the presence of the TV in the sitting room, but perhaps not in the way championed by the Council of Industrial Design. The moral purpose of honesty was something that TV cabinetmakers would have to avoid: it was disguise that a lot of people wanted. In the 1962 novel *Life at the*

Top, John Braine's follow-up to his 'angry young man' novel *Room at the Top*, the anti-hero Joe Lampton has finally arrived at full middle-class prosperity. His sitting room is his most cherished accomplishment. All it requires is a way of disguising the monstrosity of the television:

> It was the one room in the house where I felt at ease. And it was the solid testimony of how far I'd come in ten years; the parquet floor and the Maples suite alone had carried me through many bad moments. It was the sort of room I'd dreamed of when I was living in that little house in Dufton; and now I possessed it, now I was living in the dream, and flowered linen loose covers matched the curtains and cream and gold wallpaper set off the dark walnut of the writing-desk and coffee-table and sideboard and the Grundig radiogram. The great blank eye of the television was the only discordant note; but if my bonus this year came up to expectations, I'd change it for the new model with the screen door.[37]

Hiding your TV behind a screen door suggests that television was, in 1962, still a public interloper in a room that was a private space.

It seemed that TV and other electrical media would play a large enough part in most people's lives to require shaping your room around their demands. For house builders this meant that sitting rooms would require more electrical sockets. In the 1950s it was considered adequate for an entire house to function with just six sockets; by the start of the 1960s the Department of the Environment argued that a house should be built with between fifteen and twenty. Today many new-builds would have between fifteen and twenty sockets in the lounge alone. The 1950s saw a massive increase in consumer spending on electrical products: 'between 1951 and 1957 expenditure on electrical goods rose by 130 per cent, more than two and half times faster than the 51 per cent rise in consumer expenditure generally in the same period.'[38] And much of that expenditure was aimed at acquiring a television set (or more often renting one – at least, for those without the financial and technical confidence to buy outright). In a space of just nine years, between 1949 and 1958, the TV moved from being in just 1 per cent of households to gaining a presence in over half of them.[39] Since then, and with the emergence of colour television at the end of the 1960s, the presence of television in the home has gradually increased to the point where today it would be odd to find a TV-less household. Today British households have on average three televisions each – so clearly the TV has migrated beyond the bounds of the sitting room.

While the TV brought the world outside into the home (as had the radio), it also consolidated the home and the living room as a place for family and children. The birth of children's TV coincided with the emergence of TV as a popular form and did much to make television a domestic medium in a way distinct from film and radio. Indeed watching TV has consistently meant that we are often sitting in a domestic living room watching other people who are in their studio simulations of living rooms. Magazine programmes such as *Blue Peter* (BBC, 1958–2012; CBBC 2012– ongoing) mimicked the cosy setting of the lounge, albeit on a larger scale. Children's TV established a form of watching the box that often reflected back to the child the space that he or she was in. The long-running *Play School* (1964–88) began with the immortal lines 'Here's a house, here's a door. Windows – one, two, three, four. Ready to knock? Turn the lock – its *Play School*'; and there you were in a TV studio designed to mirror the room you were sitting in to watch the programme.

Soap operas, sitcoms, cookery programmes and reality TV have, throughout the decades, shown us the rooms in the ordinary British house in which the watching of TV is a central occupation. The British sitcom is a constant paean to the ordinary house, a hymn to the delights and desperation of terraced housing, to the daftness to be found in suburban semis, to the everyday skirmishes of family life and the drama and humour that often congregate in the living room. Shows such as *One Foot in the Grave* (BBC, 1990–2000), *Keeping Up Appearances* (BBC, 1990–95), *Love thy Neighbour* (ITV, 1972–76), *The Good Life* (BBC, 1975–78), *Man about the House* (ITV, 1973–76) and *My Family* (BBC, 2000– ongoing) have made the living room a central component of their comedy. TV sitcoms often demonstrate the class and social ethos of their characters through the use of rooms where the drama unfolds. For instance, in *Absolutely Fabulous* (BBC, 1992–2012) the sitting room is rarely seen: the middle-class bo-ho life is mainly lived in the kitchen–diner. In *My Family* the extravagantly large open-plan living room is the place where a more uptight middle-class normality is struggled for. One way of signalling the characters' working-class credentials is either to situate the drama in a small kitchen (for instance, in *Bread* [BBC, 1986–91]) or to show the characters talking in the front room while watching TV (as in *Till Death Us Do Part* [BBC, 1965–75]).

One of the more memorable sitcoms of the 1970s – and a compelling exploration of the contemporary house – was the series *Whatever Happened to the Likely Lads?* (BBC, 1973–74). Written by Dick Clement and Ian La Frenais, it reunites the characters Bob and Terry, who had appeared earlier in the 1960s' Geordie sitcom *The Likely Lads* (BBC, 1964–66). In *Whatever Happened to the Likely Lads?* the 'work-shy', Labour-supporting, proudly working-class, ebullient ladies' man Terry returns to Tyneside (the show left the exact location imprecise)

after five years in the army to find that his boyhood pal Bob
has become upwardly mobile and bought himself a brand-new
detached house in an edge-of-town 'executive development'.
He has also become engaged to librarian Thelma. Much of
the town where they grew up, and which consisted of back-
to-backs and two-up-two-downs, has been bulldozed in one
of the many 'slum clearance' schemes of the post-war years.
In the centre of the city old pubs and variety halls have been
demolished to make way for multi-storey car parks and office
developments.

Whatever Happened to the Likely Lads? is all about transi-
tions: from youth to adulthood, from single life to married, from
working class to aspiring middle class, from tight-knit terraced
housing to uniform suburban tract. And Bob and Thelma's house
is not simply a symbol of this transition but also its enactment.
In a tangle of cul-de-sacs Bob's house is big glass windows, inte-
grated garage, low ceilings and a kitchen with a serving hatch
through to the sitting room/diner. (The serving hatch will
feature throughout the two series as comedic device: it will trap
fingers, frame astonished faces and so on.) As Bob says when he
first shows Terry around the house: 'we decided to go completely
electric, with under-floor heating and [electricity] points everywhere.' Bob's house shows us the home where central heating is
taken for granted and where electricity is powering a new consumerism: now occupiers can concentrate on amassing the kind
of gadgetry and technology (hi-fis and fridges, Magimix food
processors and TVs) that can make use of all those electrical
sockets.

Perhaps the television comedy that has played most heavily
on the front room as the place for TV is *The Royle Family* (1998–
2000), which centres on a working-class family sitting in a front
room watching TV (a show that deliberately invokes the staging
of *Till Death Us Do Part*). We watch them on TV watching the

TV. The sofa and armchair arc round a TV that we can't quite see (our viewpoint is slightly to one side of the TV). The dad holds the TV remote as they change channels, chat, comment on the programmes or just generally watch in a half-hearted engagement with 'the telly'. In some ways this image of a family congregating around the TV is already a nostalgic image of the front room.

In the three and half decades that take us from Bob's house to now we move from hi-fi to Wi-Fi, from music centres to iPods, from electric typewriters to laptops. Such things have transformed our experience of living rooms, even if they've done little to alter the physical architecture of them (they are still brick boxes). In today's media landscape television and radio are just choices alongside a variety of entertainments that can be accessed through Xboxes and laptops. Today people watch television on all sorts of screens, often multi-tasking with mobile phones. Perhaps in one way it isn't a world away from doing the ironing in front of *The Generation Game* (BBC, 1971–82 and 1990–2002), but in another it is incomparable. The mobility of today's media technology means that living rooms can be places to work or to play, but any other room could be used like this as well. You could, if you so wished, return to the hallway for your telephone conversations. If central heating seemed to allow the focus of the room to shift from hearth to telly, its final promise seems to have been realised with mobile media: now you can be anywhere in this climate-controlled environment connected to friends, games and shows.

Over the course of a century the main reception room has changed from being a parlour room, dedicated to conversation and manners, to a room oriented by media consumption and relaxing furniture. If the parlour was a room where people occasionally were brought together to be unified, then the modern lounge is where people tend to gather on a daily basis in a more scattered and informal setting: the lounge is now a place where you can be physically together but hooked up to your own individual media networks of choice. But if technology has finally emptied the front room of its specialness – as a place for congregating for conversation or for communal viewing – elsewhere in the house technology has set up home in an even more emphatic way. The kitchen is the control room for our obsession with technology. It is where we store our industrial hardware; it is the room we mean when we say that a house comes equipped with 'all mod cons'.

In the engine room ...

4

PUT THE KETTLE ON

(Kitchens)

More than a fur coat or a hi-fi system, happiness is a modern, fitted kitchen.[1]

If, as Le Corbusier suggested, a house is a machine for living, then the kitchen is the engine room. Today's modern kitchen is stuffed with kit: fan-assisted ovens, microwaves, food processors, dish-washers, slow-cookers, toasters, kettles, washing machines and tumble dryers, fridges, freezers, electronic scales, coffee machines and the odd unused but indelibly sticky sandwich toaster. It's a world of 'white goods' and brushed steel, of gleaming pans and the latest 'mod cons'. But it is also a world of lists pinned to tack boards, of homework schedules and dentist's appointments caught on the front of fridges by magnetised toy animals. The kitchen is where calendars and colanders collide.

The kitchen combines industrial precision and homely comforts. It is the room with the most finely calibrated implements and machines in it (unless you are a hobbyist engineer and have turned your garage into a mini-shunting yard). Whereas items in other rooms in the house seem to belong more to craft (the craft of furniture, for instance), the kitchen is more fully incorporated into the world of industrial design. Writing the foreword to the 1936 exhibition catalogue *Everyday Things*, King Edward VIII told British architects that theirs was 'the great and honourable duty of educating the people of the country to better living'. Education in the kitchen would be achieved through advice but also through the design of things:

> a house, however good it may be as a *building*, can never be a fully organised and satisfying unit unless the same sense of order which influenced the design of the structure is evident in all things inside it. The window latches, door knobs, the cups, plates, forks, knives, spoons, saucepans, cookers and everything else in the house that can be both efficient and beautiful, and as this exhibition tries to show, cheap [...] there is now a simple and healthy relationship between beauty and use.[2]

Beds and sofas are of a different order from all those implements that jostle for space in the kitchen.

In the post-war period, as Britain geared itself up to 'win the peace', the war effort was redirected towards domesticity. Perhaps the most vivid symbol of this was the transformation of Britain's military prowess into a saucepan in that landmark exhibition 'Britain Can Make It' (1946). As the press release had it, the move from war to peace was to focus on such a transformation:

> A new type of saucepan is shown beside the exhaust stub of a wrecked Spitfire. In the early days of the war it was found that exhaust stubs under conditions of high speed burnt out in as little as ten flying hours. A refractory process was invented that extended the life of the stub to over 2,000 flying hours, with internal temperatures of 1,400 degrees

and an outside temperature of minus 40 degrees centigrade. This process has been applied to the manufacture of the saucepan with the result that food is less likely to burn in it, that it will wear considerably longer than the normal saucepan and that attractive enamelling will not crack under domestic heating.[3]

All that effort, all that death, all that heroism in labs and factories as well as in the field, is not for naught: our domestic lives will be enriched with food untarnished by burning. The Battle of Britain becomes the battle for Britain's prosperity, and it will be pursued in the kitchens of our modern homes.

Today's kitchen organises all its technology in a highly orchestrated selection of units and worktops. It is a choreography of ergonomic design and efficiency. That is, if you read the kitchen magazines. Yet all this technology is often, and confusingly, housed in cabinets that look as if they are from the nineteenth century: the most popular design for opulent British fitted kitchens is 'Shaker' – perhaps a little ironic given that Shakers believed in giving up worldly possessions. The fitted kitchen came late to ordinary British houses, and throughout much of the twentieth century kitchens were populated with furniture that today speaks of a pre-industrial era: the 'commodious cupboard' and the Welsh dresser, for instance, are kitchen behemoths from an age when you wanted to take your kitchen with you when you moved house.

The space of the kitchen has been transformed during the twentieth century: no other room in the Victorian terraced house has been so altered, so insistently expanded. The space of most kitchens in the by-law terraced house, for instance, now incorporates what used to be separate spaces: sculleries, outside toilets and coal bunkers. The enthusiasm for 'knocking through' found its first accomplice in the expanding kitchen. But if the space of the kitchen has altered, so too has how we think of it, what we do in it and the way we fill it. No room in the British house has been so scrutinised, so studied, and if some kitchen designers seem to want kitchens to look like science laboratories it is in part because they have been treated like this by purveyors of domestic science. It is the kitchen that bore the brunt of the new science of 'time-and-motion' studies and scientific management. Domestic reform was aimed relentlessly at the kitchen.

But if altering physical kitchens in actual houses was the labour of builders and householders who took advice from household management books and magazines, then the work of fantasising the future of these kitchens was the preoccupation of novelists, 'dream' architects and product designers. The fantasy of living in a space-age kitchen where pre-cooked dinners could be ready in seconds or where fizzy drinks were available on tap became partially realised in microwaves and Sodastreams. Today's top-of-the-range fridge-freezers offer ice dispensers and chilled water: you can now throw away the kettle and opt instead for boiling water spurting from your taps. The rag-and-bone man, the knife-and-scissor grinder, the ice-seller – all with their horse-drawn contraptions – fade into prehistory in a world replete with weekly recycling collections, self-sharpening kitchen knives and freezers. Yet many areas in Britain still supported rag-and-bone collectors and knife grinders into the 1970s. And while it is still in living memory for many, the kitchen bath must seem like a category error to today's children. One of the earliest 'fitted' kitchens in Britain (for the model cottages in Bournville, built around 1900) was fitted with a built-in bath that was housed beneath a panel in the floor of the kitchen.

To get a sense of the changing kitchen over the last hundred years we are going to have to look at changes in housework more generally (the kitchen has always been the head office of housework) as well as looking at changes in the furnishings of kitchens. We will need to look at the relentless attempts to modernise the kitchen as well as our often tenacious indifference to its most futuristic and scientific dreams.

Modernising the kitchen

The idea of kitchen efficiency became an issue for middle-class householders with the drop in the number of servants in middle-income houses. As I mentioned in the previous chapter, the growth of the servantless house had wide-ranging consequences, particularly for middle-class women, who now had to take on the chores that previously they wouldn't have considered dignified. The drop in the number of servants available can't be dated precisely, but after a little surge in the amount of servants in the years immediately following the First World War, numbers gradually dropped in the period between the wars as a consequence of more varied (and better-paid) work opportunities for working-class women. For the servantless house, as well as those households trying to hang on to servants, an efficient and pleasant kitchen became a necessity: it could make kitchen work more palatable for middle-class women; it could act as an incentive to serving women, who were now in demand.

In 1919 *Our Homes and Gardens*, a magazine that, as we have seen, was dedicated to considering these new needs, was from the start a campaigner for kitchen reform. Its number one priority was in expanding the space of the kitchen: 'Combining the kitchen with the scullery [is] an arrangement which greatly facilitates the work of cooking and washing up, and adds much to the comfort of the home.'[4] In later issues the knocked-through kitchen-scullery, the basis for 'the house of convenience', was given an international provenance in articles on Canadian, American and Scandinavian houses – countries where urban space wasn't at such a premium and housing wasn't already clogged with old

stock, and where housing was seen to benefit from larger kitchens without separate sculleries.

With a kitchen-scullery *Our Homes and Gardens* lays out the
conditions for domestic reform – 'common sense' efficiency and
a modicum of domestic comfort. The kitchen-scullery will now
become the centre of the house and a 'living-room' to tempt the
much in-demand maid:

> If there is a maid, the kitchen-scullery is not only a more
> handy place in which to do cooking, washing-up and other
> domestic work, but also when her day's labour is finished she
> has a pleasant little room of her own in which she can spend
> her leisure hours in comfort; and in the case of the house-
> wife who is without a maid, and here to do her own work,
> there are the same advantages of having everything to hand
> in the kitchen-scullery while the kitchen itself can be used as
> a place for meals.[5]

It is a moment of a considerable change in social relations:
middle-class women taking on working-class chores; working-
class women finding themselves in a position where – to some
degree at least – they can determine the conditions of their
employment (even if it means only enjoying 'their' kitchen as a
place to relax as well as work). We can also see the beginnings of
the middle-class kitchen as not just a place to prepare meals but
also a place to eat them – and not just a hastily grabbed snack but
regular household meals.

But if the kitchen was the new centre of life in the servantless
house, it wasn't going to be enough just to enlarge it: housework
itself was going to need to change. As *The Housewife's Book* put
it in 1937:

> The kitchen, the workshop of the home, is the room where

the housewife's activities are centred, and as every modern woman with common sense sees no virtue in needless work, she should so arrange its contents that her daily tasks can be carried out without any unnecessary expenditure of energy. The expenditure of energy includes every movement taken by the human body or 'machine', whether it be the taking of steps, carrying, lifting, rubbing, peeling or rolling – in brief, any movement at all.[6]

This sense of the 'housewife' as a human machine involved in a huge variety of operations that can be altered to make it more efficient is carried over wholesale from the world of industrial labour. In the United States the new science of efficiency found its gurus in Frederick Winslow Taylor and Lillian and Frank Gilbreth in the first decades of the twentieth century. The Gilbreths, in particular, developed the practice of 'time-and-motion studies', often through the use of photography, breaking down actions into segmented movement and experimenting with the placement of tools and materials to cut down on worker fatigue and speed up production. Yet, as we shall see, the idea of treating housework as a series of segmented and isolated activities – sometimes with a specialised tool to accomplish it – is not just a solution; it is also part of the problem.

Scientific management and time-and-motion studies quickly found new sites beyond the well-known arena of factory work. If the house was a machine for living, and the housewife (middle-class or not) was a worker, then what was good enough for the factory and the building site (the Gilbreths' first successes were in making bricklaying more efficient) would be good enough for the kitchen. (Lillian Gilbreth went on to research time-and-motion studies of domestic interiors in the 1920s.) The *News of the World Better Homes Book* could make the connection between factory work and kitchen work explicit a few decades later:

Many housewives work longer and harder in their kitchens than they would in a factory. For many years now time and motion study has been the basis of all factory planning. Every movement is timed and studied, and sometimes photographed, so that machinery can be provided and arranged to eliminate every unnecessary step and movement and to reduce effort to a minimum. When the same technique is applied to the arrangement of the kitchen hundreds of woman-hours can be saved.[7]

Of course, any explicit equivalence between worker and middle-class housewife would have to be hidden behind a barrage of eloquent euphemisms that would treat house*work* as something slightly different from labour, something more ladylike – something more like needlepoint on a vast scale.

Our Homes and Gardens hands out advice and euphemisms in equal measure. In an issue from 1919 titled 'Time Studies of Housework: Scheme Out Your Work, Then Work Out Your Scheme' the magazine doesn't just offer ways of cutting down on unnecessary tasks; it invites every 'home-maker' to become his or her own efficiency expert. The first problem to overcome is seeing housework as a sequence of discrete tasks:

It is difficult not to think of each household task separately just now, when we find particular devices and aids for each, every one claimed to solve the domestic riddle of getting home comfort in face of the shortage of labour and the cost of living. The plain truth is that successful home-making (a more dignified and comprehensive title than housekeeping) is *one task*, made up of carefully co-ordinated parts, with its features determined by the aims, the ideal and the conditions of the household.[8]

The labour-saving device is not, in this article, a solution; rather, it is the problem, because it too categorically demarcates jobs.

The solution offered by *Our Homes and Gardens* is to take detailed records of daily tasks, weekly tasks and more seasonal or occasional tasks and then to calibrate them into an overarching scheme, which might include grouping all upstairs tasks into one super-efficient cleaning jag. With every housewife her own time-and-motion expert (or at least, those readers of the magazine who took up the invitation), it made sense for the magazine to launch competitions for readers to show how efficient they have become in the new, servantless world. One reader has some handy hints for cutting down on washing up:

> At night after supper we put all the silver into a large jam pot filled with water and kept for the purpose, and leave to soak till morning; and the dirty places we put in the basin and leave to soak also. This saves a lot of trouble when washing up, and if you are wise you will lay your table for breakfast when the supper is cleared. Near the sink it is very useful to have two small shelves about 2ft long and 6 ins. wide on which to keep things like soda, whitening, etc., which are constantly in use.[9]

Clearly she has become her own efficiency consultant, grouping tasks together (laying up at the same time as clearing away), finding nifty ways to cut down on elbow grease and positioning constantly-in-demand products within easy reach.

Other suggestions included: eating in the kitchen and serving the food in the same dishes that they were cooked in; doing all the tasks that require step-ladders (dusting high places, window-cleaning etc.) in one go; and so on. The winning entry (and the prize was a not-to-be-sneezed-at 5 guineas) took to servantless existence in a rigorous manner: 'when it became impossible to get a maid, all superfluous ornaments were put away.'[10]

This house-worker or home-maker has taken the *Our Homes and Gardens*' message to heart: 'as far as possible I do all the work requiring the same implements at the same time, e.g., sweep, or mop right through.' Her love of wipe-clean surfaces has meant 'the use of oil baize on the kitchen table, and linoleum remnants on the shelves and tops of cupboards'.

The house of convenience, from this evidence, was not the result of buying new vacuum cleaners or other electrical appliances, but of more prosaic materials: generous use of linoleum to cover any surface, baskets full of cleaning items so that multiple tasks don't require constantly returning to the kitchen cupboard and so on. In a previous issue the magazine had taken issue with a government pamphlet on domestic efficiency because it over-estimated the amount of footfall required to make tea. The pamphlet had suggested that the whole kitchen should be rearranged to encourage convenience; *Our Homes and Gardens* had a more simple suggestion – get a trolley: 'a very great deal of walking to and fro is eliminated by the simple expedient of the wheel-table or wagon, the things being collected on this from the several places, and the wagon subsequently taken to the sitting-room with everything ready on it.'[11] Modernity was a mobile table.

The Second World War was, as we have already seen, a time for re-evaluating Britain's housing stock and what people wanted from housing in the reconstruction that would follow. Workers were vocal about what they wanted from a kitchen:

> people definitely want their kitchens to be comfortable living rooms, not simply places to cook in. The evidence [...] goes to show that in building a working-class house the kitchen should be the *first* consideration, and should be made the

largest, lightest, most cheerful room in the house. A great many working-class houses are built from the middle-class standpoint that the kitchen does not matter.[12]

The end of the Second World War led to a period of housing redevelopment and a chance to rethink the layout and size of the kitchen. In the post-war period the state of the kitchen became the gauge of a house's attractiveness.

Fuel and efficiency

At the start of the twentieth century an average kitchen in Britain consisted of a solid fuel (coal or coke) range cooker and a 'copper'. The copper was a large kettle, which was heated underneath with the same fuel used in the range. The copper was what you used to wash your clothes and sheets and to heat the water for a tin bath or – if you were fairly well-to-do and had the space – a fixed bath in a bathroom. As you can imagine, it was a labour-intensive activity keeping the fire going, filling the copper with water (which for many houses meant walking along to an outside tap shared by many houses), boiling the water and transferring the boiled water to the receptacle used for washing. The fuel used for heating the copper was dirty and smoky, and must have required constant attention. While some houses would keep their solid fuel ranges well into the second half of the century, a new world of cooking and cleaning was being imagined through the promotion of much cleaner fuels. Gas and electricity had already altered many kitchens in the first half of the twentieth century, but the post-war period saw a concerted attempt by energy companies and fuel associations to modernise the kitchen by getting rid of the copper and the range cooker and introducing new devices.

The theme of opening up the kitchen by incorporating the scullery into it was continued into the middle of the century, but after the Second World War there was much more insistence that the kitchen should be a home to all sorts of labour-saving devices. In Adie Ballantyne's *Choose Your Kitchen* from 1944 the servantless house is still something worth commenting on:

> one of the problems of the post-war home will be the lack of domestic help. This may be available only by the hour or by the day, and on many a housewife will fall the entire work of evening meal preparation, cooking and washing-up, even if she has help during the day. Labour saving thus becomes a pressing necessity if she is to have any leisure.[13]

Labour-saving will mean having to get rid of 'the old fashioned coal range which will soon be a thing of the past'. The coal range was the symbol of all that was bad: it was dirty and required almost constant supervision and feeding with fuel. Out with coal, in with electricity.

In looking to the future, it is the device, the machine, the appliance, that leads us into a brave new world:

> in the period when war is over there can be little doubt that women will want better kitchens. An increasing number of labour-saving devices make for better working conditions, and these devices will be more freely available in the brave new world to come. War conditions have made us realise the value of the things that are worthwhile, and our homes, our children and all they stand for will mean even more to us than they have done in the past.[14]

And because we value our homes and our children, we owe it to ourselves to modernise, to have refrigerators, electric cookers and electric ventilation.

In the spring of 1946, for just sixpence, you could visit the *Daily*

Herald's 'Modern Homes' exhibition in Regent Street, London. The stars of the show were a series of three kitchens demonstrating the wonders of gas, coal and electricity. A fourth kitchen backfired spectacularly, and its backfiring tells us something important about the British kitchen in 1946. This kitchen was called the 'quiz kitchen' and was designed around a series of deliberate mistakes that visitors were invited – by a housewife-compère whose kitchen it was supposed to be – to guess. It was meant to be a bit of fun, a way of engaging and involving the audience in thinking about design. The deliberate mistakes were to do with the placing of kitchen elements so that the kitchen could be efficiently used. The massive mistake the exhibition designers made was to fill this 'badly designed' kitchen with brand new appliances. To the majority of visitors it was impossible to see past the stunning discrepancy between their worn-out kitchens and this flashy kitchen replete with the latest – expensive – gadgets.

Mass-Observation were asked by the exhibition organisers to undertake a survey about what people liked and disliked, and to listen in on people's conversations as they walked round the exhibition. It was the quiz kitchen that came in for most animosity. Some didn't see that there was anything to be quizzical about: it was simply another kitchen to envy. One visitor thought that it was the 'best I've seen'. Most, of course, understood that they were being asked to spot faults, and it was this that annoyed them: 'I wouldn't mind having that just as it is'; 'if she [the housewife whose kitchen it was supposed to be] could see what I've got, she'd say this is marvellous'; 'what's wrong with that. It's better than ours.' For Mass-Observation 'the modernity, cleanliness and many fixtures' of the quiz kitchen meant that the display acted as a 'back-handed insult in presenting as an example of all that is bad in kitchens something so much *better* than most of the visitors' kitchens at home [...] people are definitely envious of this kitchen with all its faults'.[15]

The three kitchens demonstrating the qualities of different types of fuel were much more successful. They were sponsored by the British Electrical Development Association, the Women's Advisory Committee on Solid Fuel and the wonderfully named Women's Gas Council.

> In the solid fuel kitchen there is a single prefabricated unit, incorporating all the services for a small house, such as cooking, water heating, space heating, ventilation, tanks, plumbing and sanitation; the gas kitchen has a nursery recess so that Mother can keep her eye on the children while she is cooking; and the electricity kitchen has two bays – one for cooking and one for sewing. The cooking bay has a water heater and electric washing machine, and an electric fan and drying cabinet. The sewing bay is complete with electric sewing machine, iron and ironing board, cutting out table and radio.[16]

But these kitchens were not immune to being treated as 'quiz kitchens': 'No thank you! I don't want to make pastry alongside my dressmaking. I call that silly. If there is one thing you want to keep right out of the kitchen it's your dressmaking, right out of the grease.'[17] Abandoning its station in the hallway, the electric kitchen showed that for some the telephone was migrating, though clearly this wasn't always something to be welcomed: 'beautiful equipment, but I wouldn't want my telephone in the kitchen – you don't spend your life in the kitchen.'[18]

A few months later 'Britain Can Make It' opened at the Victoria and Albert Museum. As already mentioned, it was this exhibition that aimed national hope for a better life squarely at the home. Again it was visited by the survey team of Mass-Observation, and although it seems as if people spent more time in the living- and dining-room displays, the kitchen displays became the most crowded and discussed. Kitchens, it seemed,

> aroused more envy, and at the same time, less dislike, than the living rooms and bedrooms. After kitchens, bathrooms were most coveted, and received most attention. The interest in kitchens was especially high amongst women and the unskilled workers. Out of all the furnished rooms in fact, the unskilled mentioned *only* the kitchens – a striking indication of class differences in modern housing needs and attitudes.[19]

For the poor, kitchens and bathrooms offered something that might at the time have seemed beyond hope: plumbing, refrigeration, hot water – easy access to what others took for granted.

There is a sense that what is being played out across these two exhibitions from 1946 is a cultural competition about fuels: gas, solid fuel (coal) and electricity. Who is going to get electricity? Who will stick with solid fuel? How modern is gas? 'Britain Can Make It' provided much more detail in personifying fuel differences and associating them with specific people. The *Daily Herald* exhibition had already linked solid fuel to the small house; it was up to post-war advertisers to make it explicit that future users of solid fuel would inevitably be either down-at-heel or well-to-do (for instance, the ones who will install Agas). Coal was not going to be the domestic fuel of the middling masses in the immediate post-war years.

Each of the kitchen displays in 'Britain Can Make It' offered a room that was lived in and used by an imagined family. These families weren't abstract but were fleshed out with names, hobbies, jobs, children and politics. 'The kitchen of a cottage in a modern mining village' was lived in by a 'Coal miner, middle aged, active trade unionist, member of colliery choir. His wife

a member of Women's Institute; their three children.' Their
kitchen consisted of 'White glazed wall tiles, inlaid linoleum,
metal windows, draining board and kitchen units, gas cooker,
gas heated wash boiler, gas refrigerator, sink, plate racks, window
radiators.'[20] The next was 'a kitchen with dining recess in a
small modern house' and lived in by a 'young architect; paints
in his spare time. His wife, keen on amateur dramatics, their
son.' Their kitchen was decorated with 'hand painted wallpaper'
and included 'soap holder, floor tiles (compressed cork), rug, two
wooden windows, electric refrigerator, plate rack, electric cooker,
porcelain steel sink and drainer, electric space heater, ventilating
unit, coffee brewer'. The final room was 'a kitchen in a large well-
appointed house designed by Maxwell Fry and Jane Drew'. Here
the family was a 'managing director of an engineering works;
university education. His wife; lived in America for some years.
Their daughter, now at boarding school. Their staff; two maids
and a manservant.' Clearly, if you have the money, then servants
are not so hard to come by (now as then). In this kitchen there
is 'linoleum, plastic sheeting on walls, gas refrigerator, gas range,
service hatch, silent extractor, food preparing machine, electric
clock'.

While there wasn't a distinct correlation between fuel and
wealth – though coal was never going to be an aspirational person's fuel, unless it was tied to rustic Aga culture – there is a
clear relationship between electricity and being modern: it is the
architect's 'modern' house that is all electric. The association of
electricity with being modern arose gradually. In the 1920s the
properties of electricity that were stressed were cleanliness and
convenience. Adverts set the wondrous qualities of electricity to
verse:

Ah, use the Juice: – and let the Mains provide
Such Warmth as never with Cold Ashes died,

And to the Scrap Heap of Oblivion fling
The Greedy Range with blackened Jaws set wide.

Such advertising could even claim that electricity added flavour
to food:

I always think that nothing tastes so sweet
As juicy, cooked-electrically Meat.[21]

Of course, cleanliness and convenience were modern, but this
poem is just as keen to connect electricity to more traditional
notions of home. By the 1950s the message is much clearer:

Do you live in a bachelor home? An average home? A large
home? Whichever it is you are sure to be interested in THE
FOUR FOUNDATIONS OF MODERN LIVING. Elec-
tricity brings them to you of course. They are the electric
cooker, the electric water heater, the washing machine and
the refrigerator.[22]

The one thing that the middle classes share and that isn't
shared by the miner is some sort of automated ventilation.
Having smells taken out of the kitchen and dispersed outside
seems to be a prerogative of the well-to-do and the university-
educated. When George Orwell provocatively asked his reader
to consider how smell related to class, he was recognising that
the luxury of a completely de-odorised and sanitised environment was limited to the wealthy. Today the only smells that are
welcomed by housing 'experts' are the smells of fresh coffee and
baking bread – though anyone who has walked into a house
where onion and garlic are being fried will know how welcoming such odours can be.

Perhaps surprisingly, out of the three kitchens it was the miner's kitchen that was by far the most popular, and visitors had to be continually asked to move along to make way for the next group of viewers. Visitors were under no illusions that this was the kind of housing that miners were going to be living in any time soon: 'when a miner saw that, he'd pass right out'; 'the miners won't get that for forty years' (which was just at the point when most of the mines were closed down).[23] But out of the three kitchens it probably seemed the most attainable, or the least unattainable.

Kitchen conveniences

The envy that was directed at the kitchen was not simply aimed at new technological appliances. It was the cupboards that were most coveted: 'what a lovely lot of cupboards', exclaimed a twenty-five-year-old working-class woman when looking at the miner's kitchen; 'I like that white unit cupboard and dresser', said a forty-year-old working-class housewife. But the unreality of the display as a kitchen for the working class echoes in such bitter comments as: 'things wouldn't stay long like that in a miner's home, would they? It's beautifully white now.' Looking at the miner's cottage kitchen, a middle-class woman could mournfully state: 'We'll never have a kitchen like this … look at all the cupboards.' Space and built-in cupboards would characterise the modern kitchen just as much as new-fangled gadgetry.

Cupboards and gadgetry would come together ten years after 'Britain Can Make It', when the architects Alison and Peter Smithson built their 'House of the Future' in the *Daily Mail* Ideal Home Exhibition of 1956. It was a vision of what a house might look like in twenty-five years' time – in 1981. A number of things marked it out as modern. First, the entire house was structured around the kitchen as the central hub of the house. Second, like many other visions of the future that were produced in the 1950s, it benefited from an unlimited energy source. The 1950s and '60s imagined that nuclear energy would (eventually, but also quite soon) produce electricity that was so cheap no one would even bother to meter its consumption. Third, the Smithsons' 'House of the Future' was aimed at lessening women's work and at the safety of small children.

Visitors to the 1956 exhibition would see this 1981 house peopled by actors dressed in crocheted 'onesies' – skin-tight, knitted romper suits. The Smithsons conducted their futurology by adopting and adapting materials and devices that were already available. So, for instance, their use of plastic as a wall material was something that had already been pioneered by Jane Drew and Maxwell Fry in their kitchen for 'Britain Can Make It'. But the Smithsons used the qualities of plastic to produce not just a surface that was easy to clean but one where dirt simply couldn't accumulate: 'the house is moulded in plastic-impregnated plaster, a kind of skin structure built up in units comprising floor, walls and ceiling as a continuous surface. A flexible joint between each unit allows for thermal movement and provides a structural break for reducing noise.'[24] Without corners there was nowhere for dirt to hide. You could simply sluice down the entire house. *Our Homes and Gardens* would surely have approved.

This is a fuel-guzzling house: 'electric power, drawn from the nearest atomic power station, is used for heating, lighting, air-conditioning, water-heating, cooking, house laundry and refrigeration. Heated floors provide whatever warmth is required in any area of the house. Air conditioning sees to the mechanical extraction of all smells and ensures that dust infiltration is practically non-existent.'[25] This self-contained house, with an internal courtyard garden, soaks up electricity in its endeavour to provide a womb-like existence that barricades the household from the outside and expels any unpleasantness from the inside. It is a house that is disconnected from its environment – whether that is the street or the land.

The kitchen extends the idea of convenience to ergonomics;

every unit and built-in appliance can be reached without bending down, for instance. While the Smithsons' kitchen looks space-age, you could achieve some of the same effects by making ample use of a material that was being promoted elsewhere in the exhibition: 'Formica for me! What a mess! Cups upset – sticky finger marks everywhere. Lucky the mother whose table is FORMICA topped. No need to scrub – one wipe with a damp cloth and it's clean.'[26] Formica mimics the practice of covering kitchen surfaces in linoleum; it was advertised as bright and cheerful but also the perfect product for the chronically clumsy and thoroughly inebriated: 'alcohol has no effect whatsoever when spilled on a Formica surface […] no damage was caused by this careless smoker, as the table here is surfaced with cigarette-proof grade Formica plastic.'[27] The Kitchen of the Future is a kitchen of convenience that is perfect for dipsomaniacs.

In 1957, a year after the Smithsons' 'House of the Future', Formica will find its DIY equivalent in the form of 'sticky-backed plastic'. Britain took to sticky-backed plastic in a way that would have been hard for the Smithsons to envisage. Sticky-backed plastic covered kitchen surfaces both seen and unseen: in the 1960s no kitchen shelf would be free from the wild designs of Fablon. Indeed households didn't stop at covering the inside of drawers with this stuff – it was an essential ingredient for covering your school books, and if the children's TV show *Blue Peter* had its way, sticky-backed plastic was the material out of which the future would be built – or at least in which it would be covered.

The kitchen of the Smithsons' 'House of the Future' (lived in by knitwear-clad Anne and Peter) featured a set of electric appliances built for convenience and speed:

the Hotpoint refrigerator, for instance, forms one of the eye-level cupboards. Anne is greatly in favour of its shallow compartments, for with storage in length rather than depth everything in it is so readily accessible. Then there is the dish-washer, so placed that loaded trays of dirty crockery can be fed straight into it from a work surface with no previous scraping of the plates either; the machine disposes of all scraps, including bones. Now move on to the kitchen sink. This, like the bath and the hand basins, is made in glass-reinforced plastic, and is fitted with an electric waste disposal unit. The sink has only one thermostatically controlled tap. This can dispense any temperature of water from cold to boiling.[28]

Elsewhere in the exhibition a real dish-washer was being promoted. The 'Dishmaster' was the latest in convenience: 'We're washing dirty dishes in public. Dishmaster does a whole day's washing up in just 3 MINUTES. Every item is washed, rinsed, dried and polished in circular plastic cover trays. No breakages with Dishmaster.' A three-minute cycle is pretty quick: the packing and unpacking of every single item into its individual plastic container probably less so.

Cooking was speeding up too:

Notice the two ovens built in to the Galley at eye level. The one on your left is rather like a normal electric oven with preset time controls. Its special feature is that it can be converted into an automatic rotary spit. Its neighbour, Anne admits, and Peter swears, is a bit of a luxury: a super high-frequency oven for cooking at high speed. It will deal with a 3-lb roast, for instance, in less than fifteen minutes.

This piece of kit seems to be properly prophetic, foretelling the microwave. Though, of course, the microwave never really found its niche as a cooking implement and has instead soldiered

on defrosting and heating up, forgetting its energy-efficient van-
guard role of being able to cook an entire Sunday roast (with
'fake tan' varnishing – a lacquer of gravy browning – so that your
'roast' chicken actually looks roasted) in a fraction of the time a
conventional oven would take.

Appliances that were fully automated had been a feature of
the Ideal Home Exhibition two years earlier with such preset
time controls as the Smithsons were envisaging: 'Creda – the
leader! The super Comet! With the oven that switches itself on
– does the cooking – switches itself off.'[29] The cooking range is a
thing of the past in the 1956 kitchen of the future: 'Boiling rings?
You will look in vain for these. Look instead at Anne's electric
saucepans and frypans with thermostatic controls and made of
titanium: titanium because foods and fats cannot adhere to its
extra-hard, smooth surface, so a hot water rinse will clean them
easily.' Of course, with all those plugged-in pans having to all sit
somewhere while they cook, you might as well have a cooking
range.

Lastly, this kitchen has found a way of combining the kitchen-
wagon with the cooker and, hey presto, the result is the 'hostess
trolley': 'You may overlook the service trolley, it is recessed so
neatly under the two ovens. Apart from the usual warmed food
compartment, it has a built-in toaster, an infra-red griller and a
piece of mechanism that appeals particularly to Peter – an automatic hot plate dispenser.' Much loved in the 1970s, the hostess
trolley will come into its own as the prerequisite for a successful
dinner party.

Fashioning the future
The job of prediction is always a hit-and-miss affair: science
fiction at this time is much happier predicting time travel and
teleportation than imagining achievable futures. But designers
and manufacturers aren't soothsayers and, rather than being in

the business of predicting fashions, they are the agents shaping them. Technology doesn't feed our need for convenience; it creates this need. As we have seen, a good deal of the desire for convenience would be satisfied with wheel-based tables and more cupboards. For new-fangled contraptions to get off the ground what was needed was an assembly of factors including big business, advertising and shops – the whole machinery of commodity promotion.

Why is it, for instance, that today the fridge is always electric, when in the 1940s two out of the three fantasy kitchens at 'Britain Can Make It' used fridges that ran on gas? Was the electric fridge technically superior or more efficient? We might also wonder why it is that we all have clunky and cumbersome 'portable' vacuum cleaners when it might have been much more convenient to have a central sucking unit with air inlets in each room that we can attach our nozzles to? Writing about such technologies in the United States, the historian of domestic technology Ruth Schwartz Cowan is in no doubt that the crucial driver is business practice rather than consumer desire: 'the central vacuum cleaner, which technical experts preferred, quickly lost ground to its noisier and more cumbersome portable competitor, in part because of the marketing techniques pioneered by door-to-door and store demonstration salesmen employed by such firms as Hoover and Apex.'[30]

Yet if big business could simply foist expensive goods on unwilling consumers, our kitchen cupboards would have even more useless gadgets in them then they actually do. The domestic stories of kitchen technologies are best seen as 'family' stories wherein forces join hands to create symbiotic relations of machines, household practices and supporting structures. The freezer is a case in point. The freezer suggests the microwave; and without the freezer the microwave would be even more alone and unloved than it is. But without shops selling frozen chips and micro-chips (microwave-able chipped potatoes – which never really caught on) both freezers and microwaves would be less used than they are today. As the freezer became established in British kitchens, it didn't change quite as much as householders' shopping, cooking and eating practices changed.[31] In its initial introduction in the 1950s and '60s it was marketed as the solution to seasonal needs: too many plums falling from your trees? Why not freeze some? Just slaughtered your pig? Then you are probably going to need to freeze most of it. At this point the freezer's 'natural' friends were the farmer and the smallholder, its place of operation the countryside rather than the city.

In the 1970s it was promoted as efficient and liberating: no need to go shopping so regularly; now you can buy in bulk and limit yourself to the monthly shop. A monthly drive, then, to the giant out-of-town shopping centre can take care of all your household's needs. The supermarket, then, becomes dependent on people having freezers and of buying in bulk. And then all this freezing requires quick and easy ways of defrosting all your cryogenically stored food: enter the microwave. Of course, technology isn't determined in quite this way, but what we can see is a series of kitchen machines and practices that are – to some degree, at least – symbiotic and have effects on each other.

In this way domestic technology becomes a necessity because it has produced the conditions that eradicate the possibility of not using it. How often do we ask our technology: how did we do things before you arrived? How did we store stuff before the freezer? Of course, we have forgotten our old arts: the arts of storing, of salting, of pickling, of drying, of curing. But in a more prosaic way we can see that the success of the freezer was also the death knell of the local grocery store – although this is making a comeback in the form of mini-versions of superstores. The freezer comes of age as a kitchen necessity in the age of Kerry Katona, supermarkets dedicated to frozen goods, a massive range of ready meals, frozen pizzas, oven chips available everywhere and the ever-handy microwave. In its long cold march from the garage to the kitchen it has witnessed a range of other changes that it is not solely responsible for, but without which it would have remained a novelty.

At the kitchen table

The current-day association of the kitchen with shiny new gadgetry, sleek and shiny surfaces and high tech has meant that 'designer' kitchens often look like a mix of science laboratory, hospital and cottage. The cottage elements are there to mitigate the relentless unhomeliness of the modern kitchen. When kitchens go for full-on ultra modern, their effects can be alienating. June Freeman, in her *The Making of the Modern Kitchen*, conducted an experiment in relation to the modern designer kitchen. She asked her respondents to describe their feelings about an award-winning and hugely expensive kitchen design, where there isn't a shred of Shaker woodwork. One of them explained: 'I couldn't possibly live in it. It's not relaxed or comfortable. It wouldn't fit in with my character or lifestyle. Too cleaned up. I like clutter. I've deliberately introduced clutter in my kitchen. You wouldn't want to stay in that kitchen even to cook. It's for a very smart, high-powered young bachelor …'[32]

Unlike exhibition kitchens, 'real-life' kitchens are more like the railway refreshment room described by Roger Fry: a hotch-potch of different styles and different times. For those who can afford it, kitchens are the rooms most constantly redecorated and refitted (every seven years, on average) and the room we spend most money on.[33] Yet even when a kitchen receives a pretty conclusive refit, it is still stuffed with favourite old pans, mugs that hold sentimental significance as well as coffee, not to mention all those knick-knacks that have been turfed out of the living room. We get attached to those things we are intimate with: and eating and drinking are corporeal pleasures that directly connect us to the sensual world. A small pan might be perfect for boiling milk, or we may just like the way it looks and feels. Just as there is comfort food, so there are also comfort utensils.

A 'normal' kitchen is more likely to look something like the wartime kitchens described by Mass-Observation researchers than the colour supplement kitchen ads. One 'kitchen is long and narrow, contains sink, gas stove, dresser, cupboard, two tables, several chairs. Linoleum (three different kinds) pieced together on the floor, and a length of crimson stair carpet runs down the middle of the room as a rug.'[34] This is an anti-design kitchen, a kitchen pieced together out of old bits of lino.

Another kitchen consists of

> sink, gas stove, dresser, table, cupboards, chairs. Dull orange paper, ornamented by slightly lighter flowers and leaves. It is smudged and stained in many places – particularly over the gas stove, where it is almost rotted away by heat and steam. Above this stove there is a print of a Victorian drawing room, in which are a young woman standing by the mantelpiece and a little boy looking up at her. The picture is in a narrow black frame, and so spotted with damp that one has to look closely to see what it is of.[35]

Kitchens, perhaps more than front rooms, are filled with things we live with but hardly notice: part of the world that receives our daily inattention. Sometimes, when we think about it, it is these taken-for-granted items that hold our most cherished memories and deep affections.

Perhaps the item that is most taken for granted, but which finds a place in our hearts and memories, is the kitchen table. For one of the Mass-Observation diarists it was the kitchen table that was their most prized possession:

5 foot 4 inches × 2 foot 8 inches and 2 foot 6 ½ inches high. Containing 3 drawers and made of pine. I bought this table at a jumble sale in 1974 [...] I couldn't get me knees under it so added two inches to each leg. The top of the table was covered by a tacked-on piece of leather cloth and it was painted with a thick dark brown varnish. I stripped all this off and put brass finger handles on the drawers. Much of our life together has gone on round this table which sat in the back room where we ate in our last house and in the kitchen where we cook and eat in this house. We always sit at this table when we have guests to dinner, the children have lain on it to have their nappies changed, I write at it when working at home – placing the computer on it, Lin and I play chess and backgammon etc. over it, and the children sit at it to draw. I still can't completely get my knees under it. It has lots of scratches and other scars on it, some made by me, and others of unknown provenance. I suspect others have enjoyed sitting round this table, eating, talking and working.[36]

Kitchen tables hold memories beneath their oilcloth covers. They are witnesses to the daily maintenance of the household and the dramas that unfold around it. It might not be a perfect design, it might even be inconvenient, but it is there through thick and thin. A kitchen table may be designed with utility in mind, but its life story will always reveal the dramas and pleasures of the kitchen.

The kitchen table is also where we often learn our first lessons in housework: how to shell a pea; how to peel a potato; how to hold our knives, forks, spoons, chapattis and chopsticks. The kitchen is, as Edward VIII claimed, a place of education but it is often not an education in 'better living' so much as a lesson in finding your role in the house and in the wider world. In the *Daily Express*'s *Housewife's Book* that role is – surprise, surprise

– gendered. In this late 1930s' induction in mainstream femininity there is a picture of a young girl sitting at the kitchen table peeling a bowl of apples; underneath, the legend reads: 'As soon as a girl is old enough she should be encouraged to take an interest in housecraft.'[37] 'The wise mother', the book continues, 'will train her daughters as they grow up to take their share in the routine work, not to make drudges of them, but to give them work in which they can take an interest.' The sons, presumably, are out devouring snips and snails and puppy dog tails.

In her book *Kitchen Secrets*, a wide-ranging ethnographic study from a few years ago, Frances Short looks at the gap between what people aspire to in the kitchen, based on their intentions, and what actually transpires. She highlights the reality of 'microwaves, meal replacements and junk food' existing 'in a world where glossy cookbooks, celebrity cooks and innovative and refined cuisine also prevail'.[38] But within such a kitchen world the division of labour between men and women, while it might not be as stark as that detailed in *The Housewife's Book*, is hardly encouraging for anyone interested in a more equal world. Men may take an interest in cooking, but on a day-to-day routine level they are more likely to follow this male interviewee: 'I help out really because my wife is here and I sort of help her. I'm like an assistant in the family so I probably do a couple of hours a week, something like that.'[39]

But if such a division of labour clearly works in the interests of men, it is often simply too much work for already busy women to retrain men for a more equal role in the house:

I don't really trust Alec to go and do the shopping. He's no interest in doing the shopping anyway. And I suppose I prefer my cooking to his cooking, at least for evening meals. I would be happy for him to cook breakfast, like a fried breakfast, or a basic lunch. Though even sandwiches he would defer to me because he makes crap sandwiches. He really does. He's really lazy about it, he doesn't butter to the edge of the bread and he doesn't think about what he'd put in it. He'd just put cheese in it. Just cheese! I have no interest in eating a plain cheese sandwich.[40]

The ethnography of housework is filled with a sense of inequality felt by women combined with the recognition that men simply don't have the expertise and would end up making more work for women: 'John does no housework at all, I prefer it that way, except on the rare occasions when I'm unwell.'[41]

Yet across the twentieth century a large number of men were trained in household chores to a considerable degree. Any man who had done national service or who had fought in either of the two world wars (not to mention those other wars that pepper the twentieth and twenty-first centuries) was more than competent in housework. As *Good Housekeeping* pointed out in an article from 1947 titled 'Should Men do Housework?', 'thousands of ex-Servicemen have returned home with unprecedented experience of the traditional duties of washing, ironing, cleaning and cooking – qualified, as never before, to be true partners in the task of making a home. But are they gladly taking upon their newly trained shoulders an equitable share of housework? And if not, why not?'[42] Perhaps men were also trained in the perennial art of amnesia – if not, how do we explain the unwillingness of some men to utilise skills learned at summer camps, at boarding schools and in institutions such as the military? If war, for a while, bridges the gender gap by offering women 'men's work' and by making men domesticated animals, then this gap is one of the first things that gets remade in post-war reconstruction.

Kitchens, though, are not just places where we learn to labour (or not to labour) but also places for an induction into the larger world of culture. Food is perhaps our first encounter with a wider cultural world: a world quite literally of taste, of likes and dislikes, a world of routine meals and celebrations. And this world is where we might learn about regional foods from all over the world. In his memoir of growing up in south London in the 1970s, the child of immigrant parents (of Ceylonese/Sri Lankan, Burmese and Portuguese descent), Rohan Candappa comes across a book written by his aunt and uncle. Writing of the disparity between kitchens that they had known in childhood and the modern kitchens they see in Britain, they write:

> It is strange to observe the change in eating habits in prosperous countries, against the ones practised in the so-called poor ones. A look at a modern kitchen in the west gives the impression that it is geared to feeding fairly large groups of people on many occasions. All the amenities are there. In actual practice, all this expensive gear is seldom used, in comparison to its extent and the money invested. These elaborate kitchens are used to cut down the time for cooking to a minimum, not to promote kitchen culture. The accumulation of things is nowhere better shown than in the fully equipped modern kitchen, that does not serve hospitality and sharing, but is only geared to saving time – for what? Even smells suffer in the process: they are sucked away mechanically, much to the dismay of the stomach, which loses its companion, the nose, for the enjoyment and digestion of food.[43]

Technologically the kitchen has changed more than any other room in the house. Even the most modest kitchen today would have an electric kettle, a cooker that you can turn off and on, and a fridge-freezer. A hundred years ago the tasks such technology performed would have been dependent on coal-fuelled ranges and a visit from the ice cart. But in other ways the kitchen has remained a place where boys and girls find their place in the world. Yet if the kitchen is to be a place of pleasure and conviviality, then perhaps we need to lessen its technological prestige – make it less like a hospital and more like a playroom which even whiffs a bit.

Illuminated homework ...

MIND YOUR MANNERS

(Dining Rooms)

Removal day is fraught with all sorts of anxieties and frustrations. Our last move was only a couple of hundred yards, but even then the removal van managed to break down between collecting our stuff and taking it to the new house. When we arrived, we saw the previous owner driving away, sitting next to a huge crystal chandelier on the passenger seat. It became obvious after we moved in that we had bought a work in progress. A fireplace that looked fixed and workable was merely a wooden surround propped up against the wall in front of a disintegrating grate: the sides of the bath were similarly unfixed. Electricity sockets sat unsteadily in patches of crumbling wall. Clearly we hadn't examined the house too closely. The one room that was finished, though, was the dining room. It had sage-green walls, a thick green, ochre and brown flowered carpet, and a cream ceiling which was where the chandelier had hung. It isn't a dining room any more: it is something like a guest room crossed with a games room and a work room. To keep a room just as a dining room suggests a commitment to formal dining that we just haven't got. We gave a little cheer when we watched that chandelier drive off.

A large number of the Victorian and Edwardian terraced houses in Britain were built with a dining room or, rather, a second reception room. Those without a second reception room were often houses where there was no hallway and where you either had a single downstairs kitchen–living room or a parlour that you entered through the front door and led into the kitchen–living room at the back. In Belfast, for instance, small terraced houses were described as either 'parlour houses' or 'kitchen houses'. The architectural plans for 'Artizans', Labourers' & General Dwellings Estate' in Hornsey in the 1880s shows five types of working-class housing. The 'first-class' house and the 'second-class' house have two parlours with a kitchen and a scullery at the back; the 'third-class' house still has a hallway, but now the scullery has shrunk and the second parlour is now called the kitchen; the 'fourth-class' and 'fifth-class' house have no hallway and just one reception room.[1] By the 1880s hardly any houses were being built that were 'kitchen houses' – that didn't have any reception rooms – though, of course, many such houses still existed and were being lived in.

Today I imagine that most of these second parlour rooms are not specifically kept as dining rooms, or at least not only as dining rooms (and, as we shall find out, the dining room often had to earn its keep by accommodating a range of activities besides dining). Today the second reception room might be used as a den for kids to hang out in, or as a home office or as some form of hobby room. A large number, especially in the smaller houses, have probably been knocked through, creating one long room that is often zoned into table-and-chair space and sitting-and-watching space. Indeed many terraced and semi-detached houses were built in the decades around 1900 precisely with such an arrangement in mind, and instead of having a wall separating a living room and a dining room, folding panel doors were used to divide them. So, if you were feeling expansive or had a lot of people round, you could have the doors open or, if you needed discrete spaces, for warmth or quiet activities, you could close them. This was flexible space that you could alter, depending on your mood or your requirements.

The function of the dining room 'earning its keep' by having to provide space for other activities has always been an element of the flexibility of a room that is neither purely connected to practical necessities (bathrooms, kitchens, toilets) nor needed to maintain a sense of specialness (the parlour). Even in the post-Second World War period, when parlours were becoming more like living rooms, a second reception room could provide for the kinds of activity that required space or quietness. The history of the dining room's use as a hobby space has been shown by historians looking at probate ledgers and sales inventories and catalogues where items are identified in relation to rooms. Thus in late nineteenth-century dining rooms it was fairly common for there to be bookshelves. But it also might be the place for keeping sewing equipment and a sewing machine.[2]

For the early domestic goddess Mrs Beeton evening 'entertainment' was crucial for producing a pleasant mood for the house and 'to make her children feel that home is the happiest place in the world; [...] to imbue them with this delicious home-feeling is one of the choicest gifts a parent can bestow'. Her list of things to do might well have been done in the drawing room, but they are just as likely to have been carried out in the dining room: 'light or fancy needlework often forms a portion of the evening's recreation for the ladies of the household, and this may be varied by an occasional game at chess or backgammon. It has often been remarked, too, that nothing is more delightful to the feminine members of a family, than the reading aloud of some good standard work or amusing publication.'[3]

Clearly the idea of a room kept purely for dining belongs to an era when people didn't eat on their lap or snack at a breakfast bar. Of course, many people still keep regular meal times, lay the breakfast things before going to bed and have excellent table manners – but they are as likely to do this around a dining table in a large kitchen as in a separate room. In this chapter I'm going to treat the 'dining room' as both a physically discrete room (a dining room as opposed to a drawing room, or a living room as opposed to a parlour) and a space that can move around – a nomadic zone, so to speak. I'm also going to look at eating and entertaining more generally, precisely because this is what we mean by a dining room, whether we have such a designated room or not. A table in a living–dining room can be somewhere for playing Scrabble one moment, doing your school homework at another and sitting down for a celebratory banquet the next. It can sit there modestly in the back row, so to speak, while a household eats on their laps in front of the TV or it can take centre stage as the candlelit scene for an extravagant meal. So the dining room in its more recent guise is often a shift worker or a place-holder, marked by nothing more than a table.

The dinner party
The dining room (whether this is a separate room or part of a more amorphous living room) is best remembered for those special meals: the weekend roast, the dinner party, the Christmas dinner. They can be anxious as social events, as moments when you are introduced to new people or when your neighbour decides to take on the role of matchmaker and fix you up with someone entirely inappropriate from their workplace. The dinner party makes the dining room or dining zone the most public space in the house: it is where the household invites the world in (a carefully chosen selection of that world) to break bread with them. For children such concentrated moments of domestic life can also be difficult: the dining room becomes a place for dragooning young ones, policing their behaviour, instilling adequate cutlery skills and refraining from the more wild pleasures of food.

Mrs Beeton, writing in the 1860s for servant-employing households, in an era of extensive social deference, recognised how much anxiety was involved in giving a dinner party even if you didn't have to do any of the cooking:

> the half-hour before dinner has always been considered as the great ordeal through which the mistress, in giving a din-ner-party, will either pass with flying colours, or, lose many of her laurels. The anxiety to receive her guests, – her hope that all will be present in due time – her trust in the skill of her cook, and the attention of the other domestics, all tend to make these few minutes a trying time. The mistress, however, must display no kind of agitation, but show her tact in sug-gesting light and cheerful subjects of conversation, which will be much aided by the introduction of any particular new book, curiosity of art, or article of vertu, which may pleasantly engage the attention of the company.[4]

It is clear that in this period the dinner party was primarily about social mixing and only secondarily about food. Having good food simply meant you were skilled at employing.

The presumed masculinity of the dining room was premised on the idea that at a certain point in the meal – when there was no longer food to be had, but still plenty to drink – the women would leave: 'When fruit has been taken, and a glass or two of wine passed round, the time will have arrived when the hostess will rise, and thus give the signal for the ladies to leave the gen-tlemen, and retire to the drawing-room.'[5] Notions of etiquette and manners have changed since Mrs Beeton's day: no one today would expect women to retire to the drawing room after a dinner, would they? Yet the persistence of a sense of social manoeuvring is a continued aspect of dinner party planning, and advisers suggest the tactical use of women guests as distractions. 'When planning your dinner company,' suggests a book on manners from 1959, 'do not invite too many brilliant talkers. Each of them wants an audience, not rivals. Silent (though not dumb) people must be sandwiched between good talkers. Never put silly people next to learned ones, nor dull persons by clever ones, unless the former are beautiful women who can at least pretend to be good listeners.' Of course, some people are just going to be social disaster zones that just have to be borne:

> we all suffer from close friends whose husbands (or wives) are bores, or fools, or irritating people. There is nothing to do except place such people next to good-natured friends, who might be warned and asked to be forbearing! This can, of course, be done only if one is *sure* that the friend in question is discreet – and discretion is a rare quality.[6]

The social niceties of dinner parties are often based on the assumption that those attending them are from the same social milieu: work colleagues, neighbours, old school friends and so on. Dining-room etiquette, for those interested in marking and remarking on the different practices of social class, is an absolute treasure trove. For a writer like Jilly Cooper – who has made a journalistic career out of being a self-conscious snob – the dinner table is clearly somewhere to watch class differences at work. For Cooper the nuances of class are condensed in a small square of cloth:

> the ritual of table napkins is interesting. The working-class man tucked a handkerchief under his chin to protect his shirt and waistcoat (he would never eat in a coat). The lower-middles, daintily thinking 'napkin' sounded too much like babies' nappies and wanting to show off their knowledge of French, called it a serviette. The middle classes, wanting to go one up, talked about napkins, but, being frugal, also wanted them to last a few days,

so they introduced napkin rings. The upper classes, who had plenty of people to do the laundry, had clean napkins at every meal and regarded napkin rings as the height of vulgarity.[7]

There is less distance between Jilly Cooper and Mrs Beeton than there would be between many of Cooper's contemporaries.

But perhaps the greatest change since Mrs Beeton's day is the expectation that the middle-class household will prepare the meal themselves (or, at least, the hostess will). The trouble here is that the dinner party is primarily a display of hosting skills, and only secondarily about the food. How could a host cook a three-course meal and make sure that the dinner part is a social success? *The Ideal Home Householders' Guide* from 1966, a publication that not only offers advice but also names products for you to buy, is ready at hand with a labour-saving device:

> Most people entertain these days with little or no help in the home and it is important that the hostess should organize things well beforehand. If not, the guests will only see hasty glimpses of her red face as she trots between them and the kitchen at high speed! It is a good plan to have a dessert that is all ready beforehand and to choose a main dish that can be left to finish itself while the hostess is having a pre-dinner drink with her guests. A trolley is a great help. If one is ready in the kitchen with everything needed for coffee and cheese and biscuits to wind up the meal, it will only take a minute to wheel it into the dining-room.[8]

The hostess trolley will become a feature of dinner party planning and brings to actuality what had been envisaged in Alison and Peter Smithson's 'House of the Future', looked at in the previous chapter. A hostess trolley is not simply a convenience; it is also a mood enhancer:

A dinner party is the most intimate and formal type of entertaining – an event never to be rushed. A dinner for two presupposes a very special reason for celebrating, so the atmosphere must be thought about carefully. The mood of the evening should not be spoiled by jumping up from the table to supervise last-minute details. It is very easy to have two of the three courses ready prepared and one keeping warm in a low oven or a heated trolley.[9]

But while the fully functioning hostess trolley was something of an investment, the *Ideal Home Householders' Guide* suggest ways of creating your own hostess trolley by combining the heated dish or the hot plate with the ever-useful 'electric heated serving tray, comprising three or four heat-proof glass dishes fitted into a chrome-steel case with handles, can be placed on a trolley, and plugged in to pre-heat in the kitchen. […] All she needs to do is to unplug the tray from the kitchen socket, wheel the trolley into the dining area and plug in again.'[10] The following year the full hostess trolley (that is, a trolley designed as one big hot plate) is introduced – some ten years after Alison and Peter Smithson's Ideal Home display.[11] Writing at the height of the hostess trolley's reign, one sociologist will be prompted to study the relationship of technology and women's labour by 'a picture advertising an electric hostess trolley laden with elaborately prepared food, presided over by a smiling woman in evening dress. Although the trolley clearly allowed her to conceal that she had done the cooking, then dress while the dinner kept hot, it had not cooked it for her. Did this save her any labour, or only appear to do so?'[12] It may not have saved on physical labour, but it allowed the hostess or host to be more effective with their emotional work of excising anxiety and producing conviviality.

The production of convenience, as we saw in the last chapter, suggested that housewives became their own time-and-motion experts. In the attempt to achieve the perfect dinner party women are similarly invited to become their own experts by recording and deliberating on how previous parties have gone:

> a record-book of your dinner parties, guests and their comments is always a good idea. It can ensure that you don't give a repeat performance to the same people. More important, it can remind you, perhaps, that the dish that won acclaim was not the soufflé you slaved over, but the delicious way you cooked the potatoes, or dressed a very simple salad.[13]

And while the varied success of your dishes is important here, again it is the whole social scene that needs to be worried about and recorded:

> Entertaining of all kinds is one of the performing arts, and as with the others, confidence is half the battle. Even in a meal, good food is only one element of the production, albeit the main one. This notion does *not* derive from those restaurateurs whose dining-room is a stage-set, with lighting, music and costumes to match. But a touch of stage company morale does no home or hostess any harm. This may strike contrary to the prevailing wisdom […] about naturalness and relaxation, and with most guests there is no point in pretending that your cooking, your income, or your personality are different from what they are.[14]

This is advice that is contradictory and likely to send the diffident host reaching for the Diazepam: be totally honest, don't punch above your weight, be true to your ability and your pocket; but also put on a good performance, give a good show, disguise your inadequacies.

At one level a dinner party's function is to feed a group of people in a convivial manner: it is a gift from the host – an act of generosity. At another (according to the advice literature, at least) it is clearly a social ritual with endless opportunities for making mistakes – and to be judged by your mistakes. Food may be a secondary concern, but for the ambitious hostess the food would still have to be attractive. For Mrs Beeton dinner party food has to attract the palates of metropolitan types:

> food that is not well relished cannot be well digested; and the appetite of the over-worked man of business, or statesman, or of any dweller of town, whose occupations are exciting and exhausting, is jaded, and requires stimulation. Men and women who are in rude health, and who have plenty of air and exercise, eat the simplest of food with relish, and consequently digest it well; but those conditions are out of the reach of many men.[15]

Mrs Beeton's culinary response to the problem of the over-worked businessman is 'boiled half calf's head, tongue and brains', 'oyster patties', 'clear gravy soup', 'fricasseed rabbit' and 'macaroni soup'.

In the twentieth century dinner party food still has to attract jaded palates, but it has a world of culinary traditions to choose from. Since the 1960s the dinner party has been a place for adventurous hosts to show their familiarity with cuisines from around the world. Today we impress our guests with soufflés, foams, jus, not to mention all the snazzy kit for *sous vide* – 'warm bath cooking for vacuum packed food'. A few decades ago we would have fired up the fondue burner or shown daring through the use of avocado.

The various British nations are not renowned for their culinary sophistication and delicacy of traditional dishes, and it is clear that there isn't a spread of Scottish, English or Welsh restaurants abroad. Most of the invention in British cooking has meant adopting and adapting the cuisine of its former colonies (India, Pakistan, Bangladesh, Sri Lanka) and wrestling their flavour combinations into sometimes bizarre productions: Constance Spry's coronation chicken – designed for the 1953 coronation – with cold meat, spiced mayonnaise and raisins being the obvious example. Table condiments too were fashioned in colonial India: Worcester sauce, for instance, was invented in India and brought back to Britain in 1835.[16] In the nineteenth century 'curry' (which is itself a British term that runs roughshod over the wide variety of dish textures and preparation methods) would have been part of most recipe books in a variety of forms and dishes such as kedgeree and mulligatawny.

A cookbook from 1903 – *Curries and How to Prepare Them*, by Joseph Edmunds – distinguishes between regional varieties: Madras, Bengal and Bombay.[17] But even with some sensitivity towards regional differences, the tendency throughout the late nineteenth century and throughout most of the twentieth century for popular British domestic cookery has been to turn the enormous heterogeneity of tastes in subcontinental cooking into a single flavour note. Curry powder (the single flavour note), which had been marketed in Britain from the end of the eighteenth century, became so popular that by the time you reach the twentieth century there wouldn't be a grocer's shop that didn't sell it.[18] For migrants arriving in Britain from the subcontinent in the 1950s, the existence of curry powder, and the British style of producing curry (with lots of flour, as well as sliced bananas on the side) must have felt very odd indeed.

Dinner party suggestions, as well as weekly family dinners, often included suggestions for curry. As the magazine *Wife and Home* could write in 1954, 'most men enjoy a good curry, so now's your chance to win your husband's approval. KAY our Cookery Expert gives you a variety of recipes and hints to help you.'[19] Kay offers the standard route to producing a curry:

Stew tripe until tender and then cut into small neat pieces. Heat the margarine in a saucepan, add the onion and cook until tender without browning. Add the curry powder and flour and mix all together. Pour in the stock and milk and cook until boiling. Continue cooking for a further 5 minutes, stirring all the time. Season well, add the pieces of cooked tripe and allow to cook for another 15 minutes. Serve very hot with boiled rice or mashed potatoes.[20]

Tripe curry and mash – perhaps not the most sophisticated dinner party classic, but a useful example of producing food designed to titillate jaded palates with the minimum of work: add curry powder, add flour, and hey presto – curry.

But the dining room as a place of celebration doesn't require the formalities of the dinner party to bring it alive; the weekly roast or the Christmas dinner is often the dining room meal that is most memorable. In Richard Llewellyn's famous novel *How Green Was My Valley*, set in the mining valleys of south Wales, the author conjures up a weekly roast meal that is eaten on Saturdays (the nonconformist Christianity that the family espouses means no cooking on the Sabbath except in exceptional circumstances). *How Green Was My Valley* is clearly a nostalgic evocation of Welsh mining communities by an author who only had limited experience of the valleys. (He was born in London and drafted most of the novel in India; he did, however, interview many miners in preparing his novel and also worked as a miner for a few months.) The weekly roast is set out as the idyllic aspect of life in the valley against which the decline in the community can be measured:

But when we used to sit down to dinner on Saturday, it was lovely to look at the table. Mind, in those days, nobody thought of looking at the table to keep the memory of it living in their minds. There was always a baron of beef and a shoulder or leg of lamb on the dishes by my father. In front of him were the chickens, either boiled or roast, or ducks, or turkey or goose, whatever was the time of the year. Then potatoes, mashed, boiled and roast, and cabbage and cauliflower, or peas or beans and sometimes when the weather was good, all of them together. We used to start with Grace, all standing up and Mama holding me in the crook of her arm. My father used to close his eyes tight and look up at the stain on the ceiling, holding his hands out across the table.[21]

The valley was indeed green to produce all that – and while the novel focuses on men's work, here it is women's work that is clearly what maintains the community being described. And perhaps the protagonist's mother would have benefited from a hostess trolley: 'After my mother had taken out the plates with my eldest sister, my father carved the chickens or whatever was there. My mother was always on the run from the table to the stove to cover the plates with gravy and she was always the last to start her dinner.'[22]

But my all-time favourite menu for a Christmas dinner, which I can't imagine being topped in terms of range or quantities comes from Rohan Candappa's food memoir of growing up in suburban London (Norbury, on the way out to Croydon). In the 1970s Christmas dinner with his extended family in their double-fronted Victorian villa meant cobbling together a dining-room table large enough to accommodate them all: 'On Christmas Eve the table would be set for lunch the next day. Except that it wouldn't be one table, but two or three arranged in a line. Each table would be a slightly different height to the one next to it. Which would be fine, unless you were unfortunate enough to end up with your plate on the tectonic fault line between two of them.'[23] Such improvisations are practised across the country on high days and holidays – for Eid, for Passover, for Christmas, as well as for birthdays, weddings and other celebrations.

But it is the food that crosses continents and food traditions (Candappa's parents bring together Sri Lankan and Portuguese traditions by way of Burma) that makes it so special:

> So there would be roast turkey and stuffing and cranberry sauce and roast potatoes and Brussels sprouts and chipolatas and carrots and gravy and a flaming Christmas pudding with cream or custard and with a sixpence hidden inside it. Then there would be a mountain of subtly spiced rice tinted a vibrant yellow with turmeric, vindaloo made with pork and beef, two chicken curries (one hot, one mild), mulligatawny made with mutton bones, minced meat cutlets (some made with green chillies, some without), lentils, pickled aubergines, raitas, a mixed Burmese salad of cauliflower, carrots and green beans called thanat, beetroot salad, pickles, chutneys and also a salad of tomatoes and cucumber. Then after that there would be traditional semolina-based sweets like the Indian soojee-ka-metha or the Burmese tsunamaki and the small, hard, sugared pastry kul-kuls that the same uncle who had made the cutlets would have stayed up into the early hours churning out.[24]

Earning its keep

What happens to the dining room when dining is not happening? How does the dining room earn its keep? Somerset Maugham's 1915 novel *Of Human Bondage* is an overwrought account of one man's journey through childhood and adolescence, and into adult acceptance of the reality of his humdrum existence. But before you get to the acceptance, the novel is stuffed full of unrequited love, God, art and sex – I loved it when I was an overwrought fifteen-year-old. It's also stuffed full of domestic period detail.

The book starts when the protagonist, nine-year-old Peter Carey, is orphaned and has to go and live with his emotionally consti-pated aunt and uncle in the vicarage. In this vicarage the dining room is primarily a living room where meals are taken:

> The dining-room, large and well-proportioned, had windows on two sides of it, with heavy curtains of red rep [a horizon-tally corded cloth]; there was a big table in the middle; and at one end an imposing mahogany sideboard with a look-ing-glass in it. In one corner stood a harmonium. On each side of the fireplace were chairs covered in stamped leather, each with an antimacassar; one had arms and was called the husband, and the other had none and was called the wife. Mrs Carey never sat in the armchair: she said she preferred a chair that was not too comfortable; there was always a lot to do, and if her chair had had arms she might not be so ready to leave it.[25]

Although Maugham's book was published in 1915, he is describ-ing a dining room in the second half of the nineteenth century that is still going strong at the beginning of the twentieth.

In the classic advice literature during that period it seems that it wasn't just chairs that were sexed. In H. J. Jennings's *Our Homes and How to Beautify Them* (1902) the dining room was set out as a complement and a contrast to the drawing room, and this contrast was between the presumed femininity of the drawing–sitting room and the masculinity of the dining room: 'the Dining Room should be the man's Paradise, as the Drawing Room is the woman's.'[26] The masculinity of the dining room harks back to a tradition whereby women would 'withdraw' to a drawing room at the end of a meal while the men would carry on quaffing alcohol while puffing on cigars. Once they had sobered up a bit, they might also join the women in the drawing room. Of course, the vicarage in Somerset Maugham's novel isn't used in this way, but the sense of the dining room as furnished with heavy furniture and dark woods echoes this tradition.

In *Our Homes and How to Beautify Them* Jennings suggests that, while the drawing room might benefit from 'light' styles, the dining room should opt for heavier 'national' styles such as Elizabethan and Jacobean. To illustrate this he provides a photograph of a showroom exhibit from the firm Waring and Gillow that shows a 'modern' Jacobean dining room where the walls are all oak-panelled, with a large stone fireplace and heavy oak dining table. As the design historian Jane Hamlett puts it: 'these spaces were increasingly linked to national identity. The oak dining room (often imitation Tudor) was linked to masculine Englishness, the ornate drawing room (often Louis Quinze) associated with French femininity.'[27]

But the attempt to fix room decoration according to tradition came unstuck as soon as it was pointed out that those traditions had a habit of changing very rapidly:

> people whose taste is guided by mere custom sit down to dine upon an oaken chair before an oaken table, with a turkey carpet under their feet, and a red flock-paper staring them in the face. After dinner the ladies ascend into a green-and-gold-papered drawing-room, to perform on a walnut-wood piano, having first seated themselves on walnut-wood music-stools, while their friends are reclining on a walnut-wood sofa, protected from the heat of the fire by a walnut-wood screen. A few years ago, all these last mentioned articles were made of rosewood. In the early part of this century it was *de rigueur* that they should be made of mahogany.[28]

The writer here is Charles Eastlake, one of the tastemakers of the nineteenth century. Ironically, perhaps, he is alerting his readers to the foibles of fashion while at the same time promoting a version of the modern Gothic and Arts and Crafts style that, like everything else in a fashion-animated world, will soon have had its day.

During the period when the front room or parlour was reserved for 'high days and holidays' and for visits from local dignitaries, the dining room or breakfast room (which in terraced houses sat between the front room and the kitchen) was the room that was used on a more daily basis as the living room. Eating meals, reading newspapers, listening to the radio, doing school work were the routine activities that took place there. In larger Edwardian suburban villas the dining room also had a day-to-day life as the place for meals, reading, games and radio listening. With the drift towards taking meals in an enlarged kitchen and with the opening up of the parlour into a more usable daily room, the dining room's status and use became more unsettled. Hanging on to a dining room whose only function was for a relatively formal meal would be something of a luxury.

Newly built houses from the 1920s and onwards – especially those that flirted with a modernist style – often favoured the lounge–dining room: a largish room that could be used for a variety of purposes and which might be 'zoned' into little spaces for comfortable sitting or for sitting at a table. These were not just middle-class houses but new council houses: 'The nicest houses I ever saw – for council houses, that is, were at Wednesbury. There was one long living room with a circular window at each end, so that the sun was always coming in. Then they had a kitchenette. I reckon our council ought to go there and learn a few lessons.'[29]

In a house where the dining 'room' wasn't actually a separate room, then, it was the furniture alone that marked it out as a dining 'zone'. Items of furniture could show your commitments to traditional values with heavy antique table and chairs, or show your modernity with up-to-date styles of light wood and Scandinavian design. The dining set was also a substantial financial investment and could become a central focus of the house. Add to this the sideboard and dresser, and the dining room or dining zone was clearly an area of the house that mattered a great deal.

Perhaps in more subtle ways it was the sideboard and the dresser or the shelves for showing china ware that told you that a certain decorum was in order and made you aware when you were in a dining room – or in a kitchen–living room that had to function as a dining room as well. It also allowed you to know when the best china and glasses were out. For Eastlake the sideboard

> consists of a wide and deep shelf fitted with one or two drawers, and resting at each end on a cellarated cupboard. If this piece of furniture was constructed in a plain and straightforward manner, and were additionally provided with a few narrow shelves at the rear for displaying the old china vases and rare porcelain, of which almost every house contains a few examples, what a picturesque appearance it might present at the end of a room![30]

Of course, Eastlake knows that 'rare porcelain' isn't going to be found in many workers' cottages (he is not particularly interested in workers). But whether it is 'rare' or not, all classes liked to display heirlooms of crockery alongside the dining table – it showed generational continuity and the fact that you had crockery that was worth putting on show.

The displays at the 'Britain Can Make It' exhibition show us how the dining room was being imagined in the immediate post-war period. The 'Dining Room in Small Suburban Villa' was a room that consisted of table and chairs, sideboard, shelves for displaying china (blue china in this case), plants and a 'trolley book shelves'. One of the most controversial things about this display was the way that the china plates were shown: because they weren't in glass cupboards, they would be an endless chore of dusting. One woman complained: 'that's not labour saving. Open china shelves are an abomination.'[31] This dining room was 'lived in' by a curate who was a keen naturalist and great reader (hence the book-case trolley) and his wife who collected pottery: they didn't have much money. The pottery on display was a modern twist on the display of inherited crockery: what didn't seem modern to the visitor was having such a display open to the accumulation of dust. We are told that they have three children who do their homework in this room. The dining-room table – even more than the kitchen table – would always have to accommodate the studious pursuits of children – that is, until they got their own little bedroom study areas.

The dining-room display was clearly at the forefront of any negotiation of traditional and contemporary design. Wedding presents and family heirlooms were the stuff of dining-room displays. Of course, what you received wasn't always to your taste or in keeping with your sense of being modern, so the display of gifts was often difficult: if family had given you things, they would wonder why they weren't out and on display. Sometimes the best thing to do was to wait and to pass it on to another, perhaps more appreciative, generation:

> My mother gave me one of her own wedding presents, an Edwardian silver teapot, which she always prized. I thought it very ugly and was glad to give it to my eldest daughter when she had a home. She has it on display and is very fond of it. Children generally despise the treasures of their parents' generation but turn with pleasure to those of the one before.[32]

Terence Conran's *The House Book* is ambivalent about the dining room. On the one hand, in the 1970s and after, it could function in a way that was equivalent to the parlour – hardly used, kept for best and something of a showroom. This is what one Mass-Observer meant when he said: 'actually in our circumstances, our dining room comes nearest to a parlour using the word in its Victorian sense.'[33] For Conran this meant putting the emphasis on the room as a form of display:

> a single-purpose dining-room serves a very distinct function in the house; it is the room used for entertaining; the room which is 'shown off' on special occasions. Consequently the decoration should be a little special too, and the scheme can afford to be more emphatic. Traditionally colour schemes for dining-rooms tended to be dark. Today the most favoured dark colour seems to be chocolate brown.[34]

And to illustrate this Conran includes images of rooms where it looks as though a séance is about to take place.

'The dining area', writes Conran,

> must earn its keep by being put to other uses. If the walls of the dining area are covered with built-in storage units the table can become a working study, a sewing-room or area kept separate for study. It is important that clutter can be quickly put away when a meal is in the offing. And it is extremely important to plan for enough power points in appropriate places. The section might be turned into an area for watching TV or listening to music, so lighting must be suitable. If the table is to be used to most advantage, plan a ceiling light that can be lowered or raised, dimmed or brightened; for reading or study, an Anglepoise lamp can be plugged in for good, economical light.[35]

Throughout the twentieth century it seems clear that for

those that had a second reception room but not a third (or fourth etc.), then the dining room often needed to be flexible. It could be somewhere for practising a musical instrument, for playing games that required table space, for homework or for doing your tax returns and, for those that enjoy that sort of thing – jigsaws! Where better to do a jigsaw than in a room whose purpose has historically shifted and where meals are often eaten in front of the TV or on the kitchen table? The following description of a dining room as a room that seems to be used for all sorts of things except dining may not be representative but it may be symptomatic:

> The second room facing the front is the dining room. (We had servants' bells when we came here and that is what they said it was.) It has a bookcase, a nest of tables, a long low Indian type table that doesn't suit the rest of the mahogany furniture but which my husband gave me one Xmas. A large TV set, a magazine stand, another lower bookcase, a fish tank (been here for 20 years and breeds its replacements), an oak drop leaf desk, regency table and eight chairs with red and cream typical striped seats.

This is clearly more like a box-room. Perhaps the dining room was 'remaindered' by the ordinary house and has to make do with the storage of remainders: 'at the moment there is a wall-papering table there and head rest affair that I don't know who is responsible for dumping in front of my fish tank.'[36]

As the ordinary house became more and more informal over the last century it is perhaps no wonder that the dining room has had a difficult time maintaining its identity: it is, after all, a room that seems to have formality as its basic characteristic. But as a room whose identity has been in doubt it has performed particularly useful tasks for hobbies and for technology, whose place in the house has also been (at times) uncertain. It could act as a TV room for those who didn't want the TV to pollute the sitting room; or it could house the second TV when sets started accumulating (particularly after the introduction of colour broadcasting). It could accommodate a computer too, when it was unclear where that device was meant to go. It was a good place to listen to the radio in the early days of wireless enthusiasm.

When the wireless set appeared, it gravitated towards the sideboard. For many families the first wireless was a considerable piece of furniture and was usually bought by men: indeed in radio history women often seem indifferent or actively hostile to the intrusion of the radio in the household. In this Bryan Magee's family are not particularly unusual. The dad buy's the radiogram after a significant win at the betting shop, and it is installed in their dining room. The mum, however, is not a fan of the radiogram. This is Magee remembering the arrival of the music machine:

> To me it looked magnificent. There it stood a polished wooden cabinet the size of (I thought) a small wardrobe, actually a typical 1930s piece of furniture. […] both Dad and I were childishly proud of our new radiogram. My mother, however, resented so much money being spent on something that meant so little to her. It had one or two trivial teething troubles – it may well have been bought on the cheap – and when one of these took the form of a faulty electric connection that produced a red glow somewhere in the apparatus she pretended to believe that the whole thing was about to go up in flames and burn the house down, and threw a large basin of water over it.[37]

Magee's mum may have had an extreme reaction to the radiogram (which would have included a record player as part of the set), yet it is clear that as a piece of household equipment the radio was something that increased the gendered divisions of the household.

Conducting an oral history of early radio listening in northern England, the media scholar Shaun Moores finds that not only was the radio something that was mainly listened to by men, but it was also something that increased women's work: 'I remember once when a battery leaked. It was on the dresser and leaked all over the carpet and left a big white patch. My mother was furious.' Another remembers: 'We used to have the radio on the sideboard – my mother used to be going mad [...] in case it took the polish off the sideboard. My mother didn't like it on there. She was always polishing and that. Well, your home was your palace in them days.'[38]

As the modern house became more and more informal during the twentieth century and into the twenty-first, so the role of the dining room changed. In many respects the idea of a dining room as a place set aside just for formal eating has had to give way to household demands for more everyday sociable space. Dining rooms have become home offices, dens, playrooms or have simply been incorporated into the space of larger 'living' rooms: the kitchen–diner; the lounge–diner. As a room devoted to dining but also prepared to accommodate studious schoolchildren it has an unsettled character: a place of rambunctious socialising, and a place of quiet contemplation. In the dining room you could play 'fondue forfeits' (where you have to undergo a challenge should you drop your bread or crudité in the cauldron of bubbling cheese) or do a jigsaw puzzle. And after dinner, after the washing-up – what then? Upstairs – of course.

The ancient art of bellowing up the stairs.

UPS AND DOWNS

(Stairs, Landings, Corridors)

There is something both exciting and daunting about staircases in other people's houses.. What lurks upstairs? What secrets will be spied through half-open doors? A downstairs toilet in someone else's house seems like a different proposition from one upstairs; in comparison the downstairs toilet seems semi-public.

For some households the downstairs loo is used for an ironic display case for prizes, certificates, accomplishments (well, you assume there is some irony in placing them in the toilet). So while the downstairs loo may reveal something about the household's character in the form of pictures on the wall or magazines to look at (which are there for visitors as well as the household), the upstairs bathroom toilet offers a different form of evidence. There in mirrored cabinets, on shelves or in cupboards are the accoutrements to our vulnerable lives. In there are the chemical compounds that keep our skin taut, our hair lustrous, the pills that keep us child-free, the tonics that stop us falling into despair. It is upstairs that you find out that your colleague wears a wig or your boss is on anti-depressants, or your boyfriend's mum has a large collection of sex toys. Of course, you have to do a bit of snooping to find out much. And a lot of the time you'd rather not be there and you'd rather not know: you want to remain downstairs, where the escape routes are clearly marked. The stairs take you up into a different world: a world of dreams and dermatology, lust and laundry.

As a child, you might quickly scamper past the adult world of 'downstairs' to rocket up the stairs so that you can hole up in a friend's bedroom. At the turn of the twentieth century the painter Paul Nash spent the first years of his life in a large terraced house in London's Kensington. It certainly wasn't a servantless house and boasted a roster of employees: cook, maids, nurse. Such large houses have lots of 'zones', and these zones are distributed vertically as well as horizontally: the basement was a world of cooks and cooking; the ground floor of formal adult life; upper floors of bedrooms of servants, parents, children. (It is hardly surprising that the long-running 1970s' TV drama based around a wealthy Edwardian household and its staff would have stairs in the title twice – *Upstairs, Downstairs* [ITV, 1971–75, revived on the BBC in 2010]). For the child Nash it was upstairs, beyond the rooms of public adulthood, that he felt at home.

It is worth just getting a sense of the lie of the land, so to speak, of Nash's house. He describes it from the perspective of the hallway:

> On climbing its three or four steps and getting inside the front door, I see a dim room across the narrow hall. This is the dining-room which lived in a sort of warm gloom, like a jungle, and looked onto a meaningless garden, actually only an 'ornamental' promenade about twenty yards across between two blocks of houses. [...] Opposite the dining-room was the drawing-room, an entirely unreal place to me.[1]

In this house the little Nash boys were cared for by a nurse and only saw their mother for an hour a night in the drawing room (presumably they spent even less time with their father). Consequently these visits had a formal quality to them. Rooms take on the emotional qualities associated with the kind of care and concern that orchestrate them: for little Paul the ground-floor rooms have an unreal and awkward character that the upstairs nursery didn't have. The stairs function as the passport control to this emotional landscape: 'From this floor [the ground-floor] two stairways started. One down to the kitchen premises in the basement, the other, steep and branching, up to the lighter and airier apartments of the nurseries. On the way was the floor of the important bedrooms and the bathroom.'[2]

These childhood nursery rooms – for sleeping, eating, playing and learning – were not without their difficulties: the young Paul was beset by repeated nightmares. But

for all that it was thus haunted for me, this upper area of the house was by far the happiest. And although they now come only indistinctly into the focus of memory, many wonderful and thrilling happenings occurred there. Wonderful, I mean, in the gauge of a child. For instance, there were games as well as dreams. We were richly endowed in this respect, both naturally, in the range of our imaginations, and materially, by the gifts of a devoted and generous friend known as Mr. Dry. Mr. Dry's Christmas presents were on such a scale and of such a quality as to take the breath away. Soldiers arrived in battalions and army corps, superbly made, the best, obviously, that could be bought. Animals by the zoo, as it were, realistically modelled, each covered with its appropriate skin, for all we could tell, it *was* its skin. Oxen and giraffes had smooth leather coverings, bears had hard harsh hair on their bodies – tremendously convincing.[3]

For a child with family friends this generous, upstairs was a world of fantasy life, of care and play that clearly weren't a 'family life' in any biological sense. In this context the hour spent with mama was anxious; but 'then bedtime would come and we would climb the steep stairs to our happier rooms above'.[4] Paul Nash went on to become one of the few well-known British Surrealist painters, and you could see how the domestic arrangements of his childhood would have prepared him for this: a heightened reality to the world of dreams and toys, and a veil of unreality over the life of familial relations strained by feelings of obligation and emotional distance.

Two worlds separated by stairs. Ever on the look-out for ways of disturbing the niceties of conventions, Surrealist art often took the domestic interior as its subject matter. By altering the logic of our domestic rooms Surrealism revealed the uncanny potential of homely life. Artists such as René Magritte and Max Ernst took prototypical *haut bourgeois* drawing rooms and twisted them into something else. For Magritte sideboard mirrors reflect back not the visage that looks at them but the impossible view of the back of the head that is looking; for Ernst the Victorian interior is spliced and spiced with exotic animals and improbable people. But it was the much less well-known women Surrealist painters, such as Leonora Carrington, Eileen Agar, Leonor Fini and Dorothea Tanning, who did most to make evident the strange moods that are evoked, particularly in those in-between spaces in the house.

It is Dorothea Tanning who provides the most uncanny renderings of the house, and it is appropriate that in doing this she focuses her vision on the corridors and staircases of the domestic interior. The word 'uncanny' is the nearest equivalent to the German word *unheimlich* – which literally translates as 'unhomely'. It refers to the spooky feeling we have when we find something weird at the heart of what is most familiar. Tanning's two best-known paintings, *Birthday* (1942) and *Eine Kleine Nachtmusik* (1943), are both set in corridors. In *Birthday* the artist has painted herself standing, bare-chested and with a skirt made from branches, in front of what looks like an endless series of half-open doors; crouching in front of her is an animal that looks like a winged marmoset. *Eine Kleine Nachtmusik* is even more uncanny: we see the top of the stairs and four doors along a corridor. Three of the doors are closed, and one is open only a tiny amount, and light is coming from there. The walls are old and cracked. In the corridor are two young girls with long hair: one child's hair hangs down, the other's floats upwards towards the ceiling as if gravity has been reversed. At the top of the stairs lies a gigantic sunflower head. It uses the usual jolts of Surrealism: strange dislocations in scale, the displacements of items from different realms. Yet it is the setting, I think, that does all the uncanny work: we are at the top of the stairs, and we don't quite know where to go next.

The staircase can be a difficult, in-between space, especially for children. You drag your feet going up there when it is time for you to go to bed; you edge down the stairs when you know you should be in bed but you can't sleep. Stairs are where children often first glimpse the adult social world as they surreptitiously spy their parents' parties when they should be sleeping, or cautiously try to see what the babysitter and her boyfriend are up to in the sitting room. Stairs are for overhearing, for glimpsing – and it is this that gives them an uncanny character.

And stairs are also about display. The wall to which one side of a stair is usually attached is often the largest wall space in the house: it is also the wall that we get closest to. The staircase in the official house of the British prime minister uses this wall to provide a history lesson. As you ascend the stairs in 10 Downing Street you meet all the previous prime ministers. A new incumbent must feel that taking the stairs to bed is like taking your place in history. Some households offer the same effect by providing family photographs where you can see babies turning into toddlers and then into teenagers, and then grown-ups growing greyer and more portly as you climb the stairs. Going to bed there is ascending to old age.

The novelist Ruth Rendell, writing under her pseudonym Barbara Vine, has, to my mind, created some of the most unnerving stories in the English language. Her writing often centres on a disparate collection of adults living together in a house. It isn't, I think, incidental that the novel with the most apprehensive mood is titled *The House of Stairs*. It's a story of love, infatuation and ruthlessness, in which the house seems to take on the role of a character in the drama. The house that drives the narrative is owned and directed by a rich widow who runs a quasi-commune for young people. Like Paul Nash's house, this is clearly a large, terraced house that accommodates a large number of rooms scattered across many levels. But it's much poorer and narrower than Nash's – almost one room piled on top of another – where the stairs constitutes a large proportion of the interior space. The scruffy gentility and upmarket hippiedom that result seem to encourage an easy sociability, and, to begin with, impromptu celebrations seem to be a regular occurrence. Yet in the house of stairs the mood shifts as the narrative progresses.

It is the house as a place built round an elaborate set of stairs that both connects the different rooms and separates them that seems most important. When Cosette (the wealthy widow) buys the house, it initially seems unpromising. For Elizabeth, the narrator of the story, Cosette becomes her substitute mother when her real mother dies. For her the house of stairs on first sight just seems old and inconvenient: 'I saw it as big, old, dirty and cold, the stairs a curse and a handicap, the arrangement of the rooms – the kitchen was in the basement, all the best living and sleeping space loftily high up – seemingly designed to be as inconvenient as could be, the steep staircase and windows dangerous.' Set in late 1960s' and early 1970s' London, Elizabeth's reaction to the house is not unusual: Victorian and Edwardian terraced houses seemed to many – including those who actually lived in them – ugly, impractical and ripe for demolition. It will be the gentrifiers (of whom Cosette could be an early example) and their cultural agents who will shift the meaning of these houses.

It is not long before the house has been transformed, and the changes centre on the stairs. The stair windows have been 'festooned with curtains in slub silk and curtains in velvet, with Roman blinds and Austrian blinds and Chinese bead curtains that were mêlées of rainbows when they moved and showed pastoral pictures, remote and oriental, when they hung still. […] the stairs carpeted now in blood red.'[5] Perhaps the blood-red stair carpet is the clue to what will unfold in this house of 109 stairs. Much of the tension of the novel is played out in the day-to-day comings and goings of a household where footsteps echo on stairs and corridors and tell of arrivals and departures. A lover's footsteps passing by your bedroom door as they ascend to their own is the sound of foreboding.

Storage, safety and copper sulphate crystals

Unless a staircase is part of a room (as in the stairs of open-plan houses or workers' cottages, for instance), then the stairs takes you from one indeterminate place to another: from hallway to landing. And around these spaces are often nooks and crannies, cupboards and alcoves. It is here that we can glimpse something of the intestines and nervous system of the house. Most crucially there is the space beneath the staircase. In many houses this is the central storage cupboard, where mops and brooms and a myriad of household items live in a precariously haphazard fashion, with the thing you need stuffed behind a teetering mountain of clutter. Under-stair space was crucial in houses with limited room, and there you could find coal storage, ovens, bicycles and so on. A single under-stairs cupboard is unusual (how would you reach the final inner wedge?), and doors are often arranged as a small suite of differently sized cupboards – with a little wedge-shaped cupboard for tiny things perhaps. It is as if the house is planning for the three bears to take possession.

Around stairwells and landings you find a host of pipes: inlets and outlets, fuses, meters. In the days before combi-boilers the upstairs landing was often the place where the airing cupboard could be found. In newer houses in the post-war period this was often a built-in cupboard with an immersion heater in it and a number of wooden-slatted shelves. Here was where the hot-water tank lived, coated in an early form of the puffer jacket. Whether it was on or not, the airing cupboard seemed less suitable for airing (surely outside would be the best place for that?) than for very gentle steaming. The climate of the airing cupboard was like stepping outside in Singapore: a blanket of warm, slightly damp air greeted you. Lovely. It was perfect for growing yogurt, for germinating tomatoes and for the important business of growing copper sulphate crystals (a common school chemistry project), whose sapphire-blue gleam made you feel like a magician.

Airing-cupboards were a world unto themselves. In these tropical cupboards lived bedding and towels. If people came to stay and beds needed to be made up, then a trip to the airing cupboard was in order. Airing cupboards weren't just part of day-to-day life: they came into their own at special times (when you were trying to grow crystals). The philosopher Richard Wollheim remembers the airing cupboard as having a distinct annual role in marking the seasons:

> Winter came round with its own relentlessness, and it began on the day when the clothes I had been wearing for the past

few months – aertex shirts, khaki shorts, cotton underpants – were, without any discussion, taken out of my chest-of-drawers and cupboard, and replaced by another lot – viyella shirts, tweed shorts, woollen combinations – which were stored on shelves of wooden slats, surrounding a metal boiler held together by rivets, in a small, steamy room, called the airing-cupboard.[6]

During the Second World War the staircase was part of civil defence. Seen as a structurally protective part of the house, the under-stair could become a place of relative safety: 'I used to keep all the brooms and brushes in the cupboard under the stairs, but now we've a camp-bed under there for the air raids you know, for babe.'[7] The fear of air attack, which was such a crucial part of the lead-up to the Second World War and such a real part of many people's experience of that war, continued into the post-war era in a more amorphous fear of air attack and air-borne threats. In the official guides telling you how to prepare for air attacks in the late 1930s the need is to prepare both for blast and for the possibility of gas. Turning the house into a place of safety was a crucial aspect of this. From the 1950s through to the 1990s the threat changed, but in many respects it was articulated in a similar way in the advice literature that was handed out.

Government leaflets such as 1980's famous *Protect and Survive* pamphlet encouraged you to ready yourself in case of a nuclear attack. Admitting that if you lived anywhere within five miles of a bomb being dropped you would be immediately wiped off the face of the planet, it still suggested preparing a 'fall-out' room. A slightly odd naming, then, as it was 'fall-out', the nuclear radiation, which you were hoping to be protected from: it would be like calling a room designed to isolate you from illness the 'plague room'. Again it was thought that staircases would be useful and that you could incorporate them as part of your 'inner refuge'.

The inner refuge would be the place you would hide out in for a couple of weeks if nuclear war was imminent. To turn your under-stairs cupboard into an inner refuge you would need to 'put bags of earth or sand on the stairs and along the wall of the cupboard. If the stairs are on an outside wall strengthen the wall outside in the same way to a height of six feet.'[8] Of course, earth and staircase would have had little effect in protecting you from radiation – but in a society that didn't have the resources to protect the majority of its population from nuclear Armageddon it might have looked like the government was out to protect the gullible.

Up the wooden hill to Bedfordshire

The night-time saying that signalled for children that it was bedtime imagined stairs and bed in a safe suburban world of home-counties life: to go to bed was to climb 'the wooden hill to Bedfordshire'. But if stairs became 'wooden hills', and beds turned into Bedfordshire, then these were endlessly inappropriate metaphors to apply to the chronic worlds of pre-war and post-war overcrowding in the poorest areas of cities. In the worst working-class houses the stairs didn't separate distinct emotional areas so much as signal a structure that could barely function to hold up the house. In Arthur Elton and Edgar Anstey's film *Housing Problems* (British Commercial Gas Association, 1935) one of the production team – Ruby Grierson – was responsible for what was then a radical departure in documentary film: getting people to talk about their own experiences. In a set of interviews householders having to endure the worst housing talk about what their houses are like and what goes on there. One woman begins: 'this house is getting on my nerves. We're shored up in every room. There's the staircase you can't walk up if you get seasick; you need one leg longer than the other. The upstairs is coming downstairs, where it's sinking.'

The terrible overcrowding and awful state of much of the worst housing are given added indignity by the sense of the staircase being unable to separate a world of sleep from elsewhere in the house. And it is here in these impoverished conditions that space is necessarily flexible. A downstairs parlour might well be 'kept for best', but it might also have to exist as a child's bedroom at night. Landings, which are designed as simply platforms for distributing upstairs rooms, take on a different significance in overcrowded slums:

> I live in one room with my husband and child. We have no facilities or privacy when my husband wants to undress he has to go out in the corridor to take his trousers off so that our little girl shouldn't see. At night time when the child's in bed she keeps telling me to put out the light. Then my husband shouts at me to keep it on. So I just put on my coat and walk out and leave them to fight it out. I'm not complaining though – there are people not half so lucky as we are – we have got a roof over our heads.[9]

A staircase divides and unites the house. It is a place of passing. For those that live in large houses with multiple household occupancy, the staircase can be a place of nodded 'good mornings' or embarrassed mutterings. It is often a disconcerting experience to stay in those holiday houses that want to make the most of the glimpse that they offer of the sea by putting the bedrooms on the ground floor and the reception rooms above them. Our bodies seem to have been attuned to the expectation that going upstairs should take us to a private realm of dreams and desire. But before we get to rooms of dreams and desires we need to stop off to go to the place where nature calls.

To pamper or not, that is the question

NOW WASH YOUR HANDS

(Bathrooms and Toilets)

My father and my brothers used to go out in the back to the
shed to bath in summer, but in winter they came into the
kitchen. My mother filled the casks with hot water and left
wooden buckets full of hot and cold for sluicing. When they
had finished and put on their best clothes they came in the
kitchen for the Saturday dinner, which was always special.[1]

It is hard to imagine the kinds of scenario that the builders of
new 'luxury' homes – and who would dare build a home that
didn't have luxury as its main adjective? – had in mind when they
were ordering toilets and bathrooms. Toilets seem to outnumber
householders in most of these new buildings. At the same time
architectural proportions seem to be getting meaner. The new
estates mix 'social housing' (legislation demands it) with speculative profit-based housing to create domestic spaces that feel
squeezed: if you should meet someone on the stairs in one of the
new houses, then one of you has to go back and start again. The
style is, in the main, neo-old-fashioned (Georgian-Barratt or
Prince-Charles-Pastiche), and the layout of estates nods towards

garden-city culs-de-sac. In these enclaves toilets seem to be multiplying: everywhere you turn there's an opportunity to evacuate.
Perhaps the building firms involved have some inside knowledge
of new gastric viruses that will soon become so extreme that one
toilet per person is going to be the bare minimum requirement
(and it makes sense to have a spare one in reserve, just in case).
Perhaps there is a sense that in the future no one will be prepared
to see *their* toilet, or bath, or shower as something to share with
anyone.

The twentieth-century British bathroom was caught between
an idea of a room with a minimal set of amenities (bath and
WC) and the possibilities of a more luxurious room dedicated
to pampering yourself. The proliferating bathroom that you find
in new-builds is often a minimalist affair of bath (with shower
attachment), basin and toilet, placed so as to take up the least
amount of space. At the start of the twentieth century most
houses in England and Britain had no separate room for the bath
and many had no internal plumbing of any sort, and certainly no
fixed toilet. Baths were things that hung on the wall in the scullery or in the backyard: toilets were outbuildings shared between
a number of households (or chamber-pots to be kept under
beds). Today the idea of a house without plumbing wouldn't be
conceivable – it is our minimum requirement. Yet we are still
ambivalent about how we think of bathrooms and their fixtures:
should we opt for functional minimalism or opulent maximal-
ism? Do we treat our ablutions primarily as part of a strict health
and hygiene regimen (a bit like going to the gym), or do we think
our bathrooms should be primarily about indulgence?

As a place that has often had to filch space from the hallway
or is a ramshackle extension, the bathroom is not a room easily
dedicated to hedonism. But it could have been different. At the
start of the twentieth century the very words 'English Bathroom'
signalled the height of luxury:

England fashioned the luxury bathroom of the world. No other country equalled the quality and distinction of English sanitary articles between 1880 and 1910. [...] The bath of 1900 calls for a spacious room possessing a number of windows. The expensive fixtures were placed at dignified distances from one another. The central space was ample enough for moving freely about, even for exercising.[2]

For Sigfried (sometimes mistakenly given as Siegfried) Giedion, the pioneering Swiss historian of design and architecture, the squeezed bathroom is partly the result of the influence of hotels, but here his example is from the United States. The idea of the en-suite, though, is connected to a sort of standard luxury en-suite associated with chain hotels:

> as regards the trend of a bathroom for every bedroom, this has become rather accepted general practice amongst leading architects and builders throughout the country; in fact, the real requirements for good homes at the present time are a bathroom for each bedroom and a powder room or a small washroom on the main floor adjoining the living-room and the dining-room for guest use.[3]

The standardised bathroom suite and the cramped arrangement that it takes is much more likely to have developed owing to the lack of space in many older houses that were built before 'running hot water' for ordinary people could have been imagined.

Toilets and bathrooms are never simply practical places; or, even at their most practical, they also deal in phenomena that anthropologists treat as foundational for 'who we are' as a culture. While modern secular societies often pride themselves on their rationalism and pragmatism, one glimpse at a bathroom should remind us of all those arational and irrational rituals that are so common as to be almost invisible but which also define us as certain types of creatures. Do we shave off underarm hair or not? Are armpits coated in antiperspirant or not? Perfumes, tweezers, dyes, varnishes, conditioners, brushes, buffers and pumice stones – all the tools of our ritual care – reside in our bathroom cupboards. The Martian anthropologist would immediately take an interest in all the paraphernalia required to keep up our appearances, but would perhaps be even more interested in our ablutions and evacuations. Why do some people use paper to clean their bottoms after a bowel movement (as the medics say) while others wash them? What sort of cruelty was involved in designing toilet paper that was shiny and non-absorbent (the Izal medicated toilet tissue, for instance, favoured by schools, hospitals and prisons)? Why is there 'toilet humour' but not 'kitchen humour'? What is the etiquette about leaving reading material for guests who use a downstairs toilet? Is it OK to leave light-hearted journalism (especially if it comes in handy page-and-a-half chunks), but not OK to leave philosophical tomes on existentialism (slightly pretentious, or conducive to a motion)? The Martian anthropologist wouldn't have to look far, I think, to see an infant fascination with our waste product followed by an increasing disgust with bodily excreta, to the point where civilisation seems to be founded on hiding any sign of it. In this instance those who hose themselves down may have reached a higher plane than those who paper.

For most of the twentieth century the question of how and where you wash and how and where you go to the toilet was one of the surest indicators of social class: as the Mass-Observation report had it, 'whether or not a house possesses a bathroom has become a major social dividing line'.[4] Yet it was the new council houses from between the wars that introduced hot water, bathrooms and indoor toilets probably more quickly than many privately rented houses aimed at the lower middle class and prosperous working classes. And this was because the council housing was new housing stock while the private housing was often the stock from a previous century. The history of bathrooms and toilets in the modern period is a history connected to taboos and conventions, infrastructural changes and domestic technology, and money. It is also a story of uneven modernisation.

In her autobiography the theatre director Joan Littlewood, who was born in 1914, remembers washing as a baby in her house in south London:

> As a baby Caroline Emily washed me in a zinc bath by the kitchen fire, and Grandad would sit in his corner watching till she handed me to him, wrapped in a warm towel. Then I was rocked and jigged to the bawdy songs he'd learnt in the army. The adults were not so privileged. Monday night was bath night, because Monday was wash day. All the dirty washing went into Gran's copper in the scullery; clouds of steam escaped every time she lifted the lid. […] When the wash was done, the hot grey water was bailed out of the copper and lugged up two flights of stairs, bucket by bucket. The bathroom was splendid, with double doors, a wide window bordered with stained glass, a bath with claw feet – but no plumbing. My grandfather liked the bathroom; he reared his canaries there.[5]

Having a bath and a bathroom then wasn't necessarily an indication that you had the infrastructural amenities to make a bath a quick and convenient option for washing.

Indeed many people who had a bath simply carried on using the sink in the scullery for washing their bodies. In an attempt to give a fairly exhaustive account of an Exmoor village at the end of the Second World War, W. J. Turner, working for Mass-Observation, gives an account of the twenty-four cottages that make up the village to ascertain whether any of them have baths. 'There are baths in the two new council cottages', reads the report, with cold taps and drains. Mrs Howard uses hers for the children, who have a weekly tub from water heated in the copper. The next-door bath is not used, as there are only kettles for water-heating. One villager has a bath in her kitchen, but without outlet and not used; another has a hip-bath, which is not used either. None of the cottages has a water-heating system, and so far as can be ascertained it is the usual and perhaps universal practice in the village to have a strip-wash in a basin.[6]

The village had no gas supply and no electricity supply at the time, and in this it wasn't particularly unusual. The very fact that the council had built houses with fixed baths but only fitted a cold water tap suggests that the move from the bath in the kitchen, filled from the water boiled in the copper, to a bath with hot and cold running water was anything but simple.

Mass-Observation's large wartime survey about conditions of working-class housing revealed a host of concerns about levels of sanitation and the difficult practices of using baths without proper hot water – or, more fundamentally, without a decent water supply at all. For one a fixed bath was spoilt by the fact that his house didn't even have its own indoor cold running water: 'it wouldn't be so bad if you didn't have to go outside for water'. Another householder also noted that 'there's no water. I have to go down to the cellar for every drop. There's a tap in the yard, but she [the neighbour] won't let me use it.' For another, with a rudimentary pumping system between the copper in the kitchen and fixed bath upstairs, it was the length of time and effort that was the problem: 'the copper makes a mess and I don't like the pumping system. It takes two hours to get a bath ready.'[7]

Settling down and coming indoors
The long story of bathrooms and toilets in the modern age is, according to Sigfried Giedion in his indispensable *Mechanization*

Takes Command, a double story. On the one hand, it is the story of communal amenities become private; on the other, it is the story of nomadic objects (such as commodes) that stop roaming and become fixed in space. The story of communal washing becoming private takes place over centuries and isn't a straight-forward linear progression. For instance, in the last few centuries in Britain the high point of communal washing (public washing baths) was in the early decades of the twentieth century. There are still vestiges of communal washing in the popularity of steam rooms and saunas, but the historical sense of 'vapour-cleansing' as a form of hygiene has mostly been lost in Britain: today saunas and steam rooms are connected to relaxation, detoxification and skin therapy (this, at any rate, is how spas advertise themselves).

The bath is a vivid example of a portable domestic device that gets fixed in the house: 'furniture in the Middle Ages passed from nomadic to a stable condition. And in the nineteenth century this happened to the bath. The portable bath turned into a fixed bath anchored within a complex network of piping and ventilation. In medieval times, nomadicism was the result of instability of living conditions; in our own period, of the instability of our orienta-tion.'[8] Tin baths that once happily graced the kitchen floor one moment then the outside wall another finally settle down and find their place in the house. The bath achieves a room of its own. Chamber-pots, which once happily roamed domestic interiors, waiting patiently under beds at night, slopped out in the communal WC in the morning, have grown a base and stopped moving.

Before the fully flushing, main-drains-connected toilet, def-ecating and urinating involved a lot more implements and a lot more people. 'Night soil' – that wonderful euphemism for human poo – would be regularly collected by an army of workers. In the centuries leading up to the twentieth century prosperous houses would have a 'house of office' (a toilet) in the garden that would need to be emptied. In more ordinary housing human waste would flow in open drains down the street. But the nineteenth and twentieth centuries saw a revolution in plumbing and in sewerage. The massive eruption in speculative housing and housing built for industrial workers in the nineteenth century made new provision for toilets. For middling houses (the by-law terrace house of three or four bedrooms) it would be usual for each house to have its own outside toilet. For smaller houses (back-to-backs, small terraced houses and cheaper housing in general) it would be usual for many households to share the same toilet.

When in 1936 George Orwell visited the working-class housing of the industrial north, he constantly noted the length between the backdoor and the nearest toilet (50 yards, 70 yards and so on). In certain arrangements of housing (particularly the back-to-back housing) it might mean that you had to walk several hundred yards before you got to 'your' nearest designated toilet. In a memorable passage from *The Road to Wigan Pier* Orwell recounts one particular conversation:

> Talking once with a miner I asked him when the housing shortage first became acute in his district; he answered, 'When we were told about it' [...] when he was a child his family had slept eleven in a room and thought nothing of it, and later, when he was grown-up, he and his wife had lived in one of the old-style back to back houses in which you not only had to walk a couple of hundred yards to the lavatory but often had to wait in a queue when you got there, the lavatory being shared by thirty-six people. And when his wife was sick with the illness that killed her, she still had to make that two hundred yards' journey to the lavatory.[9]

The communal aspect of the toilet was obvious in the queuing as well as in the business of emptying chamber-pots. The practice of many households sharing the same toilet was a common aspect of the worst housing and carried on into the 1960s. A newspaper report about the housing in Glasgow could report in 1958 that in the Gorbals district 'less than one house in four has a lavatory, and about one in 30 a bath – the same situation as existed 30 years ago'.[10]

It seems likely that the gradual but wholehearted privatisation of the toilet has altered our relationship to the human waste matter emanating from our bodies and from others. The British were, it seems, at one time more unabashed about the communal possibilities afforded by the commode. A French American in 1810, in a state of obvious bewilderment, asks: 'Will it be credited, that in the corner of the very dining room there is a certain convenient piece of furniture to be used by anybody who wants it? The operation is performed very deliberately and undisguisedly, as a matter of course, and occasions no interruption of conversation.'[11] It should be noted that such behaviour in an obviously fairly well-to-do house would only take place among men, once the women had withdrawn after dinner. By the twentieth century such communal behaviour would have ended, not least because for this class the indoor flushed toilet would now be a part of their domestic life. But for those without inside toilets, chamber-pot use was universal. George Orwell notes the constant presence of chamber-pots in the houses where he stays. He seems to have gone out of his way to find not just the meanest housing but the dirtiest householders to lodge with: 'On the day when there was a full chamber-pot under the breakfast table I decided to leave. The place was beginning to depress me.'[12] Such practices, it would be fair to say, would have been unusual in the extreme: much more common for people to show discretion in chamber-pot use.

The practice of turning one or more of the rooms in a house into a room for a lodger was a common practice, particularly if the household was trying to eke out a living on a single wage. But this put even more pressure on limited facilities in many houses, maintaining its communal feel against the more general tendency towards private space. In tales of migration this aspect of shared living was often simply impoverished rather than convivial. In the tales of Caribbean migrants coming to Britain in the late 1940s to lodge within a household privacy was particularly hard to come by. Linda Small remembers taking a room in one of the few houses that didn't just turn her away because of her skin colour:

> He had a basement room. I walked in and there was a bed, a little stove, a sink, and a little table. I put my suitcase down and opened a door, because I thought it led to another room, but it was the wardrobe. I said to the Landlord, 'How we gonna cook and do everything in here?' He told me 'You'll get used to it. Everybody has to do it.' I couldn't get used to it. I told him that I wanted to use the toilet so he told me that I had to put my coat back on and go through his kitchen to the toilet outside. I came back and cried. I wrote my mum and told her what had happened. Back home they thought it was a joke because they couldn't understand it.[13]

The inside toilet and the fixed bath had to struggle to become incorporated into the housing stock because nearly all of it had been built without any idea that such a state of affairs would be possible for modest-income households. The early decades of the twentieth century saw the 'double shelled, enamelled tub' becoming affordable:

> around 1915 the domestic bathtub appears in its now famil-iar recessed form. But only around 1920 could the double-shelled, enamelled tub be made in one piece and put out in mass production. Its price was thus cut by some 20 per cent. Soon the five-foot tub established itself as the standard; it amounts to 75 per cent of the present output. The tub became a module determining the breadth of the cell, while the basin and toilet at minimal distances determine the long wall.[14]

But the usable bathroom needs more than a cheap bath: it needs running hot water, and it needs drainage. If these things aren't there, then the fixed bath is used in the way that Joan Littlewood's family used it: filled with hot water carried upstairs in pails from the kitchen copper. And this was the situation that many found themselves in. Like the proverbial chicken and egg, it is difficult to imagine which came first – the fixed bath or the plumbed infrastructure of drainage and water pipes. For some it was probably a massive all-in-one modernisation. But for many it would have been *ad hoc* and piecemeal.

One of the biggest problems was the affordability and capacity of hot water systems. Thus

an electric geyser was developed in 1912 that provided boiling water at the rate of 12 pints a minute. It was smaller and more compact than anything else available at the time and cost £14. 'There was just one snag', said its inventor Charles Belling – who would become one of the most successful producers of electric ovens and fires, 'it took a 10kW load which in those days dimmed the lights for miles around.'[15]

It was later in the 1930s that the bathroom became a possibility for many as the technology improved and became more affordable:

after the [First World] War there was a great and continuing boom in sales and between 1930 and 1937 the number of British houses possessing bathrooms doubled. Even today, however, in the affluent Britain of the early seventies one and half million households lack a bath of their own. The provision of such essentials has yet to match the excellence of the water service, so long perfected and so reliable that it is almost taken for granted.[16]

The massive expansion in the number of bathrooms in the twentieth century meant having to find the space for a new room or new rooms. Many of the add-on extensions that you see today on the back of Victorian and Edwardian housing were built to allow for the provision of a bath and a toilet. A bathroom often had to be squeezed in where it could: 'a bathroom could be added above the single- or two-storey "offices" at the rear'; 'a bathroom could be filched from a bedroom'; 'stair landings were sometimes just big enough to squeeze in a bath cubicle'.[17] Similarly indoor toilets were either added as part of the squeezed-in bathroom or had to find room downstairs in houses that were often lacking in space as it was. The under-the-stairs cupboard became the under-the-stairs toilet for many, as it was the only space available.

Many people had had their houses modernised through the addition of a ground-floor bathroom at the back of the house. But 'downstairs bathrooms are unpopular since people consider them inconvenient in case of illness. Baths built into bedrooms are disliked for the same reason. Another unpopular feature is the scullery bath, and some people have on their own initiative taken the bath away, while many others would like to see it removed.'[18] All houses, it was argued by one observer, should have 'upstairs bathrooms, and have water running into the bath, as we have. We did that ourselves, but most houses here have to bail water to their baths with a pail. It's so dangerous. Now and again the pail slips, and there's a nasty accident.' The lack of fixtures was also a problem: 'washbasins in bathrooms are another fixture so far absent from working-class homes, and yet very much in demand. At present, apart from the weekly bath which most working-class people take, they have to wash in the scullery. This arrangement is heartily disliked by most.'[19]

It is perhaps logical that, if human waste is an object of disgust, then we might want it as far away from us as possible. Instead we append toilets to bedrooms but favour gleaming white toilets that have to be kept spotlessly clean. In the 1940s the lavatory was not something that you necessarily wanted upstairs: 'the lavatory is upstairs. It should be downstairs where there are children. An outside lavatory would be better.' There is a suggestion among some that the house was not really the place for such things: 'the lavatory shouldn't be in the house at all. It should be in the garden.' And if there was going to be an inside toilet, then it certainly wasn't the place for receiving the evacuations of grown men: 'there should be an outdoor lavatory for a family, as well as one inside, where there's men. I think that should be done.'[20] There may well be people who still think that this isn't a bad idea.

It will be in the 1950s and through into the late '60s that there is the final big push, if you'll excuse the terminology, via new large-scale social housing developments and through the post-war 'slum' clearance schemes, when about 95 per cent of all households have fixed baths and indoor toilets. Other forms of *ad hoc* modernisation will be achieved through gentrification – by the middle classes taking on run-down and un-modernised housing in working-class areas of town and refitting them and selling them on at hugely inflated prices. While today we might think it is somehow unseemly not to have an indoor toilet, it wasn't that long ago that the idea of not having an outdoor toilet seemed fairly barbaric.

The Mass-Observation survey describes an indoor toilet where the sense of *ad hoc* building and decoration practices is clearly evident:

> Orange wallpaper, very stained and dirty. On the floor dull brown linoleum, with a faint diamond pattern, only just visible. On the floor in front of the seat is a circular small mat, made of wool, with a blue and red pattern on it. The cistern and pipes are bright green, recently painted. The chain is broken, and a piece of string has been tied to the remaining

part to make it long enough. There is torn-up newspaper behind the cistern instead of toilet roll.[21]

In impoverished housing the recent piecemeal modernisation could quickly look like the unkempt outside toilet of old.

Efficiency and luxury

In his endlessly informative *Clean and Decent: The Fascinating History of the Bathroom and the Water-Closet*, Lawrence Wright tells us that bathing has never been an activity with a single purpose or a single set of practices. For the ancient Greeks it was connected to gymnastics and was meant to be 'brief, cold and invigorating', while for the Romans and for Islam it was about 'relaxation, bodily refreshment and resultant well-being'.[22] Today British householders' washing regimens might fall into two distinct categories: those who favour showers and those who, given a choice, would prefer a bath. Those who opt for showers might argue that the benefits of a shower are that you don't wallow in your own dirty water; they might argue for the revivifying effects of getting blasted by jets of scorching water; they might say it is more environmentally friendly. Devotees to the benefits of the shower have long praised its efficiency and practicality: 'whether we consult sources of 1850 or those of 1890, we find popularisation of the shower advocated for identical reasons: showers consume less water, less space, less time, require fewer repairs. In use, moreover, they are more hygienic than the tub bath.'[23]

Bath users may be a more hedonistic bunch and don't mind wallowing in their own 'dirty' water. A bath, it would seem, offers more opportunities for relaxation. A well-known manufacturer of bath products (up-market bubble bath) calls its potions 'bath therapy', with various concoctions designed to help relaxation (with lavender and water-lily), relieve stress (rosemary and eucalyptus), aid sleep (camomile and jasmine) and rejuvenate you through 'eastern spirit' (lotus flower and orange blossom). In 1947 a well-known hot water system could advertise itself by stressing its ability to de-stress the owner of a water heater: 'How smoothly the troubles and problems of this world sort themselves out under the influence of a hot bath. How quickly constant hot water tames the bogey of washing up.'[24] The plumbing industry has, in recent times, joined forces with a New Age therapy culture: 'it's well known that a warm, soothing bath is the best antidote for stress. But what's less known is that you can enhance the already soothing effects of water by using bath products with calming essences like sandalwood, lavender, vanilla or chamomile.'[25] Aside from the New Age spin, washing has always had a luxuriating side – especially when it wasn't conducted in the scullery.

The idea of the bath as a de-stressing phenomenon may well have something to do with the relaxing abilities of hot water and pleasant-smelling lotions, but it also may have something to do with the bathroom being the one room in the house where it is OK to lock the door and where you can spend some time doing nothing without being bothered by others. For mothers with young kids a bath may offer the only way of escaping the constant demands of kids. This, at any rate, is the basis for the children's story *Five Minutes' Peace*. The over-taxed mother in a family of anthropo-morphised elephants just wants 'five minutes peace' before she has to get back to her role as Mrs Large the mother to various elephant children who constantly fight and demand her atten-tion: 'Mrs Large ran a deep, hot bath. She emptied half a bottle of bath-foam into the water, plonked on her bath-hat and got in. She poured herself a cup of tea and lay back with her eyes closed. It was heaven.'[26] Unfortunately Mrs Large doesn't have the requisite strength of mind or heartlessness to keep the door locked and ends up letting her children into the room and finally into the bath itself.

The efficiency and science side of washing has often had the upper hand, partly because it plays to all our fears about hygiene and health, but also because the British bathroom has not always been a place that has been very good at accommodating luxury. Today the trick seems to be to see the negotiation of luxury and hygiene as an endless opportunity to sell you more stuff, rather than as a contradiction. You can see it in bathroom units, with their white and chrome hospital aesthetic coupled with flowery, fluffy towels. But I always think that the conflict is most vividly caught in the advertising of bathroom products: shampoos, soaps, deodorants, skincare products and so on. The adverts for these products seem to vacillate between white-coated scientists busy at work making serums in preposterous-sounding places (Laboratoires Garnier is surely the lair of Bond villains) and images of 'lovely ladies' popping up out of crystal-clear lakes in the middle of a tropical forest with newly washed lustrous locks (and not a mosquito in sight). On the one hand, all the accoutrements of science and rationality; on the other, unspoilt and non-existent nature. Both are invented: the first through the liberal use of Latin-sounding words, the second by the absurd vision of such ludicrous nature (a place that, if it was pollution-free at the start of the advert, is now brimming with detergents – from all that hair-washing).

Claire Rayner, the famous agony aunt, managed to get efficiency and luxury to coincide in her odd little book on housework from 1967. It often adopts a feminist tone but still assumes not only that it is women who are doing the housework but also that it is women who will continue to do it. Perhaps, all things considered, it is Rayner assuming that sexual equality will be a long time coming and in the meantime women might as well do such chores with the absolute minimum of effort. So out the window go any attempts to be a domestic goddess who would keep the house spotless, to be replaced by a modern 'houseworker' who can fit in the odd bit of crafty tidying between her other commitments and interests.

Rayner's account of bathroom cleaning is worth relating in detail. It begins with a gleaming white bath:

Our house had a new bath tub put into it five years ago and I can assure readers with my hand on my heart that never once has this bath been purposely cleaned. This is not to say that there is a five inch thick ring of grease round it; far from it. It is gleaming and white and so attractive that I'm almost tempted to take people on a tour of my bathroom merely to show it off. No. The answer to this mystery is quite a simple one.

It must be magic, surely? Or some fancy self-cleaning bath imagined by Alison and Peter Smithson for their 'House of the Future' in the 1950s. But it isn't: it is hedonism turned into efficiency:

> Whenever anyone takes a bath, from the youngest up to the oldest, they are encouraged (if not *forced*) to use something in the water that will soften it, for it is hard water that causes grease to precipitate on to the side of the bath. This can either take the form of bath salts (for the older members of the family), a handful of washing soda for the really hardy ones, bubble baths for the older romantic minded and special non-eye-stinging bubble baths for the very young. When it comes to my turn I usually find that all the washing soda has been used up and all the bath salts have disappeared and the children have finished up every scrap of my bubble bath so that I am reduced to using a handful of ordinary detergent powder or the last squeezing of the washing up detergent bottle.[27]

Now those who want to luxuriate for hours at a time in a steaming bath can do so in the knowledge that they are also involved in a little bit of housework at the same time to assuage any vestigial guilt. Now 'therapy' bath products can be thought of as household necessities.

The balance between practicality and luxury in bathrooms shifts in the 1970s, when Britain was changing from being a predominantly renting population to one where the majority of households were owner-occupiers, and when central heating was found in most houses. At this point, for many at least, the bathroom becomes a room for 'ordinary' luxury. (There has, after all, always been élite luxury in the bathrooms of the wealthy.) As the 1972 *Daily Mail Ideal Home Exhibition* put it:

> Today, the bathroom is looked on as being one of the luxury areas in the modern home. More and more houses are being designed with two bathrooms – one opening off the principal bedroom, the other serving children and/or guests. Inevitably it is the bathroom *en suite* with the master bedroom that has the most luxurious appointments; the other must of necessity be simpler and more practical.[28]

If, in the immediate post-war period, it became clear that the lack of a bathroom was a significant marker of poverty and that a bathless house was a house in need of development, then the 1970s began the period when an en-suite bathroom became a way of signifying your commitment to being modern (as well as the amount of cash you have at your disposal).

The 1972 Ideal Home Exhibition went on to offer two versions of the bathroom. The first was the en-suite bathroom designed for adults. This bathroom was

> Carpeted in a new deep-pile Acrilan weave, a Persian-inspired design in off-white and lime. Walls are part tiled in a striking large-scale design in almond-green on white, part covered in pale greenish-gold vinyl wall-covering with the shimmering matt finish of pure silk. [...] the bathroom suite is in a subtle greenish sand colour with gilded controls. The bath itself is splendid, generously proportioned with wide white marble surround and fluted bath panels; twin His and

Hers oval basins, each with mirror above framed in a shallow arched alcove, are set in a marble-topped vanity unit.[29]

The 'His and Hers' twin basins suggests a growing accumulation of emollients, special soaps (coal tar for him, Pears for her), razors (His and Hers) and so on that require accumulating basins. The green bath will definitely go out of fashion in a few years, as too will the idea of carpeting the bathroom (cold, squelchy carpets are no one's idea of luxury).

For the kids and for guests things are quite different: 'the children share a colourful bathroom with pine-panelled walls and bright tangerine floor – spongeable nylon cord carpet that is warm under foot, and dries fast after splashing. Their bathroom suite is in smart two-tone donkey-brown with gleaming white.'[30] Within this explosion of colour – and if you couldn't quite stomach donkey-brown, you could always go for pale pink or yellow – it was hard not to agree with Terence Conran:

> attitudes to bathrooms have been changing. These rooms are no longer limited by Puritan traditions according to which you used them only for ablutions, if not cold baths, or groped your way through clouds of rolling steam and yards of pipes. Standards and expectations of comfort have risen dramatically. New materials like Perspex, plastics, polyurethane seals and nylon have opened up new possibilities. More important is the feeling that a bathroom should be a pleasant place where you relax and pamper yourself.[31]

Of course, it might turn out that having a chocolate-coloured bath wasn't much use in helping you relax: however much bubble bath you chucked in, it always stayed looking streaky and grubby.

In a 1976 publication by the Design Council we are told:

> a bathroom can be anything from the all too familiar minimum of a bath, basin and possibly WC, all grouped together in an alternatively chilling and steamy confined space, to a room a good deal larger than many living-rooms, lavishly equipped and luxuriously furnished to cater for every ablutionary need and many more besides – including making up, hair drying, keeping fit, dressing, telephoning and just relaxing, to name but a few.[32]

The authors also note that the: 'more expensive baths often have some extra features, including non-slip shower areas, built-in soap holders and grab handles. These are well worth having but some expensive baths seem to vie with each other in bad taste.'[33] Bad taste or not, many of the bathroom innovations that came out during the 1970s now seem just gimmicky and excessive: the corner bath, the jacuzzi bath and so on.

The 1970s' home makeover business often had to face the reality that most people's bathrooms were indeed the smallest room in the house and that, if they could squeeze in a separate shower as well as a bathroom suite, people felt that they were doing well. The one bathroom fitting that never really took off but would have been a useful addition to the bathroom was the bidet. The bidet, it seemed, was as likely to cause consternation to the British as it was to be welcomed: 'although they are now becoming more popular in this country, bidets in the past were only known to intrepid Continental travellers as objects of mystery and imagination. Were they for washing feet? Why were the French so particular about their feet? Later it dawned that there were more "adult" uses.'[34] As a standard household object, the bidet never achieved anything like the popularity of the duvet (another 'continental' item which we will explore in the next chapter): it seemed that Britain was only ready for so much continental life. Indeed today sales for bidets in Britain have dropped (the high-street giant B&Q only sold 500 in 2010, prompting the *Daily Telegraph* to announce the 'Death of the Bidet').[35]

Today's bathroom has settled down since the immoderate design decisions of the 1970s. The only place that you find two-tone donkey-brown bathroom suites or green baths with gold taps is in our nightmares. Certainly avocado bathroom suites, once the height of style, or the indulgent jacuzzi would be one of the first things to get ripped out of a house restoration. They may come in all sorts of shapes and fittings, with different patinas and different surrounds, but they will be white. Innovation has mostly concentrated on the shower and those who have the space and money opt for 'wet rooms' or enclosed power showers with various nozzles that hose you down from every angle, which steam you and then blast you with warm air. Alternatively, like millions of others, you might just end up with a bath, a bog and a basin, with a shower attached to the bath.

Training centre

Toilets and bathrooms are places where we learn fundamental lessons about social values and manners, about how to look after our bodies and about the nature of our material world. They are there for those significant moments that are rites of passage in the life course: the first period, the first shave. For the humorous science fiction writer Douglas Adams a hot bath was a constant way of managing the writer's block that always gnawed at his self-confidence. When 'the long, dark teatime of the soul' descends (a mood that we can think of as a banal existential boredom that can come upon many people as they recognise that another Monday morning is looming), we know that even another bath will no longer do the trick:

> it was the Sunday afternoons he couldn't cope with, and that terrible listlessness that starts to set in about 2:55, when you

know you've taken all the baths that you can usefully take that day, that however hard you stare at any given paragraph in the newspaper you will never actually read it, or use the revolutionary new pruning technique it describes, and that as you stare at the clock the hands will move relentlessly on to four o'clock, and you will enter the long dark teatime of the soul.[36]

For Adams a hot bath became a legitimate form of procrastination and a way of gathering inspiration.

But perhaps the bathroom furniture – so intimate, so blank – offers us other life lessons. 'Potty training' is a small phrase for what is a profound moment in our lives: suddenly we can control parts of the body that seemed to have a life of their own, to open and close at will. For the child psychoanalyst Donald Winnicott recognising when a 'motion' is about to occur is a chance for connection and reassurance between parent and baby. It is my favourite description of a bowel movement:

> If you wait you will sooner or later discover that the baby, lying over there in the cot, finds a way of letting you know that a motion has been passed; and soon you will even get an inkling that there is going to be a motion. You are now at the beginning of a new relationship with the baby, who cannot communicate with you in an ordinary grown-up way but who has found a way of talking without words. It is as if he said, 'I think I am going to want to pass a motion; are you interested?' and you (without exactly saying so) answer 'Yes,' and you let him know that if you are interested this is not because you are frightened that he will make a mess, and not because you feel you ought to be teaching him how to be clean. If you are interested it is because you love your baby in the way mothers do, so that whatever is important to the baby is also important to you.[37]

Of course, not every parent reads Winnicott or has the patience for this sort of sensitivity towards baby poo.

In houses where there was no indoor toilet there is a sense that potty training continues throughout childhood, or at least a sense that your business is everybody else's business, that 'going' is in the public domain. In 1930s' London, Bryan Magee remembers that the chamber-pot was a way of teaching shame about the fact that bodies expel:

> because we had no indoor lavatory, the use of chamber pots was part of our everyday life, and I took them for granted. There were always two under each bed upstairs – my sister and I had our own, as did our parents. They were referred to as 'the po', as in 'I want to use the po', and were the first focus of repression I can remember. I was supposed to try hard not to use the po, and to use it only when I had to, and to crap in it only when I *absolutely* had to, and given clearly to understand that the whole thing was really a bloody nuisance, which obviously it was.[38]

Toilet training is our biggest lesson in learning to distinguish between good and bad, between cleanliness and dirt, between the mentionable and the unmentionable.

But toilet training can also be a lesson in freedom and achieving independence. Richard Wollheim, for instance, remembers the first time he was allowed to go to the toilet unaided: 'Up till that moment, I had been required, when I was ready to do so, to get off the lavatory seat, hobble to the door, open it, and shout "Ready".' But then comes the preparation for going it alone:

> I was told that I could clean myself, that I would be initiated into the mysteries of how, and that from that time onwards I would be on my own. First, I was asked to observe how the roll of lavatory paper was divided into separate sheets with

perforated lines between them. Then I was instructed how to hold the roll, and that I must first tear off three sheets in one, then fold them so that the fold ran through the middle of the middle sheet, and then I wiped myself. Then I folded that whole piece in two, and wiped myself with it a second time. Then I tore off just two sheets, and folded them along the perforated line, and wiped myself with them. When I tore off two sheets, there was no second folding, no second wiping. I was to go on using just two sheets until I was clean, and I was shown what a clean piece of paper looked like. Then I stood up, and, for the first time in my life, I could take it on myself to pull the chain: it was my decision.

We soon take for granted those achievements that will become part of our habitual world: learning to walk, being able to wash ourselves, cleaning our own teeth. For Wollheim such achievements should be at the foundation of our understanding of what responsibility is: 'this small incident was probably the single greatest increase in personal responsibility that my childhood had in store for me. It is what I think of when I hear moral philosophers discuss responsibility.'[39]

Wollheim's freedom seems to be offered in a fairly regimented way, but it is a freedom. A more dictatorial sense of toilet training was prescribed in America by the child psychologist John B. Watson. Although American, his *Psychological Care of the Infant and Child* from 1928 made a big impact in Britain among those who today we might say wanted to practise 'tough love':

a Watson baby [...] after he [*sic*] was eight months old, [...] was strapped into a special toilet seat and left alone in the bathroom, with the door closed and with no toys to distract him. Within twenty minutes Watson felt that a bowel movement should occur. If the door was left open, or the mother or nurse stayed, it would lead to 'dawdling, loud conversation, and generally unsocial and delinquent behaviour'.[40]

For Marie Stopes in 1939 tough love doesn't need to be too tough because 'babies, loved properly and well-bred, do not like to be soiled, and do not take that perverted pleasure in ordure which the aberrant mind of Freud has smeared on the social consciousness.'[41] Whether or not 'smeared' is the most fitting word in this attack on Freud, it certainly conjures a vivid image.

Toilets and bathrooms have much to teach us, and they perform their pedagogic function on a daily basis. Their relatively recent introduction into our domestic interiors has altered the cosmology of the home. But while the changes that we encounter as the bathroom is fixed and connected to the world may encourage us to forget that we are creaturely beings with creaturely needs, the bathroom and toilet will always confront us with the materiality of our bodies. For W. H. Auden – the modern poet of the domestic interior – the toilet is a privileged room in the house because it connects body and mind:

> Revelation came to
> Luther in a privy
> (Crosswords have been solved there).
> Rodin was no fool
> When he cast his Thinker
> Cogitating deeply,
> Crouched in position
> Of a man at Stool.[42]

I have no idea if Auden favoured the donkey-brown toilet or the gleaming white one. I'd be keen to know.

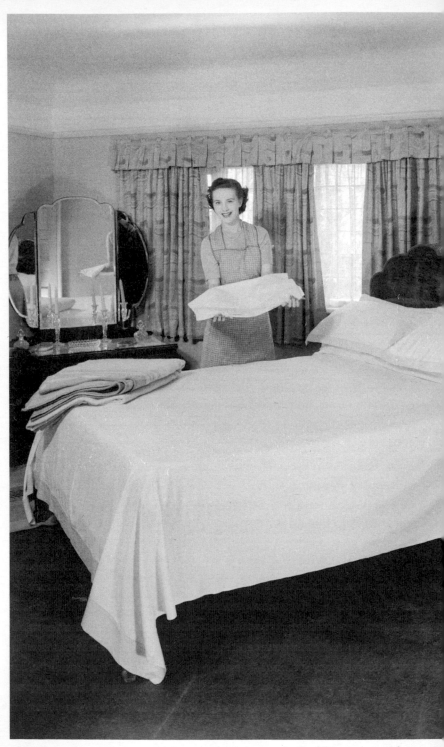

Bedding in a pre-duvet age

PUT THE LIGHT OUT

('Master' Bedrooms)

Bedroom: Think 24hr sanctuary for you and those you love to spend special time with. Well organised, calming and luxurious, make it everything you've dreamed of. Make it IKEA.[1]

In the world of modern housing, and in the language of estate agents, the 'master bedroom' is to the upstairs of the house what the living room is to the downstairs: it is the first-floor showroom, the room upstairs that should have the biggest 'Wow' factor. We can measure the swagger of a house by the grandiosity of its best bedroom. It, of course, deserves its own en-suite bathroom, it craves walk-in closets, it longs for thick pile carpets and heavy curtains. Slightly shamefacedly, it longs for luxuries that might seem to belong more naturally to other rooms: but why not have a flat-screen television that pops out from the bottom of the bed with the touch of a button? Household gadgets have worked hard to make sure that you don't need to travel too far to get a cup of tea: why not get woken up by an alarm clock that makes you tea and coffee while playing you your favourite radio station at the designated minute you have set it for?

A major theme of this book is the changes in the ordinary house that technology has brought about. When we get to the bedroom, we need to broaden our perspective. Of course, the sort of circuit-board technology is there, in items as diverse as radio-alarm clocks and vibrators; it is there in all the accompaniments to comfort, from dimmer-switch lighting to beds that massage you. But some of the most distinctive changes to the bedroom have to do with soft technology: high-tog duvets, memory-foam mattresses, sleeping tablets. In other ways technology – this time as technique – is there in the way that we might think about something as seemingly natural as sex, or how we bring up a baby. The twentieth century is awash with self-help literature, and nowhere is this more evident than in the realm of sex. Alex Comfort's *The Joy of Sex* was, in the 1970s and '80s, a night-stand favourite for many heterosexual couples. With its upfront and unashamed hedonism (primarily from the male's perspective), it is a book that treats sex as technical craft: the greater the range of techniques you have at your disposal, the better you are it and the more fun and satisfaction you're going to have.

The very term 'master' bedroom should make us pause. It seems to suggest that this room is primarily the province of males. Yet any quick consultation with the design advice about bedrooms seems to suggest that the adult bedroom or the 'parental bedroom' is a room where an unabashed femininity can be let off its leash. Only in the bedroom could the ultra pink-aesthetic of someone like Barbara Cartland (where everything is floaty and flirty, flouncy and flowery) be deemed appropriate to main-stream tastes. The 'masculine' look for a main bedroom is promoted in magazines like *Playboy*, but only as something suitable for the 'bachelor pad' (and there 'masculine' means a lair geared towards seduction). Most actual bedrooms, of course, negotiate such fantasies with the pragmatism of necessity, idiosyncrasy and personal interests – which means that for the most part they would eschew much of the advice given by trend-setters. Yet, for all that, the parental bedroom is often a fantastical space for children. The French writer Michel Leiris speaks for many when he describes his parents' bedroom as a place that was perceived as 'simultaneously attractive and dangerous, prestigious and outcast'.[2] Leiris grew up in the first decades of the twentieth century, in a culture where parental authority was absolute. The parental bedroom was somewhere you went when you suffered night terrors, not a place where you might wander unannounced.

In this chapter we are visiting unannounced to look at the banality and bliss of the bedroom. The daily life of dressing and bed-making will be as much our topic as the bedroom as the theatre of love and passion. The night-time routines of couples rehearsing hopes, fears and frustrations that are a staple of domestic dramas and comedies (from *Morecombe and Wise* to *My Family*) are just as important as their ecstatic cries. But whether it is the shift from blankets to duvets or from the missionary position to 'Feuille de Rose' (and you'll have to read *The Joy of Sex* to get the details of that technique), the 'master bedroom' is a place brimming with secrets and unreality. The closets of the bedroom are deep and take children into other dimensions: they are also the place where Christmas presents are kept.

In 1962, in John Braine's *Life at the Top*, we find Joe Lampton ensconced in a brand-new house in the expanding suburbia of a northern town. He has done well for himself, married 'above himself' and landed a high-paying job with his father-in-law. But his bedroom is a constant reminder of the social treadmill he is on in a never-ending circle of expense. When his child cross-questions him about why he is tired and why he has to work all the time, he replies: '"Daddy has to earn pennies to keep Harry at school. And pennies for pyjies and frocks and bicycles and all sorts of things."' He continues his listing in his head: 'And the light grey fitted carpet and the grey and primrose yellow wallpaper and the built-in wardrobe and dressing-table and the candy-striped sheets and the divan bed with the Continental headboard; we were always buying something new, the house itself was only three years old.'³ For the dedicated follower of fashion, for the persistent moderniser and for the unfettered social climber, bedrooms, like all the other rooms in the house, are a constant financial drain.

Joe Lampton is ambivalent about the lifestyle he has bought into: this is his tragedy. His house – new, executive, fitted out with all mod cons – is a constant irritant that scratches his melancholic nostalgia:

> I went back into the bedroom to fetch my own slippers and the fuzzy dressing-gown. […] Its thickness had been welcome enough in the draughty corridors and icy bathroom of the house in Pudney Lane; it wasn't really necessary now. The oil-fired central heating, in fact, kept the house so warm that we hardly needed clothes at all; I didn't object to this, but there were times when, perversely no doubt, I missed the comfort the dressing-gown had given me on winter mornings, just as I missed the open fire in the big kitchen.⁴

If there is one piece of furniture that defines the bedroom it is, of course, the bed. This puts the bedroom on the side of those most functional rooms such as the toilet and the bathroom. But how beds function, and how they should be dressed, has been changing in the last hundred years.

Going continental

The bedroom has been at the centre of debates about hygiene and health – about what is best for the well-being of the human organism. Is it better for a bedroom to be warm, or to have gale-force arctic winds blowing through it – and how can you find a compromise if one of you demands fresh air but the other can't stand being cold? Should a bedstead be made of metal or wood? Should couples sleep together or in separate beds (or even separate rooms)? Should bedding be heavy enough to almost force 'deep' sleep on to you, or should it be light and airy? Should mattresses and pillows be luxuriously soft and giving, or hard and unyielding? Underpinning such debates has been a concern with hygiene and well-being in all its shapes and forms. Some of the debates have been fairly crackpot – such as the belief that, should a grandmother and granddaughter sleep in the same bed (which would have been fairly common in poor neighbourhoods at the start of the twentieth century, say), then there would be an adverse magnetic effect. Much of the advice about a healthy bedroom is based on scientific ideas that had been proved wrong long before they died out as folklore. The idea, for instance, that illness was carried in the air and that stale air and miasma (super-stale air) were either unhealthy or deadly can account for the obsession with the idea that an arctic breeze wafting through a bedroom is the only healthy option.

Throughout most of the twentieth century it was usual for bedding to consist of blankets and sheets. Starting from the bottom, a standard arrangement of bedding might go something like this: immediately on top of the mattress you might have a cheap blanket to add some extra comfort and offer some protection should a stray horse-hair or spring poke out from the mattress below; then you would have the bottom sheet; on top of this you would put the pillow at the end with the headboard (if it had one); then you would have the top sheet. Depending on the time of year, you might have some or all of the following: various blankets (including cellular blankets, for instance); an eiderdown (basically a small quilt, traditionally filled with eider feathers and covered by silky, shiny material); a counterpane or bedcover (which might involve patchwork, quilted or not). Given that for most of the twentieth century the British bedroom wasn't heated, and given that winters in Britain will always have many freezing days and even more freezing nights, such a weight of material was needed to stop frostbite setting in. As already mentioned, when central heating was introduced after the war, many people who had it fitted simply didn't include bedrooms as rooms requiring radiators – such was the association of cold air and health.

A requirement for any bedroom was that you slept with the window open all year round so that you didn't suffer the ill effects of breathing 'stale' (already breathed) air in your sleep. If the stacking of sheets, blankets, eiderdowns and counterpanes was to guard against indoor frost, now there was the danger that you might well overheat while you sleep. Luckily the blankets were usually so ill fitting and the eiderdown of such slippery material that, unless you slept as still as a corpse, most of your bedding invariably fell off during the night. The trick was to use the counterpane, which was designed to reach the floor on either side, as a way of holding all the rest of it in place.

The 1930s' *Housewife Book* declares that

> Modern ideas of hygiene dissuade from the use of feather beds, not because they are uncomfortable, but because they allow the body to sink into them, with the result that free circulation of air is not possible. Heavy sleep is not necessarily perfect sleep, for it may be the result of insufficient ventilation and too heavy bedclothes, which prevent the body heat from escaping.

Instead it suggests that hygienic people will get 'foundation mattresses composed of a number of vertical spiral springs'.[5] It is this shift from the heavy weight of traditional bedding to something much lighter that establishes some of the conditions for the eventual success of the duvet in Britain. The shift to the duvet is a domestic revolution in British culture that is worth spending some time on. It wasn't sudden, and it wasn't without its detractors, but it did alter not just the way we slept but also the conduct of housework – the cornerstone of which was the daily round of bedmaking (for those housewives who hadn't persuaded the remainder of the household to make their own beds).

According to legend (which today means the internet), the *Daily Mirror* ran a headline sometime in the 1930s that read 'Fog in Channel: Continent Isolated'.[6] Of course, given the puny size of Britain in relation to the enormous scale of continental Europe, the headline is meant as an example of Britain's gargantuan conceit. Culturally, it is rare that you hear Britons refer to Europe with the sense that they include themselves in this category. Britain is a place where pasta could still be thought of by some as fairly exotic even in the 1980s, and where the bidet would often be thought of as an alarming item to find in a bathroom. While it was a slow process, Britain did eventually follow European fashions in bedding by adopting the duvet, or 'continental quilt' as it was often called, just to remind you of its exotic paternity. For anyone who has grown up with a duvet, where making the bed consists of shaking your quilt a bit and making sure that it lands roughly flat and central, the pre-duvet history of British bedding must seem like the Dark Ages. I think you get some sense of what the duvet meant to bedding from this pre-duvet exclamation from a housewife in the 1940s (mentioned previously in the kitchen chapter): 'I love scrubbing, and I love polishing, but I don't like making beds. I hate making beds. Funny, isn't it?'[7] To a duvet-user this would seem like the comment of a self-confessed domestic masochist (though washing and changing your duvet cover are another matter altogether).

The intricacy of the pre-duvet bed meant that bedmaking was a fairly involved affair. Here is an example of bedmaking (and sheet- changing) being described in 1942 by a Mass-Observer witnessing a working-class woman of thirty engaged in the process. She starts by going into the bedroom and then

> bends down, and drags out parcel from beside the foot of the bed. Opens it (pulling the string aside, without either breaking or untying it). Pulls out sheet and pillow-case, without disturbing other things. Throws them on bed, then looks at list. 'Six and threepence halfpenny! Good Lord!' Takes sheet and pillow-case off bed, puts them carefully on the floor, beside the parcel.[8]

We should note, in passing, that the weekly laundry delivery was not reserved for the rich but was a part of ordinary people's lives. Indeed, if you were poor and lived in a small house with a small copper, sheet-washing and sheet-drying were almost impossible. The account of bedmaking goes on:

> [She] takes blue and white striped pyjamas, folds them carelessly, puts them on the floor beside clean sheet and pillow-case. Throws pillow on the floor. Strips off blankets and top sheet, one at a time, and throws them in a heap on the floor, on top of other things. Then takes off bottom sheet, folds it and puts it on the floor beside the other things.
>
> Under the bottom sheet are four or five blankets, folded double; she stores them there for the summer. Takes them all off, turns the mattress. 'I like to make it properly twice a week,' she comments. 'Once on laundry day, and one other time, if I can.'
>
> Puts back spare blankets, folding each one double, laying it on, and smoothing it carefully. Fishes among the heap on the floor for erstwhile top sheet, puts on now as bottom sheet. Smoothes it, tucks it in carefully. Comments on the blankets underneath:

'I'm fed up with these blankets every time. They're waiting, really, to go to the laundry; but I can't afford to send them yet.'

Fishes for pillow, takes dirty case off it, puts on clean one. Unfolds clean sheet, spreads it over the bed. Stops to examine two holes, about an inch across, in the middle:

'I can't understand how the laundry does that. They must drag it through something. I'll have to patch the darned thing now.'

Tucks it in carefully all round. Puts on two brown blankets, both at the same time. Bottom one has a large scorch mark and a hole.

Stops and blows nose. Tucks in blankets. Folds sheet over at the top. Puts on counterpane. Then remembers pyjamas, pulls back counterpane at the top, pushes in pyjamas. Pulls counterpane over again.

Finishes bed-making 10.17 a.m. Total time taken, 12 minutes. Has worked briskly and efficiently the whole time.[9]

Bedmaking was heavy, tiring work, with learned techniques such as making 'hospital corners' when tucking in sheets and blankets. In classic Mass-Observation style this is incredibly detailed, but it is the detail that matters. The slightly dirty and dingy blankets that need a visit to the laundry; the scorched marks (from a coal fire, from candles, from cigarettes – scorched blankets were not uncommon); the feeling that the laundry service was getting one over on you; the lack of space for storing winter blankets in summer: all of this was the daily grind of bedmaking.

In this book I'm particularly interested in how seemingly banal changes are symptomatic of a more substantial social change. More importantly, perhaps, the banal change may well turn out to be at the centre of what we see as the more profound world of social changes. Changes in chairs and beddings, in how we wash, weren't the result of other more profound changes (to do with technology, say, or social beliefs); they are the vehicles of profound social change. People bought beanbags not because they were suddenly more relaxed but because they wanted to be relaxed, and needed the materials to achieve this. In this way domestic appliances and paraphernalia are objects that teach us.

I get a sense of the changes in social life when I think that in a few decades we can move from the situation described by the Mass-Observer above to one where Terence Conran's Habitat can proudly encourage us to 'make love not beds with the help of a duvet and fitted bottom sheet'.[10] It is a significant shift – both in terms of how we imagine ourselves and in actual terms of what we do. We physically sleep differently under a duvet; we do different kinds of things with it; we sail through bedmaking at such speed that even men are encouraged to make the bed. If this book charts a history of domestic informality, then the duvet isn't just something that was adopted as we became more informal – it was an agent in all this; it helped us to become more informal.

Habitat's slogan riffed on a countercultural, anti-war slogan. Habitat's duvets can simultaneously evoke sexy and 'alternative' eroticism along with stress-free, labour-saving practicality. As usual with Habitat, this is sex mixed with easy-clean surfaces (which may well account for their former success). By the 1980s the duvet was an object of sophistication, a sign that you probably preferred a blob of mayonnaise and some vinaigrette with your salad rather than a monsoon of 'salad cream'. It meant that you were *au fait* with metric weights and measures, might not be adverse to a bowl of muesli and might possibly be open-minded about an open relationship. The duvet was European, and by 1973 so was Britain (in principle at least).

The phenomenal rise of the duvet in Britain in the 1970s and '80s (consolidated by the end of that decade), though, didn't come without a struggle. First of all there was the difficulty of the name. The word 'duvet' not only referred to bedding from overseas: it sounded French (it was). Now, while many Britons could recognise France's gastronomic genius, its philosophical experimentation and panache, and its lyrical sensitivity, it didn't necessarily follow that Britain was ready for French-ness in the bedroom, so to say. By the 1970s the term 'continental quilt' was standard operating procedure for someone trying to explain why it was that a bed seemed to be missing nearly all of its crucial ingredients while being submerged under an over-large eider-down that had lost its shiny patina. But campaigners in the 1960s who proselytised on behalf of the duvet in Britain had yet to agree on 'continental quilt' as the default euphemism it would soon become.

Adverts from the mid-1960s have all sorts of names for the duvet. The company McLintock Europa, for instance, offers 'lightweight warmth' with the 'quiltie' (a 'unique Scandinavian idea'). Promising 'all the natural night-time warmth you'll ever need with just one sheet, the Quiltie and you', it works because 'you generate the warmth and lightweight Quiltie, with its unique pocket construction, surrounds you in it the whole night through'.[11] Good old quiltie. In the 1960s duvets were sold to the British as a modern novelty item, a sort of 'you won't believe your eyes' phenomenon. Thus the 'Puffin Downlette' starts out with the practical 'no more dreary, dusty bed-making!' but soon opts for the you're-not-going-to-believe-this: 'The Puffin Downlette, designed and made in Denmark, is used just with sheets – even in Winter! Filled with softest duck's down, light as air, it keeps you gloriously warm. The Scandinavians enjoy this luxury – now they send it to you.'[12] Good old Scandinavians and good old Puffin Downlette. The term 'continental quilt' suggests a more knowing and less specifically Scandinavian approach to bedding. A 'Slumberdown Continental Quilt', for example, is 'the new way to stay warm in bed' and, rather than being unfamiliar, it seems as though Britons might already know its comforts: 'you may have seen them on the Continent – down-filled quilts that dispense with the need for blankets. Marvellously warm … bed-making banished! Snuggle up warm in a Slumberdown – and sleep like you've never slept before.'[13]

But while the duvet – in the shape of the quiltie, downlette or continental quilt – is trying to introduce what is obviously some-thing new to the British market, good old 'sheets-n-blankets' are fighting back with their own take on modern technologically advanced bedding. For instance the 'captivair' blankets are 'So luxurious … yet so much warmer and lighter than you dreamed any blanket could be! The secret is in the dense "air-trap" pile – a slim layer of soft fluffy comfort – shutting cold air *out* locking warm air *in*. Allergy-free, mothproof and stain resistant. *Super soft too!*'[14] This is fighting talk to anyone who is thinking of jumping ship and opting for a 'quiltie' precisely because it is light, warm and dust-free. Similarly the cellular blanket is in the fight, taking on the duvet as an item that is a-seasonal: 'Smart sleepers know there's nothing so nice as a Lan-Air-Cel blanket. That's because Lan-Air-Cel is softly woven from Scottish spun wool. Woven into a unique pattern of little cells. It's the air trapped between those cells that gives Lan-Air-Cel it natural air-conditioning. That keeps you warm in winter, cool in summer.'[15] Even the old-fashioned eiderdown is in on the act, though confusingly, because of its new synthetic filling, it can't quite brand itself as an eider-down: 'The most luxurious thing she owns … her "Terylene" filled quilt. Every woman needs one, every bed is better dressed with one – a warm-as-toast, always luxurious but always practical "Terylene" filled quilt.'[16] This is a quilt perched precariously on top of a stack of sheets and blankets.

Habitat probably deserves to be singled out as providing the shock troops in popularising the duvet in Britain (though a range of other high street shops and mail order services were also doing their bit). The 1970s was when Habitat was at its most populist and cheap. In 1974 it could rightly claim that the duvet revolution was under way: 'Habitat has revolutionised bed-making. What with fitted bottom sheets which lie smooth and flat without a wrinkle from one wash day to the next, duvets which only need a quick shake out and plumped up pillow, it need only take a quick ten seconds to make a bed.'[17] By 1978 it felt that Habitat customers might like to know something of the history of the duvet:

> As with other basic and simple good things in life, Duvets were not invented, they evolved, mainly in colder Scandinavian and Mid-European countries where they had been the standard form of bedcoverings for hundreds of years. Originally just a farmer's bag of feathers, the Duvet progressed from down and feathers to the present day refined and improved product which is completely hygienic and provides the right amount of warmth with the minimum of weight, thus allowing the body to relax and concentrate on sleeping instead of having to fight the weight of the blankets.[18]

In telling such a story Habitat locates the benefits of the duvet in the language of health and hygiene, which knows that lightness is a value connected to fresh air and healthy pursuits.

In British bedrooms the duvet eventually won out. But to some it still smacks of a continental drift that needs to be resisted in the name of a nationalism that takes its xenophobia pretty seriously:

> SIR – The duvet is an invention of the misguided Continentals and should be sent back where it belongs, along with the ridiculous metric system and chilled lager. Any normal, vigorously sweaty Englishman will know that the duvet generates an overheated, fetid, jungle-like atmosphere in the

marital bed where peace, not French or Italian hyperactivity, should reign.

The proper bed cover for an Englishman must be a woollen blanket. The temperature can be regulated by using more, or fewer layers. Blankets, unlike duvets, do not need to be hung out of the chalet window every morning to rid them of the night's charge of perspiration.

England's greatness was founded on wool. The sheep of Leicestershire, Northamptonshire and Sussex deserve our continued support: sleep under wool and not under duck feathers.[19]

So, at any rate, writes one letter writer to the *Daily Telegraph*. As some of the citizenry of the UK lurch to the right and blame immigration for most of the country's ills, perhaps we will see duvet-burning in the streets of middle England.

Habitat prepared the way for a continental way of sleeping:

Less then fifteen years ago it is probable that fewer than five per cent of the British population had ever heard of a Duvet or Continental Quilt. Now in excess of 20 per cent of the population actually use one every night. These cold statistics understate what is in effect a massive change in sleeping habits of some 10 million people who have after centuries of tradition, disregarded the warmth and weight of the blanket in favour of the warmth and lightness of the Duvet.[20]

That was in 1978. Today that 20 per cent is probably more like 80 per cent, if not higher. Today the only place where you are really likely to find hospital corners is in a hospital (or in the homes of some *Daily Telegraph* readers). But if Habitat prepared Britain for continental tastes in furnishings, then the continent came to Britain not only in the form of lightweight bedding but also in the form of shops such as IKEA. Unknowingly, Habitat was digging its own grave.

The birds, the bees and the bedroom

Today it is taken for granted that couples, straight or gay, young or old, would share a bed. How else would you keep up the healthy sex life that, according to what all the magazines and self-help literature tell you, is your right and your duty (to yourself, of course)? But the shared bed has had lots of doubters, even among those who seem to champion the healthy properties of regular sex.

In the late eighteenth century the inventor of the Celestial Bed, Dr Graham, could ask:

> Is there anything in nature which is more immediately calculated totally to subvert health, strength, love, esteem, and indeed everything that is desirable in the married state, than that odious, most indelicate, and most hurtful custom of man and wife continually pigging together in one and the same bed to sleep, and snore, and steam, and do everything else that's indelicate together, three hundred and sixty-five times every year.[21]

His hatred of the habit of sharing a double bed was based on a fear of miasmic contamination which he thought was part of the cause of all sorts of maladies but which might be cured by the use of magnetism. Dr Graham's Celestial Bed sought to marshal the power of 'Electricity, Air, Music and Magnetism' to cure male impotence, infertility and anything else that should stand in the way of procreation. The Celestial Bed was not a domestic bed. You went to the 'Temple of Hymen' in London's Pall Mall, and for £100 (it later dropped to £25) you could spend the night 'pigging' together with your companion with the certainty that conception was pretty much guaranteed by the use of gigantic powerful magnets designed to generate 'inconceivable and irresistibly powerful tides of the magnetic effluvium' and to unleash potency and fertility. Dr Graham, who also favoured bathing by being buried up to his neck in earth, could be seen as one of Britain's first sexologists and sex therapists.[22] But he died poor – perhaps the world wasn't ready for the Celestial Bed.

But while this sort of fairground quackery was not promoted in such an unabashed way in the twentieth century, there are echoes of it in some of the more rational contributors to the shaping of the modern bedroom. For instance, even Dr Marie Stopes, the guru of birth control and the female orgasm, wrote in 1928 'that men and women can affect and enrich and to some degree interpenetrate each other in some subtle way depending on electrical or magnetic currents characterising each sex and mutually affecting them'.[23] And like Graham, but for different reasons, Stopes argued against married couples 'pigging' together in a shared bed.

In the early decades of the twentieth century the modern 'master' bedroom for a young married couple would as likely contain twin single beds as a double bed. E. M. Delafield's 1927 novel *The Way Things Are* has the protagonist longing for twin beds: 'Alfred lay sleeping on the far side of the double bed. They ought to have had modern twin beds, of course – much more hygienic, and Laura could not help thinking, much more comfortable as well. They often talked about it. Or, rather, Laura often talked about it. Alfred, like so many husbands, was of a silent disposition.'[24] It is this association of twin beds with a sense of the modern that seems old-fashioned today. Yet within the context of the early decades of the century 'the tyranny of the twin bed amongst middle classes after 1900 no doubt had something to do with women at last asserting their independence and, if they wished, freeing themselves from the persistent attentions of their husbands.'[25] And women's independence in the early 1900s was the epitome of what it was to be modern.

The twentieth century is the century when advice gets personal: problem pages, agony aunts and self-help manuals are all aimed at you. These are the inheritors of the 'conduct books' that started getting popular in the eighteenth century. But if the eighteenth-century conduct books were aimed at advising you about the best way to behave in company, the twentieth century extends this to advising you how to 'realise yourself' or 'fulfil yourself', whether you're in company or not. This was, after all, the century of the self. And for modern twentieth-century types this meant the production of a whole industry dedicated to sexual advice. Marie Stopes can be seen as one of the first professional sexologists who took sexual advice out of the world of innuendo and quackery and gave it the gloss of science and health. Sexual advice, perhaps unsurprisingly, has had repercussions for the 'master' bedroom – its image, its use and even its existence.

We can get some sense of the distance that heterosexual advice literature travels during the twentieth century if I pick out two hugely popular books from different moments in the century: Marie Stopes's *Married Love*, from 1918, and Alex Comfort's *The Joy of Sex*, from 1972. *The Joy of Sex* was a phenomenal success and is still being read today in various updated formats. Its illustrations have forged a generation or two who think that men with trimmed beards like to experiment in the bedroom. Both Comfort and Stopes had a varied literary output (both wrote poetry, for instance), and both achieved notoriety for their advanced views and/or their unusual lifestyle. Alex Comfort, a committed anarchist, became a naked biologist in a communal science community in California. Marie Stopes's legacy has been 'Marie Stopes International', a global network of clinics and advice centres promoting sexual health all over the world.

Marie Stopes's dislike for the routine practice of married couples sharing a bed night after night wasn't because she was a prude. Far from it: it was because she was a romantic to her core. It is hard not to like someone whose description of post-coital bliss is at once both coy and transcendent:

> when the sex-rite is, in every sense, rightly performed, the healing wings of sleep descend both on the man and on the woman in his arms. Every organ in their bodies is influenced and stimulated to play its part, while their spirits, after soaring in the dizzy heights of rapture, are wafted to oblivion, thence to return gently to the ordinary plains of daily consciousness.[26]

But it is harder to see how this would come about when the pair are in separate beds or rooms.

For Stopes the passion killer in 'married love' (and love and sex *in* marriage is her only topic) is habit and presumptuousness. Stopes describes the results of bedroom-sharing for married couples:

> the married pair share a bedroom, and so it comes about that the two are together not only at the times of delight and interest in each other, but during most of the unlovely and even ridiculous proceedings of the toilet. Now it may enchant a man once – perhaps even twice – or at long intervals – to watch his goddess screw her hair up into a tight and unbecoming knot and soap her ears. But it is inherently too unlovely a proceeding to retain indefinite enchantment. [...] everyday association in the commonplace daily necessities tends to reduce the keen pleasure each takes in the other.[27]

It is crucial to remember that, when Stopes was writing this, the bedroom would have been a place where washing was performed as well as the use of the chamber-pot. Ear-washing is, of course, shorthand for all those earthy intimacies that arise when people live in close proximity.

Her advice about bed-sharing, or rather her advice about not sharing a bed, is ultimately to do with achieving consensual as well as sensual unions and couplings and of elevating lovemaking to celestial heights without the aid of strong magnets: 'escape the lower, the trivial, the sordid', she demands.

> So far as possible (and this is far more possible than appears at first, and requires only a little care and rearrangement in the habits of the household) ensure that you allow your husband to come upon you only when there is delight in the meeting. Whenever the finances allow, the husband and wife should have separate bedrooms, failing that they should have a curtain which can at will be drawn so as to divide the room they share. No soul can grow to its full stature without spells of solitude.[28]

Solitude allows for private ear-washing and for gaining some control over when sex occurs.

Much of *Married Love* is taken up with the satisfactions (and lack of them) of the wife. The book describes how the ebbs and flows of desire are not due to 'women's capriciousness' but connected to the menstrual cycle. She also discusses how the sexual frustrations of women cause sleep disturbances: 'many married women have told me that after they have had relations with their husbands they are restless, either for some hours or for the whole night; and I feel sure that the prevalent failure on the part of many men to effect orgasm for their wives at each congress, must be a very common source of the sleeplessness and nervous diseases of so many married women.'[29] To women she suggests that they need a 'room of their own'; to men her advice is to have some self-control: 'it should never be forgotten that without the discipline of self-control there is no lasting delight in erotic feeling. The fullest delight, even in a purely physical sense, can be attained *only* by those who curb and direct their natural impulses.'[30]

The separate bedrooms scenario, though, is not without its dangers. On the one hand, it could simply lead to more distance both physically and emotionally for the couple; on the other, it might make sex even more business-like and perfunctory. To guard against this, Stopes, the endless romantic, has some rules:

> It is true that the use of separate rooms has often presaged a break in the happiness of a marriage, but that is because things are otherwise wrong. *Every night*, unless something prevents, there should be the tender companionship and whispered intimacies which are, to many people, only possible in the dark. Men, too, are at heart eternally children, and such tender petting as comforts children warms and sweetens a grown man's life. The 'good night' should be a time of delightful forgetting of the outward scars of the years, and a warm, tender, perhaps playful exchange of confidences.[31]

Married Love was a revolutionary book for the time and was banned in the United States until 1931. Alex Comfort's *The Joy of Sex* is from a different era and for a different sensibility. Gone is the sense of coyness and the romanticism, but gone too is the overarching concern for women's well-being. In the 'anything goes' of the permissive society hedonism is seen as the main democratic principle. The subtitle of the book is crucial – *The Joy of Sex: A Gourmet Guide to Lovemaking.* The cooking analogy works on a number of levels. Comfort was initially drawn to it because it suggested that you could write and talk about sex in the same way that you could about food, and that he could write a book that would be as ordinary and as everyday as a cookery book. It also suggested that sex was an accomplishment, like cooking, that could be learned, practised and developed. Just as you might start out by boiling an egg and eventually cook something *cordon bleu*, so the sex we start out with could be improved through learning some skills and adding to our range of ingredients and processes (as they say on *Master Chef*). But there is also the sense that sex has become like food and, like food, is simultaneously a need, a pleasure and now something that is liable to the caprice of fashion and the market. (What? You're not still doing it like that, are you?')

The Joy of Sex takes its cookery book analogy pretty seriously, dividing the book into sections such as: 'Starters – the basic ingredients'; 'Main Course – which everyone needs'; and 'Sauces and Pickles – for special occasions'. And, as with many a cookery book, you are encouraged to buy some new equipment before you get started. Like *Married Love*, *The Joy of Sex* is an invitation to alter your bedroom furniture. For Comfort, beds are

still the most important piece of domestic sexual equipment. Really enthusiastic sex usually involves at one time or another almost every piece of furniture in the house, at least experimentally, but the bed is its commonest venue. Most beds on the market are designed by people who think they are intended to sleep on. The problem arises from the fact that the ideal surface for most kinds of intercourse needs to be rather harder than is comfortable for a whole night's sleep. One solution is to have two beds, one for sex and the other for sleeping, but this is a counsel of luxury, and in any case the need to move disrupts the best part of the night, the total relaxation which follows complete love. The best advice is probably to settle for a compromise and have a mattress on the floor as well.[32]

The bedroom with two double beds, one for sex and one for sleep, is a considerable investment in hedonism and certainly not available to most – but perhaps cheaper than Stopes's encouragement to sleep in separate rooms.

For Comfort, bidets too are a necessity. But if *The Joy of Sex* seems to be recommending that you need to spend-to-transcend, there is clearly one commodity that you will no longer need: deodorant. *The Joy of Sex* is permissiveness exemplified: all is allowed, though same-sex love seems to be just an exotic experimentation rather than something to commit to or to be driven to or to simply enjoy on a regular basis. Amid all this heterosexual permissiveness, though, there is a strain of hippie intolerance about smell: you simply must smell. Deodorant is 'banned absolutely: the only permitted deodorant is soap and water, although the unfortunates who sweat profusely may well have problems. A mouthful of aluminium chloride in a girl's armpit is one of the biggest disappointments bed can afford, and a truly deodorized woman would be another – like a deodorized carnation.'[33] Alex Comfort's 'joy' is in the natural smells of his lover (Jane Henderson). You get a sense of how *The Joy of Sex* is addressed to men by the fact that here is one of the few female interventions (by Jane Henderson): 'she says "Some men *should* use deodorants if they can't learn to wash".'[34]

Smell is a dominant sense in *The Joy of Sex*: unless your lovemaking is creating an odour, it seems that you haven't really got the hang of it:

Because it is so important, a woman needs to guard her own personal perfume as carefully as her looks and learn to use it in courtship and intercourse as skilfully as she uses the rest of her body. Smoking doesn't help this. It can be a long-range weapon (nothing seduces a man more reliably, and this can happen subliminally without his knowing it) but at the same time a skilful man can read it, if he is an olfactory type, and if he knows her, to tell when she is excited.[35]

The jokey tone of *The Joy of Sex* means that this piece of information about 'personal perfume' is written under the heading 'Cassolette'. We are told that 'cassolette' is French for 'perfume box' rather than the French for a small cooking implement.

Compared with Marie Stopes, Alex Comfort's book has the great advantage of being incredibly matter-of-fact about sex. But this is its disadvantage too. In the end it seems to equate lovemaking with any aspirational lifestyle. *The Joy of Sex* could be sponsored by Nike – 'just do it'. For all its boyish enthusiasm at thinking of all the possible ways of doing it, and the glee in its unabashed tone, there is also a sense that *The Joy of Sex* is a chapter in a domestic management almanac. In an entry that seems to exhibit the same blindness that Queen Victoria showed with regard to lesbianism, Comfort writes about semen:

> There is no lovemaking without spilling this, on occasions at least. You can get it out of clothing or furnishings either with a stiff brush, when the stain has dried, or with a dilute solution of sodium bicarbonate. If you spill it over each other, massage it gently in – the pollen-odour of fresh semen is itself an aphrodisiac, which is why the smell of fresh grass or thalictrum flowers turns most people on.[36]

Mrs Beeton would have been proud of him.

But the whole industry of self-help hedonism requires time and space. It is hard to imagine what use many poorer households would have for *The Joy of Sex* when the point of having two beds in a room was not to accommodate two mattresses with different firmness but simply to accommodate all the bodies that need to sleep there. The journalist Tim Lott, for instance, looking at photographs of his grandparents in between-the-wars London, comments that, for all their upward mobility, his grandfather 'is also poor, extremely poor by my standards, but not by those of his time. He lives in a two-bedroom flat above the shop, with his three boys, Ken, Jack and Arthur. He shares the flat with Floss and Charlie and their two children.'[37] A bedroom for each family. Stopes's and Comfort's suggestions for how to keep the sexual spark alive imagine a different domestic setting from what was available to many working-class households.

Furnishing the bedroom

At the end of the nineteenth century Arthur Conan Doyle's 'The Adventure of the Speckled Band' (first published in the *Strand Magazine* in 1892) can describe a bedroom as:

> a homely little room, with a low ceiling and a gaping fireplace, after the fashion of old country houses. A brown chest of drawers stood in one corner, a narrow white-counterpaned bed in another, and a dressing-table on the left-hand side of the window. These articles, with two small wicker-work chairs, made up all the furniture in the room, save for a square of Wilton carpet in the centre. The boards round and panelling of the walls were brown, worm-eaten oak, so old and discoloured that it may have dated from the original building of the house.[38]

In a 1947 study of a small village in Somerset, the author W. J. Turner describes the impoverished circumstances of many of the households. He describes one house where the 'two occupied bedrooms contain mere necessities – bed, dressing-table, chest of drawers, and two tin trunks for storing clothes'.[39] Both accounts offer us a room with rudimentary furnishings, and it is probably true that the bedroom – at least, the adult bedroom – has always been more limited in furnishings than many other rooms in the house. Yet both insist that a 'dressing-table' is a necessity. Today the only people I know with dressing tables are either in their eighties or else about five and think that they are princesses.

But what is odd about the descriptions of both rooms is not so much what they include as what they exclude. In Charles Eastlake's *Hints on Household Taste* from 1868 the standard piece of furniture that would be included in 'the upper bed-rooms of a moderately-sized house' was a wash-stand for the 'unlovely' practice of ear-washing and much else beside. The 'wash-hand-stand' or just 'wash-stand' is 'fitted with two shelves, the upper one cut to receive the basin, the lower one "boxed" to receive a drawer', and on top it has jugs and bowls for washing.[40] Clearly the bedrooms in Somerset don't have a bathroom, and it would seem unlikely that the country house in the Sherlock Holmes story would have had such a convenience. The wash-stand in some form would have continued in many houses until it was replaced by a bathroom. Perhaps, though, the Somerset house is too poor and small for such a piece of furniture, and the occupants have to wash in the scullery. Perhaps the 'Speckled Band' room is too well-to-do (perhaps it is in a small separate room). Or perhaps this was not something you noticed or drew attention to, and water jugs and bowls were simply sitting unobserved on top of chests of drawers.

In the 1920s the wash-stand was clearly a common enough object. This, for instance, is from a book of stories for very young children. It is describing an adventure by a young child who has yet to get her own bedroom. She wakes up early in her parents' bedroom:

> And then she crept to the wash-stand, but she didn't think
> she could manage the big water-jug without waking Father
> and Mother. So she took up her shoes and her pink-striped
> cotton frock, and she creepy-crept to the door and opened
> it, only making just one tiny little click. And then she
> creepy-crept down the stairs, without disturbing Grandpa or
> Grandma or Uncle or Aunty, into the kitchen. [...] And then
> Milly-Molly-Mandy went into the scullery to wash.[41]

Here, then, is a piece of furniture that would have been standard
in any bedroom but which becomes almost completely forgotten
as soon as bathrooms become a fixture of domestic housing.

For small boys as well as for little girls dressing tables have
held an uncanny fascination. If for girls the dressing table offered
a dedicated place for learning the intricate art of femininity,
for boys it often seemed to signal the feeling that women (and
mothers in particular) were distinctly mysterious. The lotions
and potions, pastes and powders which are the periodic table
for a form of femininity that many little girls see as the 'open
sesame' to womanhood are laid out on the dressing table. The
artifice of this material performance of gender was no different
in scale from the studied masculinity of the playground, with its
powerful push-and-pull of bravado: I dare you too, you coward,
you chicken. Here, at the laboratory bench of femininity, was an
alchemical formula that would need dedication and commitment
to learn.

While dressing tables were once a necessary piece of furniture for the bedroom, their assured place in the room has been
gradually put in jeopardy. Where has the dressing table gone? Is
it lurking in bathrooms, or has it spread out, taking up a drawer
here, a cabinet shelf there, a mirrored area for this, a table-top
for that. In 1936, at the 'Everyday Things' exhibition, which was
determined to see that aesthetic consideration was given to daily

domestic items we come into contact with, much was made of the dressing table and its equipment. It specified that 'dressing table equipment' should normally include the following in some form as basics:

Cotton-wool holder
Bottle holders
Toilet bottle
Large jar
Powder bowl
Military brushes (natural ebony)
Military brushes (synthetic glass)
Manicure case
White xylonite [an early form of plastic] set (hand mirror,
    hair brush, dressing comb).[42]

It might seem that, in losing the dressing table, we have also lost a good deal of dressing-table equipment.

Throughout this book one of the crucial things I am keen to highlight is the way that central heating and other seemingly banal changes are in a symbiotic relationship with other, more socially significant, changes. Central heating opens up the house, expands it. But it also connects, making the distance between bedroom and bathroom seem closer. No longer do you have to 'brave it' to move from one room to the next: perhaps there is no point in having a dressing table when you can pad along to the bathroom to fix your hair and put your mascara on?

Freezing British houses were an invitation to inventors. In the days before central heating a Teasmade alarm clock may have been more of a bedroom necessity than it is today, when central heating can be set to come on automatically before you wake up. The first Teasmades may also account for the burn marks on the blankets we noticed before: the mechanism for an early version of this convenience from 1902 was such that 'when the alarm clock triggered the switch, a match was struck, lighting a spirit stove under the kettle. When the water came to the boil, the steam pressure filled a hinged flap, allowing the kettle to tilt and fill the teapot; then a plate swung over the stove and extinguished the flames.'[43]

Once a commonplace accessory for anyone wishing to abate the open-window policy of bedroom practice, central heating has also made the electric blanket obsolete. Electric blankets, like a good deal of other domestic equipment, turn out to have an intimate connection with the military (remember the saucepan made out of old Spitfire exhausts?):

In 1929 in Britain the Ex-Services Mental Welfare Society started making electric heating pads as they were a simple sewing job for the patient members. They used a German design whose inventors may not have been pleased to learn, after war broke out, that RAF maintenance staff adopted their idea for an electric blanket to keep night fighter aircraft engines from freezing up in the winter.[44]

The electric blanket came in various forms: 'electric heater that circulated hot water through flexible plastic piping forming a grid sewn into the blanket. There was also the electrically heated mattress and a bed heater made by Belling from left-over parts of a wartime incendiary bomb.'[45] But all seemed to have their own particular dangers: 'the first of the post war blankets were made with asbestos insulated resistors but they were only safe if they were kept dry. If the asbestos became wet there was risk of a shock and there were a number of fatalities.'[46] The general agreement seemed to be that, as long as you didn't wet yourself, you might well be all right and make it through the night – although a hot water bottle might be a lot easier: 'Any blanket up to the

British Standard is safe, provided a few simple rules are observed: do not fold or crease it, or pile clothes on it, when switched on; do not put pins in it; and unless it is of the low voltage type, do not use it if it is wet or worn, and switch it off before getting into bed.'[47]

Bedroom furniture holds a particular place in the memory archives for British householders. Bedrooms are, as Dr Alex Comfort thought, places where smell takes centre stage, but it isn't always the erotic intoxicants that Comfort has in mind. Smell is the sense that is often the most powerful in invoking memory. In Somerset Maugham's great sprawling and cloying novel *Of Human Bondage* the first thing that Philip does when he hears that his mother has died is to go and hide in her wardrobe:

> Philip opened a large cupboard filled with dresses and, stepping in, took as many of them as he could in his arms and buried his face in them. They smelt of the scent his mother used. Then he pulled open the drawers, filled with his mother's things, and looked at them: there were lavender bags among the linen; and their scent was fresh and pleasant. The strangeness of the room left it, and it seemed to him that his mother had just gone out for a walk.[48]

But if bedrooms are powerfully connected to memories – especially to childhood memories – through smell, they are also connected to the future through the practices of collecting that are associated with the bedroom. The very term 'bottom drawer' indicates the portion of the chest of drawers dedicated to the future:

> On the day we became engaged we started our collection of items to set up home together. My bedroom was soon overflowing and it seemed sensible to buy a chest of drawers to

store things in neatly as we knew we would have more than two years to wait before we could get married. So off we went and bought a chest of drawers for around £17. It seemed a lot of money in 1973. But what service it has given us, and only now is beginning to show a few signs of wear and tear. The children have climbed all over it and overstuffed it with their toys. It held my bottom drawer collection, all the clothes I collected before my first baby was born, and then I used it for the children's uniforms. So it is proving its worth to the whole family as we grow.[49]

And when the children have grown up and left, what happens to the bottom drawer then? Are these bottom drawers now filled with memories, with the baby clothes that are no longer any use but can't be let go of? Or empty except for old socks, jumpers and toys for grandchildren's visits? Or perhaps they are used to store the outmoded devices that were once bedroom necessities (electric blankets and old Teasmades)?

Across a hundred years the message has been the same: bedrooms should be restful. What has changed has been the insistence that the bedroom should take on a personality. When Charles Eastlake tells us that 'a room intended for repose ought to contain nothing which can fatigue the eye by complexity', he is also promoting his particular commitment to Art and Crafts furniture and decoration.[50] When Terence Conran a hundred years later argues that 'decoratively speaking, bedrooms should be restful, welcoming and uninhibitedly personal', he is also promoting his aesthetic; it is just that this aesthetic is omnivorous in range. Conran advises bedroom decorators that 'if you see yourself surrounded in flowers and frills, then stick out for it bravely. The atmosphere of the room is more likely to come off for being authentic than it would be were you to curb your inner longings and end up with a half-baked compromise – or a style that's plainly not you.'[51] Such words of wisdom will find the most receptive ears among those souls that hate compromise with a vengeance but who flirt with the half-baked on a daily basis: teenagers.

An identity laboratory – gonna make you a star

NO ENTRY

(Kids' Rooms)

The modern kids' bedroom, stuffed with toys and gadgets, decorated with giant posters of pop stars and football players, is a relatively recent phenomenon. Today the stereotypically denigrated teenager can be imagined festering in a miasma of hormones and whiffy socks while listening to loud, mournful music and contemplating the failure of the adult world to understand them. Generally they are imagined in a room of their own. Earlier worries about kids and their predilections might have imagined them sitting goggle-eyed in front of the TV or devouring comics, but they would, most likely, have been doing this in the shared spaces of living rooms and kitchens. The Lego-crazed kid who builds a miniature town that fills their bedroom or the morose teenager who sleeps through most of the day and stays up at night requires a house that allows them space to occupy a room all on their own.

From the perspective of the early years of the twentieth century, the contemporary notion of an ordinary child's bedroom occupied by a lone child would seem to be an extraordinary and, probably for most, an unimaginable and unnecessary luxury:

why would you put two brothers into separate rooms? When the 1935 Housing Act was introduced, with the idea of addressing serious overcrowding, a formula was established for judging how many people could be housed in different sizes of accommodation before it was overcrowded.[1] Thus a three-roomed flat or house was big enough for a maximum of five people. But 'five people' within the terms of the act didn't include children under one year old, and children between one and ten only counted as half a person. Similarly three rooms meant that any 'living' room could count as a room for sleeping in (and this could include the kitchen, if it was big enough). So a five-person household could have two adults, a child over ten, and four children under ten living in a two-bedroom house and not be seen to be officially overcrowded.

For many family houses the distribution of space among the members of the household might mean that siblings simply had to share rooms, or that living rooms would also become rooms for sleeping in. In the 1930s Bryan Magee, for instance, had to sleep in the living room: 'It was chiefly for reasons to do with sex, but also partly to reduce the amount of disturbance at night, that our parents decided eventually that Joan and I should sleep in separate rooms. She being older, and a girl, was to have a room to herself, the one we had shared, and I was to sleep in the living-room.'[2] But this didn't mean that the living room simply became his bedroom: 'a divan was bought and placed against the wall immediately to the left of the living-room door, to function as a settee during the day and a bed at night. My clothes went on being kept in my sister's room, because there was nowhere else to put them.'[3]

Other households were arranged in ways that would today seem decidedly odd. This is a description of a working-class household from the early 1940s:

Both bedrooms open off a small landing at the top of the stairs, which lead out of the living room. On this landing there is also a separate w.c. The bathroom is a small annexe off the kitchen, which also contains the copper. The parents live in the smaller bedroom, at the back of the house, which contains a double bed, a dressing-table, a small bedside table and bookcase full of books, prominent among which is a large family Bible. Both the children sleep in the larger bedroom, though their mother says that the girl is naturally wanting a room of her own now. Both have single beds in opposite corners of the room, and there is a small dressing-table with a mirror next to the girl's bed. A large built-in cupboard over the stairs is used for keeping toys in.[4]

When we find out that the daughter is seventeen and the son is eleven, we are given a scene that by today's standards many would find unacceptable. Of course, many found it unacceptable in the first half of the twentieth century. In *The Road to Wigan Pier* George Orwell describes rooms that can't be considered 'bedrooms' in the sense that we often give them today – more like dormitories or lodging houses: 'In one house, I remember, three grown-up girls sharing the same bed and all went to work at different hours, each disturbing the others when she got up or came in; in another house a young miner working on the night shift slept by day in a narrow bed in which another member of the family slept at night.' Alongside this shift-sleep system Orwell notes that the desire to separate adolescent male and females often meant cross-generational sleeping: 'In one family I visited there were a father and mother and a son and daughter aged round about seventeen, and only two beds for the lot of them. The father slept with the son and the mother with the daughter; it was the only arrangement that ruled out the danger of incest.'[5]

The modern kid's bedroom, in theory at least, is a place of

single occupancy and is fashioned to reflect the identity and interests of the occupant. To get there required a number of things to change across the twentieth century. As the three-bedroom house has remained something of a standard in terms of average housing stock in Britain, the one-room-per-child ideal has required the size of families to decrease significantly.[6] But, just as importantly, there had to be a change in domestic culture which meant that bedrooms could become more like living rooms for young people. Significantly, for this to be a viable proposition in a country such as Britain required the help of central heating. Yet we can't simply say that central heating caused bedrooms to be used during the day. While it might be tricky to stay in an unheated bedroom in winter, a culture had to emerge that might think that this would be a good thing to do and not just slightly odd (unless you were poorly and actually were in bed).

Nursery times

At the start of the twentieth century, relatively wealthy families with space enough for multiple guest rooms, who might also employ live-in servants, might well chose to have children sleeping together in a single bedroom (or nursery) until they were about eight or nine (at which point the well-to-do often packed them off to boarding-school). In J. M. Barrie's classic children's story *Peter Pan* the Darling family, living in London's Bloomsbury in what would probably be a four- or five-storey town house, have a nursery room rather than bedrooms, where all three children sleep watched over by their 'nurse', who happens to be a Newfoundland dog: 'The fire was warm, however, and the nursery dimly lit by three night-lights and presently the sewing lay on Mrs Darling's lap. Then her head nodded, oh, so gracefully. She was asleep. Look at the four of them, Wendy and Michael over there, John here, and Mrs Darling by the fire. There should have been a fourth night-light.'[7] *Peter Pan* (which began life as a stage play) imagines a world where dreams and imagination are actualised. The novel that Barrie wrote in wake of the success of the stage play is hardly a conventional children's book: it is written in a knowing, mocking and highly allusive adult voice looking back on pre-pubescent childhood.

The conceit of Barrie's story is to render the dream worlds of children and babies as concrete reality. The reality of children's imaginative worlds, in their dreams and in their play, differs only in degrees:

> Of all delectable islands the Neverland is the snuggest and most compact; not large and sprawly, you know, with tedious distances between one adventure and another, but nicely crammed. When you play at it by day with the chairs and table-cloth, it is not in the least alarming but in the two minutes before you go to sleep it becomes very nearly real. That is why there are night-lights.[8]

Neverland is the imaginative space that children occupy, and it is realised with the help of the underneath of tables, or a sheet spread over the backs of chairs.

The classics of children's literature across the twentieth century often demonstrate children's seeming ability to make manifest what is imaginary. It's as if the distinction between pretend and actuality, between dreams and reality, is something that is only established when a child reaches a certain stage in life (puberty): literature often frames this as a fall from grace. In children's literature whole worlds are created from stuffed or sentimentalised animals (*The Wind in the Willows* and *Winnie-the-Pooh*, for instance, or Beatrix Potter); new worlds are discovered on the edges of this one (*The Chronicles of Narnia* or the series of 'borrower' books by Mary Norton). While these books have very different moods, they all take seriously the imaginative power of children to create an elsewhere in the midst of a domestic setting. The anthropomorphism of these books, and their understanding that children psychically invest in the objects around them (particularly old bits of blanket and stuffed toys), will chime with the work of object-relations psychoanalysts such as Donald Winnicott in the 1950s – who will show that children use toys to rehearse their changing relationship with the world beyond themselves.

But if 1950s' psychoanalysis and children's literature seem to have a fairly liberal attitude towards children's fantasy life, the same can't be said about the advice literature aimed at bringing up babies in the first half of the twentieth century. For John Broadus Watson, whom we saw at the end of Chapter 7 suggesting that infants need to be strapped to toilets to make sure that they are properly potty trained:

> The sensible way to bring up children is to treat them as young adults. Dress them, bathe them with care and circumspection. Let your behaviour always be objective and kindly firm. Never hug and kiss them. Never let them sit in your lap. If you must, kiss them once on the forehead when they say goodnight. Shake hands with them in the morning. Give them a pat on the head if they have made an extremely good job of a difficult task. Try it out. In a week's time you will find how easy it is to be perfectly objective with your child and at the same time kindly. You will be ashamed of the mawkish, sentimental way you have been handling it.[9]

The present-day anxiety about how to bring up baby is echoed across the twentieth century. The debates in the twentieth century seem larger and more violently antagonistic: to breastfeed or not; to feed in the night or not; to wrap the child tightly or loosely; to comfort children or not; to feed on a four-hour or six-hour rotation. And while breast-feeding is a fairly democratic process, prudishness and the belief that formula was more scientifically concocted made poorer mothers particularly visible. Should you be both posh and a believer in the properties of breast milk, there was some help at hand:

> the epitome of the anti-breast-feeding trend was the patenting of an 'anti-embarrassment device for nursing mothers' in 1910. This was a massive harness which cupped the breasts and provided rubber-tube extensions for the nipple, ending with a rubber teat by which the baby could be fed in public places 'avoiding the necessity of exposing the person'. If you weren't using artificial milk, you could at least appear to be doing so.[10]

The debates about fresh air (and 'fresh' air often meant 'freezing' air) are, as we have seen already, tied to an idea of health and hygiene (and to children's literature – the open window is what allows Peter Pan and Tinker Bell access to the nursery). With infants the invigorating properties of fresh air were seen as a matter of life and death. Parents in 1922 were told, for instance, that 'infants should hardly be indoors at all between 8 in the morning and 5 at night in the winter, and from 7 a.m. to 10 p.m. in the summer'.[11] I think you get some sense of how dogmatic advisers were about fresh air when you read some of the words of people who wanted to temper this enthusiasm. Thus Ethel Brereton, writing in 1927, in a book called *The Happy Nursery*, would write against the 'fresh air' dogmatists while seeming to prescribe a level of 'fresh air' that to today's kids would seem pretty extreme:

> my personal opinion is that 'fresh air', the catchword of the day, has become an absolute fetish with the careful modern

mother. In the summer, I agree, it is worse than a crime – it is a blunder! – to be indoors for one unnecessary minute from getting-up time to going-to-bedtime, but in winter – no thank you! The healthy child only needs about three hours a day in the open air, as long as the day and night nursery windows are always open.[12]

For those who were marooned in a block of flats 'a special cage could be attached to an ordinary window by a friendly builder, so that cot, pram or play pen could be pushed out to greet the elements, even in a high-rise flat'.[13] In these conditions a nursery was fairly redundant as anything more than a place to sleep.

Whether children inhabit their own 'private' bedrooms or have to make do with more shared and improvised arrangements – an hour or so at the kitchen table before it is commandeered again – the need for somewhere for children to play has been constant in the twentieth century. Houses with space to spare and children who could use it might name a room the 'playroom' as a modern and slightly more grown-up term for the nursery. But whether there is a room dedicated to play or not, toys can animate spaces in the house, turning, potentially, any room into a playroom. As anyone knows who has found a Lego brick embedded in the sole of their foot when they are stumbling around half-awake, this isn't necessarily a good thing, and much of the twentieth century has been geared to containing the space of children within the home. It is only in more recent years, when outside space seems more treacherous, that children and their toys have a freer rein.

It is hard to imagine a sensory experience more evocative of childhood than the clammy touch and distinctive smell of Plasticine or the sound of Lego bricks connecting and disconnecting. The minuscule clothing of a Barbie doll or the hit-and-miss detailing of a Matchbox car reminds you of the multiple dimensions in which children's lives are lived. For children a table is not at first a surface to do things on – well, not without training – but an obstacle to navigate. Children often experience the underneath of the adult world: the behinds of things. What better place to play with dolls than under a table or behind a sofa? A doll or car can animate a domestic space, turning the indoor world of bedrooms or sitting rooms into vistas for speeding cars to travel and for big-haired dolls to totter.

Wooden bricks, rag dolls, hula hoops and bobbins-on-a-string are the age-old precursors of what in the twentieth century will become a fully fledged industry. A simplified taxonomy might divide toys into toys of skill (yo-yos and roller-skates, for instance), toys for mimicry (doll's houses, toy cars and such like) and toys of construction (from building blocks to Airfix models). It is an over-simplified schema – all toy use develops skills, for instance – but it does have some attractions for understanding domestic space in relation to children's playthings. For instance, we could suggest that toys that are predominantly about physical skill tend to take children out of the house; we might also say that toys for mimicry and toys of construction have been unevenly aimed at boys and girls (the 'girl' version of Meccano is shocking pink and shockingly limited).

Of course, dolls, as little human or animal avatars, are not necessarily more male or female, and the market for boys' dolls in the shape of lead soldiers or Action Man figures has always been strong. But the very word 'doll', as a figure for playing with, conjures up female babies and female children to be dressed up and mollycoddled (usually by little girls). Similarly, there is nothing inherent in building blocks that would be directed more at boys than girls; and educationalists who have insisted on the educational value of construction toys have sought to encourage children of both sexes to play at making and building with blocks. It is hard to think of any items more invested with the weight and expectation of gender than children's toys. In an age of endless consumerism the specificity of gender seems even more pronounced, as TV adverts parade sets of tiny domestic environments or work environments that seem entirely dedicated to the task of reproducing gender roles.

As educationalists and psychiatrists tell us, children use toys for making sense of the world, and perhaps particularly for making sense of the physical home and their relationship to it. A doll's house, for instance, one of the oldest and most elaborate of children's toys, is a world within a world. It is a set of rooms that you play with, within a room that is part of a set of rooms in a house. To complete the picture, there should be a playroom in the doll's house with a tiny replica of a doll's house within it. Classically the doll's house conjures up a world much grander than the average house that it will go into: the suburban villas of the between-the-wars era might well have had a doll's house based on the dimensions of a Georgian manor house. In some sort of primal way the doll's house teaches us a practical form of dreaming as a way of extending ourselves into grown-up realms. At the same time it could be seen as the first step on the property ladder: a down payment to pass on the love of home ownership.

When these toys are extended out into the post-Second World War period they look like down payments on super-gendered identity. In the 1960s Britain copied varied US dolls to provide children with little avatars to prepare them to go out into the world fully armed either with guns or handbags. The American GI Joe action figure became Action Man in 1966, while the quintessential Barbie became Sindy in 1963. The coupling of Joe and Barbie and Action Man and Sindy has fuelled both the toy and the film industry ever since.

But if dolls and doll's houses can mimic the world as it is, but in miniature, toys could also be used to develop it and invent a future for it. Throughout the twentieth century one major success of the toy industry in Britain has been construction kits of one sort or another. One of the toys with the greatest longevity has been Meccano, which was started in Liverpool in 1901 and continues today. Meccano provided minuscule engineering kits so that children could put together cars, cranes and crankshafts made out of standardised parts. Later they introduced engines so that these could become powered. Meccano was also used informally as a marker of child development: boys and girls who were not interested enough in being mini-engineers would simply be seen as under-developed. Some of these were particularly prescriptive, showing you exactly what it is you were going to make. Thus Airfix models, which began on the eve of the Second World War, showed you exactly what to make and how it would look: their business was verisimilitude. Of course, this relied on levels of dexterity that most children didn't possess, and the consequence of many initial attempts at model-making was a model Spitfire that looked like it had been dug up in Pompeii.

When all this comes together as a room full of toys, it could potentially replicate a whole social world in miniature. There, on the floor of bedrooms and playrooms, elaborately (and expensively) equipped children could physically recreate rooms, houses, people, jobs, traffic, infrastructure, landscapes and cityscapes. Psychiatrists like to see children playing out their psychodramas with toys: the train that is being attacked by the dinosaur is really daddy. But perhaps it is human history and human future that are being played out in scenarios that take us from primordial times to endless war, while boy dolls and girl dolls keep on keeping on life and love, domesticity and violence. But at some point children put their toys away. For good.

Teenage bed-sits
The transformation of a child's bedroom from being a functional space occupied by more than one sibling to an individual space

that the child could shape to fit her or his own emerging identity is a huge shift in how we think about houses and the rooms in them. You can get a sense of how the attitude towards bedrooms is changing in Mass-Observation's 1943 survey on workers' housing: 'bedroom satisfaction is an important factor to be taken into account. The size and number of rooms often calls for criticism, and people with growing children especially demand at least three bedrooms. In many homes, possessing three bedrooms, the third is found to be so small as to be almost useless.'[14] But even if houses have three decent-sized bedrooms, the possibility of allowing a child a 'room of their own' would mean that a family would need to be limited to two children.

For many, of course, the dream of having your own bedroom was precisely that – a dream – and sharing with siblings was the reality. But family sizes in general did decrease in Britain (and elsewhere) over the twentieth century, and this is usually explained through the availability of family planning advice and the introduction of contraception for women. But the idea of a family as a household made up of two heterosexual parents and their offspring is not something that can be treated as the norm for households. It might exist as the 'ideal' in the land of gravy commercials and estate agent publicity, but in the actuality of British housing such a family unit now accounts for a minority of households. Households generally have shrunk, with the biggest increase in household types being in people who now live alone. Indeed the size and presence of the family as a unit consisting of a couple and two or more children have so drastically diminished that it is now very much in the minority of households:

the proportion of households consisting of one family with children decreased from 54 per cent to 38 per cent between 1961 and 2011. Over the same time period the proportion of households containing couples with one or two dependent children went down from 30 per cent to 18 per cent (from about 4.9 million to 4.5 million) and those with 3 or more dependent children from 8 per cent to 3 per cent of all households (from about 1.3 million to 0.8 million households).[15]

When we talk about a 'family house' and this conjures up an image of heterosexual couples with two and a bit kids, we are not looking at the majority of households but at a significant minority: about the same as the number of people who live alone. Yet even if many children now split their week between two households, the idea of having a room of your own is a powerful one, and more and more likely to be a reality.

In the rest of this chapter I'm going to look at the way that the kids' bedroom emerged into a place that is closer to a living room than a functional sleeping and dressing room. Children are now much more present in the home than they have ever been. But they are also more independent within the house, having access to powerful communication devices that were unimaginable even a decade or two ago. Culturally the house has oriented itself to the needs of children like never before. If the house through most of the twentieth century was dedicated to the requirements of adults – with rooms set aside for adult-only use (which makes the parlour sound a lot racier than it undoubtedly was) – then children, when they are part of a household, seem to be everywhere: their toys are found in every room; their 'artwork' is stuck on fridges and hung on walls; the rhythm of the house beats to the timetable of its youngest people. The often voiced complaint from parents to teenage children that 'you treat this place like a hotel' is not always particularly accurate in describing classic teenage behaviour. The image of a teenager scuttling out of the kitchen with a sandwich and a drink, and heading off for their bedroom to consume it away from the prying eyes of adults and siblings, does not describe the action of a hotel guest, or at least not one comfortable with their role. It is closer to the actions of a prisoner (admittedly in a fairly open prison). Or, more pertinently, this image of the teenager is a cross between a prisoner, an awkward hotel guest and a tenant who is constantly behind with their 'rent' (chores, homework, promises). At least, so it sometimes seems.

Something happens in the world of teenagers and bedrooms in the 1960s and '70s. You can gauge this by the way the punishment of 'go to your' room gradually seems to disappear throughout the decades after the 1970s. The admonition 'go to your room' only makes sense if the room in question is undesirable, uninteresting and takes you away from where you'd rather be. If you'd rather be out or downstairs watching telly, then going to your room is a punishment, especially if the room in question has sub-zero temperatures and you were in the middle of watching *Wacky Races* or the last few minutes of *Tomorrow's World* while awaiting the start of *Top of the Pops*.

While it would be a mistake to think that the teenage bed-sit arrived overnight, we still might think of it as an event in the history of the domestic house. The teenage bed-sit was taken up unevenly – with some households being able to achieve it because they had the space and the money, while other teenagers lived in a world of freezing bedrooms and sibling dormitories. To begin with, it wasn't established as a room for displaying your teenage identity and escaping from the purview of parents. The teenage bed-sit, which you can see quite clearly in the mid-1970s, is eased into family space on the back of a major incentive in post-war education. After all, what better way to persuade a parent of the necessity of turning a room for sleeping and dressing into 'your mini pad', so to say, than by holding out the promise of some return in the shape of unrivalled A-level passes or being able to take up educational opportunities that were never available to a previous generation.

The dining/living room, with its busy to and fro, was OK for knocking out homework prior to O-levels or CSEs (Certificate of Secondary Education) and, before 1951, School Certificate, but if you were going to get serious about studying, then the bedroom as study would have to be the way to go. In the 1961 Department of the Environment booklet *Homes for Today & Tomorrow* there were clear recommendations that point towards the teenage bed-sit:

> Given adequate heating, children's bedrooms are made available for a range of activities other than sleeping and dressing. They may be used for study, or leisure activities; or they may be used to some extent as bed-sitting rooms. Besides room for a bed or divan, a bedside table, clothes storage, and storage of personal possessions (as will be required in the ordinary single bedroom), a room designed as a study bedroom needs space for a desk, a chair and a book case. A bed-sitting room needs in addition space for at least one easy chair.[16]

In 1961 this suggestion would have echoed with the brave new world of an expanding higher education provision that was being put in place. Between 1961 and 1965 seven new universities were opened, the so-called plate-glass universities (Sussex, York, East Anglia, Lancaster, Essex, Warwick and Kent), with the promise of a large increase in university places. This expansion of education was a combination of political perspectives – the 'one nation' conservatism of the 'never had it so good' Macmillan government and the 'white heat of technology' vision of Wilson.

By the early 1970s the children's bed-sitting room appeared to be less a 'study' and more a 'squat', or that is the way it can seem in a novel like *The Buddha of Suburbia*. While Hanif Kureishi's novel came out in 1990, the narrative is set in the early 1970s, a period when Kureishi (who was born in 1954) was studying for

his A-levels, before attending the plate-glass University of Lancaster (and subsequently leaving after a year). Early on in the
novel the main character, Karim, is visiting the wealthier, more
middle-class and bohemian Kay family and is taken to Charlie
Kay's bedroom:

> On the upstairs landing of the house was a ladder which
> led up to Charlie's attic. 'Please remove your watch,' he said.
> 'In my domain time isn't a factor.' So I put my watch on the
> floor and climbed the ladder to the attic, which stretched out
> across the top of the house. Charlie had the whole space to
> himself. Mandalas and long-haired heads were painted on
> the sloping walls and low ceiling. His drum-kit stood on the
> floor. His four guitars – two acoustic and two Stratocasters
> – leaned against the wall in a line. Big cushions were flung
> about. There were piles of records and the four Beatles in
> their *Sergeant Pepper* period were on the wall like gods.[17]

Charlie might well be doing homework here, but he is just as likely
to be doing drugs and having sex. Charlie is as much a figure of
fun as he is someone to be envied. Filled with self-importance, he
is a personality that can adapt to the latest fashion as he trades in
off-the-shelf psychedelic clichés for ready-to-wear Punk prov-
erbs and mockney (mock-cockney) rhyming slang. The arc of
the novel follows Karim's changing attitude towards Charlie as
it changes from love and envy to bitterness and pity to, finally,
some form of rapprochement as Karim accepts Charlie with all
his faults for what he is. In this journey the 'chill-out pad' at the
top of the house is both something to envy and faintly ludicrous.

Charlie's space is substantial, and it is also culturally and
physically separate from the space of the grown-ups. The
teenage bed-sit marks a significant shift in the cohesiveness of
the domestic house in the social imagination. But its significance

doesn't just lie in the way that it alters the consistency of the house. We could see the teenage bed-sit as a major symptom of a number of social changes that impact on the culture of the house in significant ways. For instance, throughout the twenti-eth century children's use of the outdoors altered: as one news-paper reported in summer 2010, 'the distance our kids stray from home on their own has shrunk 90% since the 70s; 43% of adults think a child shouldn't play outdoors unsupervised until the age of 14 [...] 21% of today's kids regularly play outside, compared with 71% of their parents.'[18] For anyone who grew up before the 1980s most of childhood was spent outdoors, whether that was in the countryside or in cities.

That sense of shrinking space (whether we totally trust the figures or not) is connected to a number of factors: the exponential increase in traffic, which often means that a house is surrounded by a potentially threatening and malevolent force (high-speed cars and lorries); the increased perception of crime, particularly relating to children ('stranger danger'); and, of course, some real fears from children that the local park is full of bullies who will mug you for your mobile. These are some of the forces that might stop you going outside so much, but it would be wrong to assume that this is all that is going on. There are more reasons for kids to stay inside, and the bed-sit is part of this: since the 1960s children have become a growing consumer group, with more and more products aimed at them. The home becomes somewhere where children can consume the myriad of products aimed at them, from music to TV, from games to gadgets. Kids, it seems, were becoming powerful consumers but also needed environments where they could be safe and 'free', lest they turn to drugs and cults (fears about young adults joining cults such as the Children of God were particularly prevalent in the 1980s).

In *The House Book* Terence Conran discusses the design of older children's bedrooms in a manner that is different from the way the rest of the house is discussed. His tone is confessional and melancholic, but also practical – suggesting that Conran has had his fair share of living with stroppy teenagers over the years. Teenage kids need space to live, space to express themselves and space to fill with their culture. So, adults – stand back. It is sage advice:

> The best way to prevent yourself from constant worry as to the whereabouts of your older children is to make it easy for them to bring their friends home. This means arranging for conditions in which they don't have to make conversation with you all the time, so a room that isn't just a bedroom is all-desirable. The bed will have to serve as a sofa/lounging area for entertainment purposes.[19]

Of course, the Conran-like parent might well find that giving kids the freedom to fix up the room in their own way results in a style clash. But this is also part of the sense of mentally separating off the teenage room from other parts of the house:

> By the time that children have reached the bed-sitter stage, they will have a taste of their own. It may be frightful, but it must be considered; to ban everything that you don't consider impeccable does not guarantee that they'll grow up with faultless tastes of their own; they're that much more likely to rebel against yours as soon as they have the opportunity.[20]

Ah: the future style-conscious Conran-ites will need to spend a few years out in the taste-wilderness of tacky posters and grotty furniture before they can return to the faultless style of pine tables and chicken bricks.

But a style clash might be insignificant compared to a tidiness clash or hygiene clash:

It is also useless to expect your children to have the same feelings about neatness as you have. So don't blanche at displays of whatever they collect – just keep the door shut and realize that a tidy room is far more unnatural to most young people than an untidy one. Messiness, in any case, is a passing phase, and provided that there is enough storage space, strewn floors and heaped chairs will miraculously clear – in time. All you need is patience and understanding.[21]

This was Conran in agony-uncle mode: accept the floor-drobe, it is just a phase. Charlie's bedroom is its own world of taste and its own world of hygiene.

But the teenage bedroom really came of age when televisions started multiplying and when the age of the home computer meant that the ownership of computers wasn't limited to the one nuclear physicist in the house. The bedroom as media hub shifts the arrangement of the house once again: now the child can be physically ensconced in the room upstairs while the parent is downstairs worrying where they are in that often tawdry cosmos of the internet. 'Stranger danger' is no longer confined to the local park and the walk home from school. In some ways it is the final shift in the cohesiveness of the home: the physical unity of the house contains a multitude of other spaces, many of them in the form of the countless screens that today's houses often contain. Sonia Livingstone's research from 2007 claims that

For many young people now, a personalized media environment is taken for granted, in striking contrast with their parents' upbringing. In interviews with children, some have lost track of their possessions. One six year old boy told us, 'I've got two computers in the house, I've got Sega, and a Nintendo. No, I've got three, Sega, Supernintendo and the normal Nintendo.' In another family, the children disagreed on the number of television sets they possessed – was it 9 or 11, they wondered? – although they were clear that every room, especially the bedrooms, contained a set.[22]

In her interviews with children Livingstone shows how today's kids' bedrooms are often media hubs. Here is a nine-year-old girl imagining her ideal bedroom and the girl that inhabits it: 'She's got all these comics on the bed, and she likes to read them, and she's got a computer next to her TV so if she gets bored she can just move around quick, and she's got like a computer booklet on computers and TV, and she's got a telephone with a hi-fi midi system sort of thing.'[23] You could imagine this nine-year-old quizzing an estate agent about the forms of connectivity a possible future house has.

The novelist and journalist Will Self describes his sons' rooms as places dedicated to computer gaming: 'the 15-year-old in particular excels at all gaming, and having outgrown the man cave last month has moved his command centre upstairs, from where he now directs operations from in front of a battery of VDUs that would put Nasa – *c.* 1969, admittedly – to shame. He switches from game play to web searches for so-called "cheats" with effortless fluidity.'[24] These rooms are high-tech control towers where all sorts of operations can be performed: the kids might be playing at slaughtering Nazi zombies, or building the New Babylon on Minecraft; or they may be being groomed by the inexhaustible internet advertising algorithms into a new breed of super-consumer.

The sense that these rooms are their private property is palpable. For one fifteen-year-old from Sonia Livingstone's interviews the worst sin of parenting is to mess with your children's stuff:

last year I went to Austria and erm, I came back and I nearly had a heart attack because my mum had completely cleaned

my room ... She had completely blitzed my room and I was
so angry about it ... It is my own private space and I really
don't like her touching it ... She just goes on and on about me
cleaning it and I mean, I try to tell her that it is my personal
space and let me have it how I want.[25]

Perhaps this mum is blitzing the room precisely because she is
worried that the child will live there for ever. Another of Livingstone's interviewees, also fifteen, looks like she has no intention
of ever leaving home:

I'm usually in my bedroom ... I think that I like to be by
myself really. I don't know. I suppose it's just because at the
moment I have got all my furniture arranged like in a sitting
room area, a study room area and my bedroom and it is just,
like, really cool and I just like to go there because I know that
that is my room ... I mean I have decorated it how I want it
and it's just like a room I don't think I will ever move out.[26]

This is also the bedroom that Griff Rhys Jones remembers
from his teenage years in the late 1960s in suburban Essex:
'When I went to her house she introduced me to her startled
mother and led me straight up to her bedroom for a bit of torrid
fumbling. There wasn't any actual sex. None of us seemed to get
sex, however much we boasted, though we discussed the possibility endlessly. The girls were generally far too canny.'[27] In a
crucial sense the teenage bedroom wasn't about whether you had
a beanbag or a chair but about whether your parents would knock
when they wanted to come in or whether they would come in at
all unless expressly invited.

But this sense of a bed-sit in amid a shared family home might
not be just reserved for kids. Some adults might also be enjoying
a private realm within the fairly public space of a shared house.

Virginia Woolf's sense that every creative woman needed 'a room of one's own' might be extended to apply to anyone who wants to hang on to an identity distinct from their role in a household. So here is a woman with grown-up children (who visit a lot and bring round their children) who grew up as a servant girl where she shared a bedroom with a cook:

> My special room where I sleep is a 'glory hole' which is really quite organised. It would take me a month of Sundays to describe it though. There are books, tapes, photographs, snaps, Xmas cards, files, a large metal desk with a typewriter on it, a needlework box, a TV set, a radio, a jar with umpteen kinds of scissors and a pen container, an out-going letter rack, a magazine stand. Sometimes it gets in a mess but then I just have to tidy up and put things in their places. The floor is carpeted. There is a big old fir tree right next to the window that darkens the room.[28]

Perhaps this is someone who has followed Marie Stopes's advice to sleep apart from her husband; perhaps this is someone living both together and separately in a house that you could imagine being made up of bed-sits held together by communal rooms such as kitchens. Or perhaps we could simply say that here is someone who has seen the child's bedroom turn into a bed-sit-pad and decided to have some of that for herself.

The 2004 IKEA catalogue employed a child-centred viewpoint as that year's promotional gimmick. In its introduction to the bedroom section it has what looks to be an eight-year-old boy saying: 'My big brother's room is the business. He's got a whole den under his bed. There are just two rules: no spilling the popcorn – and no sisters allowed. No way!'[29] The bed in question is one of many 'loftbeds' that IKEA sell. They are like bunk beds but without the bottom bunk, but they are also much wider than the utilitarian bunk bed. Under the platform is the den: some chairs, a rug and a TV. On the other side of the room is a 'work station': a desk with a computer. Little brother says 'even though he doesn't like to admit it, I'm as good on the computer as my older brother is. He lets me go on the internet to check out stuff for homework. And we play games on it, too, of course. He's got his own desk and everything.'[30] In the pages of the IKEA catalogue the teenage bed-sit/bedroom is also a home office. The generations that were the first to enjoy the teenage bed-sit would be the generation who would be taking their work home with them in the form of computers and mobile phones.

Holding on to the once loved, once needed.

MIND YOUR STEP

(The Expanded House)

This book has been looking at the interior of the ordinary house as it has been imagined and lived in the twentieth century and in the fledgling twenty-first century. But we can't escape the fact that 'the great indoors' – our domestic landscape – also includes other spaces that might not necessarily be inside the house but are intrinsically part of our homes. Gardens and yards aren't, of course, just the plot of land your own house resides next to but a space that a household might use on a daily basis and tend and care for perhaps as much as, if not more than, any inside room. The house itself also contains spaces that might not be part of our day-to-day living but which nonetheless are part of the world of the house. Spaces such as attics, closets, cellars, spare rooms, box rooms, garages and sheds are part of the practical world of the house: they are often part of the world of storage, of things-no-longer-in-circulation; or they are practical housing for coats, cars and lawn mowers. But as well as being practical, they are spaces that often resonate with something symbolic or just plain spooky.

Attics and cellars or basements are the spaces that most

vividly vacillate between the practical and the symbolic, the rational and the supernatural. Attics are where we store things: memories, childhood things, the things of the generations before us. In some senses any attic is always 'haunted' by things that are past. The act of putting something in the attic is the act of putting something into the past, into storage, into the archive. It is no wonder that a bibliographic study of horror and super-natural literature in Britain during the nineteenth and twenti-eth centuries is called *Shadows in the Attic*.[1] But gothic literature and supernatural fiction are not often interested in the ordinary house. It is the large manor houses set out in the middle of nowhere, such as Usher's House in Edgar Allan Poe's story 'The Fall of the House of Usher', from 1839, that is quintessential for the genre. M. R. James, for instance, concocts a story where the gothic grand house enters the ordinary house as a supernatural presence. In 'The Haunted Doll's House', from 1931, the Doll's House in question (a grand manor house, of course) performs a little play each night showing how a murder had taken place. But in trying to find the provenance of the Doll's House the antique dealer who has bought it and has spent a terrified night watching its murderous events unfold inquires where it has come from: 'of course, it came out of the lumber room of a country 'ouse – that anyone could guess'.[2] The lumber room is another name for an attic or box room used for storage: haunted doll's houses should rightfully live in attic rooms – and stay there locked away.

The French philosopher Gaston Bachelard once claimed that attic rooms take us towards rationality, whereas cellar rooms take us towards subterranean forces: 'As for the cellar [...] it is first and foremost the *dark entity* of the house, the one that partakes of subterranean forces. When we dream there, we are in harmony with the irrationality of the depths.'[3] While subterranean forces do live in the cellars of both fictional narratives and real ones, it would seem that there isn't necessarily any respite if you head for the attic. Bachelard, it would seem, wasn't entirely *au fait* with the British ghost story.

Grand houses have the sort of spare space that allows for supernatural events to take place: most houses are just too cramped to imagine other worlds within them. The land of Narnia might be accessible through a very ordinary wardrobe, but the wardrobe itself has to be found in an out-of-the-way back room in a very large house:

> It was the sort of house that you never seem to come to the end of, and it was full of unexpected places. The first few doors they tried led only into spare bedrooms, as everyone had expected they would; but soon they came to a very long room full of pictures and there they found a suit of armour; and after that was a room all hung with green, with a harp in one corner; and then came three steps down and five steps up, and then a kind of little hall and a door that led out on to a balcony, and then a whole series of rooms that led into each other and were lined with books – most of them very old books and some bigger than a Bible in a church. And shortly after that they looked into a room that was quite empty except for one big wardrobe; the sort that has a looking-glass in the door. There was nothing else in the room at all except a dead blue-bottle on the window-sill.[4]

It is not in the under-stairs cupboard of a terraced house but there at the back and at the top of a large labyrinthine house that you find the portal to Narnia.

During the eighteenth century and for much of the nineteenth the standard town house would have presented a class sandwich: middle- and upper-class life sandwiched between the workers living in attics and working in basements. For many houses this would change in the twentieth century. Maxwell

Hutchinson and a team of television researchers took one Georgian terraced house in Bristol and traced its history and what this had meant for the various rooms in it.[5] The ground-floor 'basement' rooms remained as a kitchen (though the scullery room changed into various workrooms). The top-floor attic rooms, though, were constantly changing. The house was built in 1786, and from then until the mid-nineteenth century the attic rooms were for live-in servants. From then until the 1930s the attic rooms are either spare bedrooms or lodgers' rooms. From the 1930s to the 1990s they are storage rooms. The house is going through hard times, it is becoming unfashionable in a down-at-heel area, but by the 1980s it is becoming gentrified. In a wealthier area the attic rooms would have been maintained as servant rooms for much longer into the twentieth century.

Houses that had once been prosperous and lived in by one household were falling into decline precisely because such households were not in the ascendancy and well-to-do households would more likely live in suburban splendour. Attics and basements in these town houses were becoming flats and maisonettes. This was happening in a piecemeal way. Robert Louis Stevenson's novella from 1886 *The Strange Case of Dr Jekyll and Mr Hyde* describes the process of the change in use of town houses:

> Round the corner from the by-street there was a square of ancient, handsome houses, now for the most part decayed from their high estate, and let in flats and chambers to all sorts and conditions of men: map-engravers, architects, shady lawyers, and the agents of obscure enterprises. One house, however, second from the corner, was still occupied entire; and at the door of this, which wore a great air of wealth and comfort, though it was now plunged in darkness except for the fan-light, Mr Utterson stopped and knocked.[6]

Who knew that map-engravers and architects were low life? But Stevenson's story is precisely about showing something or someone disreputable existing within 'polite society'.

In Virginia Woolf's 1925 novel *Mrs Dalloway*, we see a fifty-year-old woman who is living in what seems to be a fairly stale marriage and where separate rooms aren't part of Marie Stopes's recipe for maintaining the ecstasies of married love but make for a more frosty arrangement. The Dalloways' attic room is a spare room for Clarissa Dalloway to sleep in. This is her ascending to her room:

> Like a nun withdrawing, or a child exploring a tower, she went upstairs, paused at the window, came to the bathroom. There was the green linoleum and a tap dripping. There was an emptiness about the heart of life; an attic room. Women must put off their rich apparel. At midday they must disrobe. She pierced the pincushion and laid her feathered yellow hat on the bed. The sheets were clean, tight stretched in a broad white band from side to side. Narrower and narrower would her bed be. The candle was half burnt down and she had read deep in Baron Marbot's *Memoirs*. She had read late at night of the retreat from Moscow. For the House sat so long that Richard insisted, after her illness, that she must sleep undisturbed. And really she preferred to read of the retreat from Moscow. He knew it. So the room was an attic; the bed narrow; and lying there reading, for she slept badly, she could not dispel a virginity preserved through childbirth which clung to her like a sheet.[7]

It is a dense passage, as you'd expect from one of the most famous modernist novels, but the association of the attic room with a mood of depression, of the feeling that life has passed you by, is palpably evident. Perhaps it is the association of the attic room with storage – as if Mrs Dalloway is herself in storage in some sense.

Woolf was writing about London town houses that were changing. And they were changing everywhere. The sort of town houses Woolf describes were built for large households, which were often large in both the size of the family and the number of people involved in the upkeep of the family. So a financially comfortable couple with young children would probably be likely to have a nurse, a cook and a maid as standard and living in. The suite of rooms on the top floor would be servants' bedrooms. The rooms at the bottom of the house were given over to the material labour of the house. The upstairs rooms would include various reception rooms but also bedrooms, which would be for children and their parents but might also include other relatives. By the 1930s much of this housing had fallen into disrepair. The now much-desired grand Georgian terraces that you find in cities such as Bristol, Bath and Edinburgh were too big for middle-class households and had been turned into *ad hoc* flats and maisonettes. Through much of the twentieth century such housing could form the basis of the cheapest of lodging houses.

The conversion of houses into separate units or into small hotels and hostels was the fate of much of the single-occupancy housing from the Victorian and Georgian times. The attempt to do this in an organised fashion was also an attempt to maintain this housing as usable for middle-class households but also as discrete units: 'Immediately after 1945 there may have been some justification for these adaptations to help to meet the dearth of accommodation, but anything short of self-contained flats, maisonettes or houses should be discouraged and even prohibited for their inadequacy and inconvenience of arrangement.'[8]

The sort of piecemeal adaptation of these town houses into

flats meant that one family might be living in attic rooms or basement rooms having to share a bathroom with other families living on other floors in the house. In an attempt to keep these houses from ruination, and in an attempt to maintain the 'class' specificity of these conversions, one document from the 1950s advises that 'conversions should be of a scale suitable to the neighbourhood. People are more at ease living amongst those of their own status, and to introduce families of an altogether different class tends to destroy the neighbourhood pattern'[9] – and bring down house prices. Making sure that tenants were 'suitable' was achieved through keeping rents at a certain level (as today, you paid a premium to live among those who can afford to pay a premium) and through word of mouth and networks.

For those houses 'attic' meant usable space in one form or another. Today it means much the same thing. Since the 1970s designers and tastemakers have been arguing that an attic is wasted space and that there is a real opportunity for transforming your house through a loft conversion. In the 1970s tastemakers went to great lengths to tell you just how tricky this could be. Today it is just assumed that, if you can convert your loft, you will: 'If you ask estate agents which home improvements add the most value to a home, the answer is always the same – loft conversions.'[10] To see attics and basements as opportunities for extending the usable space of your house and increasing its value, rather than as spaces where ghostly presences could be felt, is a shift from thinking about domestic space symbolically to thinking about it practically and economically. In the early years of the twenty-first century this shift was recognised by a host of TV shows dedicated to buying, selling and doing up your house. The endlessly perky property experts Kirstie Allsopp and Phil Spencer started the ball rolling with *Location, Location, Location* (C4, 2000– ongoing), which was joined by their *Relocation, Relocation* in 2004. Both programmes have Kirstie and Phil showing people their choices of properties and telling them why they are such great buys.

But perhaps the most explicitly profit-driven TV property presenter is Sarah Beeny. Her *Property Ladder* (C4, 2001–06) made no bones about making hard decisions based on finances, and she constantly berated members of the public who came on to the show as neophyte property developers who made decisions based on aesthetic considerations rather than economics. Her most recent show is prosaically titled *Double Your House for Half the Money* (C4, 2012– ongoing) and is aimed at helping 'people achieve their property dreams without breaking the bank in these recession-hit times'. This is TV for when the property market is stagnant and suggests that, rather than move house, people who are searching for a dream home might turn 'the most modest property [the one they are currently living in] into a sensational home by extending, converting or drilling down'. It is property TV for a country where the housing stock is often cramped and where there isn't always the possibility of extending. Damp, dark and unused basements become light-filled bedrooms and kitchens; attic rooms become home offices. 'If you don't have the space to extend upwards or outwards, another option could be to go downwards'; here 'basements can be used for a huge variety of purposes – playrooms, home cinemas, music rooms, wine cellars.'[11]

One of the reasons for turning basements and attics into usable space is to make room for a home office. The idea that we are all (potentially) working from home is an idea often mooted by Sunday newspaper journalists. Of course, for most people working from home is an impossibility: however virtual the world becomes, bus drivers, nurses and rubbish collectors would have a hard time working out of a basement office. According to the Telework Research Network, 'only 2.5% of the workforce consider home their primary place of work'.[12] For those that do chose to work at home the benefits can be huge. For Natalie in Essex:

> The difference between working from home and at the office was simple. Day in office – Stagger in after 2 hour commute. Gossip and moan with colleagues, try to work but fail to do so due to hot desking problems and noise in open plan office. Give up after required hours, commute 2 hours home. Cry with exhaustion and feelings of failure. Day at home – Get up, boot up PC, start work. Plough through work mountain with clarity & drive. Realise it's midday and I'm still in my nightie. Get dressed, eat, start washing machine. 10 minute chat with colleagues online. Return to work mountain. Finish work mountain by 17:00. Spend evening reasonably awake and happy with life.

For others, though, the experience is more ambiguous. For Fiona from Southampton:

> My husband & I both work from home – it's a nightmare! I have teenage kids which technically should make it easier but they forget stuff & assume that because we're at home we can drop it into school. Then when they get home we have to get involved in every dilemma. Facebook calls me A LOT of the time as does the dishwasher/washing/ironing etc. Time with my husband is no fun as we just have work life & home life to talk about. That said I LOVE that I can meet up with my friends whenever & go for sneaky breakfasts with my husband![13]

Working from home turns your labour into a form of housework, and the major problem there is to know when to quit: 'there's no natural point at which to go home, because you are home.'

Dig it

In describing the city as being like a body, urban planners have, in the past, suggested that parks are the city's lungs. If this metaphor is applied to housing, then we would need to look at the outdoor space belonging to a house as a measurement of its lung capacity. From such a metaphorical vantage point we would have to say that much of the working-class housing inherited from the nineteenth century consisted of wheezing asthmatics set amid smoggy industrial landscapes. The 1930s' semi-detached house, on the other hand, seems, in comparison, like a keep-fit fanatic with expanded lung capacity.

Associating the garden with health is still a living aspect of gardens. For instance, this is one Mass-Observer describing her garden: 'It's an end of terrace on a semi-main road, where we have a front and back garden. The front is about 14 foot square and is *mine*, where I grow my flowers, etc. The back is about 20–30 feet and belongs to the children and pets, so not a lot grows there except healthy children and pets.'[14] Today we are also likely to think of gardens as a place for hobbies, relaxation and consumption. Gardens in Britain are big business: 'Garden ownership in Britain has expanded to the point where there are now over 20 million private gardens – by far the highest number per capita of any nation in Europe – and gardening is the nation's most popular and widespread leisure activity.'[15]

Throughout the twentieth century the domestic garden has been a place where relaxation and work coexist: it is a place for delighting in the colour and perfume of nature and for growing prize-winning marrows and odd-looking carrots. The emphasis on work or leisure has fluctuated, and the long history of the back garden has seen a drift towards comfort and relaxation – towards convenience and low-maintenance gardens – and away from gardens as a provider of food. Such tendencies may well alter in the future as fashion and necessity dictate. Today, for instance, there is a return to the sort of small-scale farming of a bygone age where even people in urban areas with tiny gardens keep chickens and try to grow as many vegetables as they can.

The garden as a requirement of healthy life has had a symbolic life that exceeds the sense of merely physical health. One of the most famous examples of this is Oscar Wilde's Christian parable about the virtue of generosity and the moral corruption of some versions of private property. In his tale about 'The Selfish Giant' the giant decides not to let the local children play in his lovely garden and, to this end, erects a tall wall around it and a notice telling the children to keep out. The result of this is that the garden is kept in an eternal winter:

> then the Spring came, and all over the country there were little blossoms and little birds. Only in the garden of the Selfish Giant it was still winter. The birds did not care to sing in it as there were no children, and the trees forgot to blossom. Once a beautiful flower put its head out from the grass, but when it saw the notice-board it was so sorry for the children that it slipped back into the ground again, and went off to sleep. The only people who were pleased were the Snow and the Frost.[16]

The giant, you'll be pleased to hear, learns the error of his ways and ends up letting the children play in the garden (though he gets his heart broken in the process).

Children playing allow the fecundity of nature to appear in the garden: selfishness renders nature barren and throws the garden into a permanent winter of decay. Such associations are part of an age-old cosmology that associates spiritual values with the cycles and seasons of nature. This strong association between nature and spiritual meaning may well account for the way that gardens are often made to represent the state of the soul of a household. If, for a person, eyes are the window to the soul, then the family or household's window to the soul is the garden. At least, you could think this by looking at the way that gardens figure in children's literature.

Frances Hodgson Burnett's *The Secret Garden*, from 1911, is perhaps the story that has most extended the metaphor of the garden as a form of spiritual barometer. It tells the tale of Mary Lennox, a daughter of Empire who has been brought up in India as a feckless, selfish child as a result of having parents who were more interested in themselves than in their child. Child-rearing was left to the Indian servants. The story is set in motion by the death of both of Mary's parents (as well as the servants) in a cholera epidemic, and Mary is sent to live in her uncle's house in Yorkshire. Her uncle is also bereaved by the death of his rose-growing, garden-loving wife. The secret garden in the story, then, is the walled garden that Mary's aunt had tended but which has now been locked up after she died. It also turns out that the uncle and aunt have a child who is Mary's age and is suffering from ill health – he appears to be unable to walk. Mary, then, is an unhappy and spoilt child who goes to live in another unhappy household.

Leaving aside the servants (who seem generally strong, healthy and happy), this is a household in decline through both physical and spiritual maladies. Physically, for instance, Mary is lethargic and generally allergic to the benefits of fresh-air activities. Gardening and a skipping rope will fix this aspect of her degeneracy. But Mary, the invalid nephew and the uncle are also suffering from a grief that is 'stuck'. The maladies of the soul for this household are so involved and so extensive that Frances Hodgson Burnett has her work cut out to describe the garden in such a way that it is able to show the extent of the family's decline while also holding out the promise of what physical and spiritual good health might look like:

It was the sweetest, most mysterious-looking place anyone could imagine. The high walls which shut it in were covered with the leafless stems of climbing roses, which were so thick that they were matted together. Mary Lennox knew they were roses because she had seen a great many roses in India. All the ground was covered with grass of a wintry brown, and out of it grew clumps of bushes which were surely rose-bushes if they were alive. There were numbers of standard roses which had so spread their branches that they were like little trees. There were other trees in the garden, and one of the things which made the place look strangest and loveliest was that climbing roses had run all over them and swung down long tendrils which made light swaying curtains, and here and there they had caught at each other or at a far-reaching branch and had crept from one tree to another and made lovely bridges of themselves.[17]

The garden is simultaneously wonderful and vile, glorious and disgusting: 'Mary did not know whether they [the roses] were dead or alive'. As in 'The Selfish Giant', we get a sense that the sprucing up of the garden is going to coincide with a sprucing up of the soul.

Frances Hodgson Burnett's story was informed by the ideas of Christian Science, and the symbolism of gardens is such that it is hard to escape the super-symbol of the garden as Eden. But perhaps it is something that we shouldn't try to escape. Certainly it seems to me better to think that, when neighbours are quizzing you about the state of your garden, they are concerned only with your spiritual well-being and not at all interested in what your clutter and dead flowers are doing for local house prices.

The moral aspect of gardening came into a much more prag-matic focus in the late 1930s. During the Second World War the 'Dig for Victory' campaign made it clear that it was your patriotic duty to grow food: one of the first media gardeners came to prominence at this time, advising the Kitchen Front on how to squeeze the most out of their plots of land. C. H. Middleton, known simply as 'Mr Middleton', had started broadcasting gardening advice on the radio from the early 1930s, but it was after war broke out that his broadcasting and publications became a national institution. Mr Middleton's publications are filled with wistfulness about the loss of gardening-for-pleasure in relation to the current necessity of gardening as a way of pursuing war aims:

> There is no more peaceful spot on earth than an English garden, and for some years you and I have been building up our little flower gardens, making them more beautiful, more intimate, and more than ever an essential part of our homes. But grim times are with us, and under stress of circumstances we are now called on to reorganise those gardens, and turn them into munition factories; for potatoes and beans are munitions of war as surely as are bullets and shells; and the gardeners of England can do much to help the nation in its hour of need.[18]

As part of the war effort, the gardener becomes a sort of munitions worker. But you get the sense that national pride is to be found not in churning out carrots and spuds but in the wish to see the sensory pleasures of the garden return: 'For the moment potatoes, onions, carrots and so on must receive our full attention; but we may look forward to the time when this nightmare will end, as end it must – and the morning will break with all our favourite flowers to greet us once more.'[19] However much the garden could be a sanctuary from war, the requirements of total war leave little untouched:

It seems a pity to introduce the spirit of war into our peaceful gardens, but I'm afraid there is no help for it, the invaders are forming up their battalions, and we shall have to be on the defensive. This year, above all years, we must do everything possible to keep our crops and plants free from pests and diseases, and the best way to do that is to tackle them early, before they have a chance to dig themselves in.[20]

But alongside the metaphors of embattled gardens the war could provide in material ways too: 'If you can pick up a load of old brick dust, or mortar rubble from a demolished building, it is excellent stuff for heavy clay soil, so are the dead leaves from the trees.'[21] Bomb sites could provide material for aerating your soil. Mr Middleton was bombed out of his house during the war: he died from a heart attack two weeks after the war ended.

The garden as a munitions factory producing vital sustenance for survival in hard times was not a condition that would have been particularly new to rural agricultural workers. Indeed for rural labourers the cottage garden wasn't a hobby but a crucial way of making ends meet, as Mass-Observation's 1947 study of an Exmoor village demonstrates. This was part of a Mr Tame's routine just after the end of the war. Tame was a carter, who looked after and drove the farm horses. After a day of work that starts on the farm at 7 a.m. he

arrives back at Porch Cottage about 6.30 p.m. to find Mrs Tame putting the finishing touches to a two-course evening meal; so he takes off his jacket, rolls up his sleeves, turns in the neck of his shirt and has a good wash and shave. They then have supper – stewed steak and onions, potatoes, cauliflower, and rhubarb tart, on a typical evening. Water is drunk with the meal, and later on, about 9.30 p.m., they both have a cup of Bovril before going to bed. After supper Mr Tame goes straight out into his garden, for there is always plenty to do there.

Mr Tame also works on Saturday mornings: 'On Saturdays he gets home about 1.30 p.m., so they have a hot meal at 2 p.m., and Mr Tame is busy in his garden for the rest of the day. […] he doesn't reckon to do any real gardening on a Sunday.'[22] Perhaps not gardening on Sunday is crucial here: where many hobby gardeners might see Sunday as the perfect day for gardening, for Mr Tame it is associated too much with work for this to be something he should do on his day off.

While the garden-for-sustenance continues all over the country, for many urban householders such gardening would require an allotment. But the emphasis today (as with much else) is on the garden as a place for contemporary living, which means that it has to match up somehow to the psychological needs of householders as much as their material needs. On the one hand, this has meant that the garden is part of a world framed by fantasy and memory:

> Most of us have an image of our ideal backyard. Part nostalgia, part myth, it is a place composed of memories and daydreams coloured by childhood fantasies, remote from the practicalities and cares of a real yard. Nevertheless, it is this image which we often unconsciously recall when planning and designing our actual yards and gardens. Our enduring love affair with yards and gardens is a reflection of an instinctive desire for communion with nature. On the simplest scale, this is manifested in colourful window boxes which appear on even the narrowest city ledge, but it can and has taken many forms.[23]

But while the idea of a garden as corresponding to a dream image might shape the way that you first set out your garden, what matters to many householders today is the garden as a place to relax. In this it is seen as just like any other room within the house:

If the weather is up to it, then it [the back garden] is an additional room for me – I eat and work on the bench: read and lay around on the seat. My garden is my retreat. The front garden, like the rest of the street is lawned and open plan … it is very plain. This is intentional … I don't want the front to provide an expectation of what the back is like. The public and private image kept separate![24]

The association of the suburban garden with the over-stressed office worker might lead to a number of images: the wine-quaffing couple sitting on the newly decked backyard that leads out on to lawn and flower beds, or the hobbyist gardener as driven by gardening as by work. This gardener is, like Mr Tame, someone who will go out in the garden every night after work. But this has less to do with the need to provide than with the need to de-stress: 'I do nine hours at work in a busy pressurised office. It is actually quite a small office and it is just fantastic to go out in the garden in the evening. It is so different.' The questioner then goes on to ask whether this allows him to forget work and the 'daily stresses': 'Well yes I sometimes mull over things when I'm out in the garden … but that doesn't really matter, I mean I sometimes take the radio out there, err, but um, yeah, I mean, I can switch off or I can think about work. I think that in that lovely environment you do put things more into perspective.'[25] De-stressing may mean working through your anxieties about your job in an environment that alters its significance.

But for most of us the garden is a compromise: rather than creating a perfectly manicured garden we find something that fits our requirements:

My idea of a garden is a place that looks reasonably attractive, is reasonably well looked after, a reasonable show of colour throughout the year. Lawns cut as is practical. Weeding the same, a safe and practical place for my 2 year old son to lay and run around and enjoy his slide and toy car. We enjoy sitting out on the patio when the weather conditions permit and enjoy the colourful and varied plants around us and like to see the variety of visiting insect and occasional animals, hedgehogs and frogs. The cat enjoys hiding and playing in the shrubs and bushes so I hope I've found the right balance for all of us and nature.[26]

This sense of a garden as a place of calm, as a retreat away from the pressures of a busy working life, is very much associated with the growth of the suburbs. Indeed an itinerary of the sounds and smells of Sunday afternoon in Middle England wouldn't be complete if it didn't include the buzz of lawnmowers, the smell of bonfires and the sound of kids playing. In Julian Barnes's novel *Metroland* (1980) the suburban houses of the Home Counties are seen as living for Sunday:

Sunday was the day for which Metroland was created. On Sunday mornings, as I lay in bed wondering how to kill the day, two sounds rang out across the silent, content suburb: the church bells and the train. The bells nagged you awake, persisted with irritating stamina, and finally gave up with a defeated half-clunk. The trains clattered more loudly than usual [...]. It wasn't until the afternoon – by some tacit but undisputed agreement – that a third noise started up: the patterned roar of motor mowers, accelerating, braking, turning, accelerating, braking, turning. When they fell silent, you might catch the quiet chomp of shears; and finally – a sound absorbed rather than heard – the gentle squeak of chamois on boot and bonnet.[27]

Motor mowers have to be kept somewhere, as do the vehicles that require a Sunday evening shine.

The out house

Today the most common 'out house' that belongs to ordinary housing is the garage – with sheds coming in second. At the beginning of the twentieth century garages were relatively rare: luckily, so was car ownership. Recent (2008) statistics suggest that in Britain 81 per cent of the population have some access to a car because they live in a household that has a car (though 'access' here will certainly depend on the largesse of the owner if the household doesn't consist of just one person). In the mid-1960s the number of car-owning households reached 44 per cent, and this figure has remained constant for households owning one car: what has risen is the number of households owning more than one car, as well as the number of households – many of which are one-person households.[28]

The first car owners were, like any early adopters of technology, enthusiasts with an intimate relationship with the car as a machine. As with the first wireless enthusiasts, or the first computer owners, to own a car in the early years of the twentieth century meant either knowing what went on under the bonnet or employing someone who did. Just as the first freezers couldn't offer the benefits of packets of oven chips and ready meals, so the first cars were around before the network of petrol stations, mechanics and other services were in place: certainly before a world awash with 'Kwik Fit Fitters'. In a world where car ownership was necessarily associated with some level of amateur mechanics the garage was less the glorified shed or tent that it is now, and more a fully functional mechanical workshop.

In a 1919 issue of *Our Homes and Gardens* a feature on domestic garages raises the question that, from our vantage point in the twenty-first century, may seem odd: is a pit necessary? This isn't some gothic allusion but a reference to the practice of driving a car over a large hole so that you can look at the bottom of the car from inside this hole. But it seems that the modern way isn't to encourage such an old-fashioned practice:

> no one can visit many modern private garages without being struck by the comparative rarity of the pit. In the old days a pit was regarded as an absolute essential in any garage, but modern garage designers appear to have become wise to the fact that the pit often defeated its own object and was almost superfluous. It was always dirty and often contained a few inches of water which was invisible owing to the darkness of the depths in which it reposed.[29]

But if in 1919 a car pit was seen as old-school, this wasn't because a host of cheap mechanical businesses had suddenly sprung up, making the amateur 'gentleman grease monkey' a thing of the past: 'in my opinion, far more useful than any pit are two hefty beams in the roof to which sliding pulley blocks can be attached, with ropes capable of supporting the weight of the complete car, if need be'.

In 1919 the car was something still new to the middle-class home and would require space: space that was not available in most inner-city houses. Of course, the question of whether the domestic garage was going to be part of your house was an open question. In many ways it was because you had to work in the garage to do the ceaseless tinkering that cars required back then that garages had more reason for being part of the house than they do today. Today the idea of a garage that is connected to a house has more to do with convenience and security than anything else: the garage isn't thought of as a room. But in 1919 there was some evidence that it was being treated as something like a room among rooms: 'having settled that the walls and roof of the garage may be either wood, corrugated iron, or whatever takes the fancy, there is the question of heating for cold weather. Open fires are out of the question.'[30]

It is the post-war period that sees the massive expansion of car ownership among middle- and working-class households. In the mid-1950s the urban sociologists Peter Willmott and Michael Young were watching and studying the dramatic changes in the lives of working-class Londoners as various sections of the East End were demolished. The so-called 'overspill' was rehoused in estates of council houses in more rural locations in Essex and Kent. The East Enders now live in places like 'Greenleigh', Willmott and Young's invented name for what was most likely the council estates of Debden, in Essex, and find that what once were absolute luxuries have now moved into the realm of necessities. For one Mr Berry, 'There are two things that I think are essential when you live on an estate. One's a telephone, the other's a car. [...] You need a car for travelling about. We're so far away from everywhere out here that it's actually cheaper to run a car than it is to pay fares.'[31] The point for Young and Willmott is not that people have changed their values now that they have been rehoused in what are clearly better houses. It is that the conditions dictate that they need to buy into another set of technologies: telephones and cars are needed to maintain the connections with the kinship groups that were part of their pre-overspill life.

A common theme among critical historians of technology is that the great social benefits that a technology is trumpeted as providing are only a benefit in as much as they solve a problem that has been caused either by that technology itself or by another technology (so it is constantly righting the wrongs produced elsewhere along the line). The housing at Greenleigh was 'technologically advanced' – the houses were all fitted with hot and cold running water and indoor toilets – but now the problem is that there is no longer the environment close at hand to sustain the household. So while the new houses were marketed as self-contained in terms of services, they were in other ways

> less self-contained than ever. Greenleigh is part of a larger world. A person's shops are a mile off, his work six miles away, and his relatives ten or twenty miles away, some of them on the suburban circuit of housing estates – Oxhey, Debden, Harold Hill, Becontree – along which no buses ply. Distances to shops, work, and relatives are not walking distances any more. They are motoring distances: a car, like a telephone, can overcome geography and organize a more scattered life into a manageable whole.[32]

In the light of rehousing policies, technological progression is required to maintain old ways of life. But the increase in car ownership is not immediately accompanied by places to house the cars: 'a garage, now as rare in twentieth-century Greenleigh as an indoor lavatory was in nineteenth-century Bethnal Green, could be as much a motive for migration in the future. Cars, telephones, telegrams, and letters represent not so much a new and higher standard of life as a means to clinging to something of the old.'[33]

If old ways of life couldn't be maintained, there was always another option – for men at least, or so it seems: retiring to the garden shed. A mythology has arisen around the shed which has given birth to its own popular literature and designated by invented terms such as 'shedism' and 'shedmen'.[34] The gendering of this building is insistent: a shed is where men go to get away from it all – a feeling made vivid by the title of one book on sheds – *The Joy of Sheds: Because a Man's Place Isn't in the Home* – and, continuing the references to erotica, *Fifty Sheds of Grey*.[35] As represented in the world of cartoons, a man who wanted to get away from a nagging wife would flee to the sanctity of a shed, which might well contain girlie magazines, home-brewed beer and other manly pursuits. Interestingly, in the literature, even men who live on their own might want to have a shed 'to get away from it'. Today it may well be the idea of a shed without a telephone or an internet connection that is attractive: a place outside the requirements of daily life. So alongside the shed as representing British men's eccentricity in their obsessions with collecting soda-siphons or dressing up in armour is perhaps a desire to be off the grid in some way.

Divergent styles of upkeep – or a lesson in gentrification

DO COME AGAIN

Conclusion

This trip to the great indoors is nearly through. We have traipsed through the shag-pile prairies of reception rooms and wandered the tropical rainforest of kitchens and bathrooms. We climbed to the mountainous plains of 'upstairs' to find a cloudy dream world of bedrooms, and came back down to the wilds of the backyard. Before we go, it is worth thinking about the future of domestic space, not as a set of individual functioning rooms but as a building among buildings, a unit among units. What is the future of the house? To get to that question we might also ask: what was the future of the house as it was planned and imagined in twentieth-century Britain?

Yesterday's tomorrow

As you might imagine, in the world of planning, especially in relation to housing, the term 'tomorrow' looms large: after all, if you're not planning for tomorrow, then when are you planning for? Thinking and imagining the future have, throughout the twentieth century, meant necessarily confronting a society, its industries, its technologies and its geography. The question that might be in the background, as planners and architects have been shaping the future of housing, is whether the industrial and technological are to be embraced or whether housing should run a mile from such forces. Should housing take on the look and feel of the most technologically advanced aspects of life, or should it be a safe haven, resting on more traditional values and materials?

In 1898 Ebenezer Howard published his book *Tomorrow: A Peaceful Path to Real Reform*: it was revised in 1902 and re-titled in its more familiar form *Garden Cities of Tomorrow*. Howard took some of the values embedded in places such as Port Sunlight and Bournville and extended them into generalised schemas. Places such as Letchworth Garden City, which was built between 1903 and 1919, and Hampstead Garden Suburb, begun in 1905, followed Howard's schemas. It was a powerful idea and would inform the planning of housing throughout the century and into the present. The New Towns that were built after the Second World War, places such as Milton Keynes and Stevenage, are, for better or worse, indebted to Howard's ideas.

A few streets from where I live now there is an area of housing designed according to Garden City principles. It was built in the 1930s to rehouse the inhabitants of Bristol's inner-city slums, which were being torn down. The new houses were, for the most part, either semi-detached or built in micro-terraces of four houses. They are all extravagantly set back from the straight wide roads that were built to service the area. Between the road and the pavement is a generous grass verge, and there is another one the other side of the pavement. The front gardens leading up to the house are fairly large, and the back gardens are considerable. All the houses have three bedrooms and were built with inside toilets and bathroom facilities.

On a sunny day, and if you don't look too closely, the whole place feels expansive, airy. It has the highest unemployment in Bristol (and it is staggeringly high); it has the highest number of children who are sent to live in care homes, and the highest crime rates. The mini-supermarket looks like it's been closed down: it hasn't, it has just incorporated the metal security blinds as a permanent feature that are never opened. The local secondary school was closed some time ago. There are strong communities there, and many people have very good memories of growing up there, but success is measured by how quickly you can leave and how far you can go. It is not a place where opportunity comes knocking. Housing design alone could never solve the problems of social inequality.

'It is extraordinary how adaptable human beings are', claimed the 1958 *Daily Mail* Ideal Home Exhibition catalogue. With the end of the Second World War as a not so distant echo it went on:

> During the war people settled cosily into dugouts and under-ground stations. People live quite happily in cliffs and trees, they set up huts on stilts over the sea or build skyscrapers, or live in igloos and caves. How they live is partly dictated by society, partly by latitude, partly by income. The way of life corresponds to the needs and possibilities of the people who live it – and it is infinite in its variety.[1]

No doubt the war was far enough away for the Ideal Home Exhibition to remember dugouts and tube platforms nostalgically as 'cosy'. Britons haven't tended to opt for tree-dwelling or for igloos and caves – well, not recently at any rate. It would be hard to look at the history of British housing in the twentieth century and suggest it was heading for infinite variety. For the vast majority the choice of housing is fairly limited in form: terraced houses, workers' cottages, semi-detached villas, town houses, detached 'family' houses and such like. These may vary in scale, but they mostly follow a pretty similar pattern.

But the other choice in Britain is between the individual

house and the multi-household building made up of flats and maisonettes. This could include an old town house converted into flats or a purpose-built set of flats as in the tenement buildings from the nineteenth century in cities such as Glasgow, Belfast and London, or the mega-complexes of flats that were pioneered after the Second World War. Perhaps, then, the choice is between 'stacked households', 'sandwiched households' and separate ones. At the same time as the variety of housing was being championed at the Ideal Home Exhibition, housing in Britain was going through the revolution that was producing the mega-housing complex.

The 1950s and early 1960s are the moment when two of the most iconic high-density housing developments were built. Between 1951 and 1958 the London County Council decided to house 10,000 people in woods and fields in the south-west of London, between Richmond Park and Putney. The various Roehampton clusters of mixed development housing included some of the first skyscrapers in London as well as low-level blocks made up of maisonettes. One of the major accomplishments of this project was that when the first estate (Ackroydon) was opened, its 23-acre plot included 400 mature trees that hadn't been damaged by the build. It was in many ways a form of vertical Garden City design.

The mixture of housing was designed to accommodate a range of households with different requirements and different abilities (the elderly, those with infants and so on). The show flats, though, clearly gave the impression that, young or old, with or without children, the housing was dedicated to the modern. They were furnished in the contemporary style, 'with their Scandinavian-inspired natural finish door frames and dining suite, plain carpets and wallpapers, and the low, straight lines of the sofa and not-so-easy chair'.[2] Given that these council houses were usually rehousing established households, and that they didn't come as furnished, it is hard to imagine that the residents would have similarly adopted what in the 1950s was quite an *outré* style choice. Whatever the long-term success of this as a form of mass housing, when it opened, it offered residents unrivalled facilities and housing qualities outstripping anything available in the non-luxury private rented market.

The other development was in Sheffield: Park Hill, which in 1998 was awarded (to the consternation of some, perhaps many) Grade II listing. Park Hill was decidedly not vertical, though it rose to fourteen floors at some points. To begin with, at least, it was a reply to vertical housing, which one of the architects, Jack Lynn, described as 'bungalows stacked one above the other ... [like] tidy solutions of a storage problem'.[3] The area that Park Hill was built on had formerly been an area of back-to-back housing notorious for the amount of crime it generated. The back-to-backs had started to be demolished in the 1930s, but the war had interrupted the development of the site. Park Hill was an attempt to recreate the close-knit community life of working-class housing by mimicking aspects of old terraced streets, but this time situating them in the sky.

The buildings in Park Hill are like serpentine ribbons connected by 'sky decks' that were wide enough for an electric milk float. The first part of the development was opened in 1961, with 995 dwellings that mixed two-storey maisonettes with smaller flats. In 1965 the Hyde Park section was opened (this time with more vertical buildings) and added a further 740 flats and 582 maisonettes. To begin with, it was fantastically successful and received enthusiastic endorsement for its amenities (streets of shops were built into the plans) and its suitability for young families.

I was in Sheffield in the early 1980s, and by then Park Hill was suffering. Most of the shops that were part of the original scheme had closed down. Some of the flats were vacant; others were let by the council to groups of students. At the base of the buildings were painted lines and notices telling you not to cross them. I later found out that these marked a danger zone that you had to keep outside of if you wanted to remain free from falling debris: a water bomb if you were lucky, a broken TV or a fridge if you weren't. Now the flats of Park Hill are getting a makeover and are no longer being offered just as council houses. Now they are aimed at high-end urban chic.

If the Park Hill flats and the Roehampton ones are an answer to the massive problems of housing, then they could be seen as only partially responding to this wish-list of a working-class woman during the war:

I should like a house with a kitchen-dining-room – you know, one room where you eat and cook and a scullery. And a sitting room, not too big. Three bedrooms and a bathroom, and *two* lavatories, one upstairs in the bathroom and one downstairs. I'd like large windows, very light and airy, and of course, a garden. I like bow-windows really, the modern type that let in all the light. In the scullery I should like a sink and draining board all in one piece. Like those steel ones, I think they are. And I'd *like* – of course people in our circumstances can't have it, but I'd *like* a refrigerator. I would like a coal fire in the sitting room, with a nice brick fireplace, and gas or electric in the kitchen. Gas, I think; electric dries the air up worse than gas, I always think. Gas fires in the bedrooms. I'm not keen on central heating. I'd like paint, definitely. So you can sponge it down, and I'd like a nice warm colour – or one of those nice plain parchment shades, with just a touch of colour on the top – a coloured picture rail or something like that. I'd like linoleum looking like tiles or else real tiles in the kitchen, and linoleum and rugs in the sitting room. It would be quite nice to have a balcony to put window boxes on, but I don't really mind about that.[4]

Such a modest proposal was answered by Roehampton and Sheffield – yet there is no indication that there was a desire to be sandwiched into a high-rise. If this Mass-Observer had moved to Park Hill, she would have got most of what she wished for. And yet such housing would quickly turn into some of the most denigrated and impoverished housing in Britain. Was this the fault of the architects? Today the flats in Park Hill, Sheffield, are being sold off as luxury urban apartments by the redevelopment firm Urban Splash.

Living the future

We are living the future of housing not as someone imagined it but as it actually came about, with all the contingency and unpredictability that that implies. We have central heating, but the hot-air system, which was the one imagined to be most popular, is not the version that most of us have. Central heating allowed some of the largest social shifts in the culture of the home that I've been charting here: it would be hard to imagine households where the occupants can be so scattered about a house in winter without it. But one of the important messages of this book is that, while technology is a hugely important agent of change, alone it is not a sufficient cause of change. A bedroom doesn't move from utilitarian dormitory to teenage crash pad just because of central heating; a downstairs doesn't get knocked through into a large open-plan space just because central heating allows it to be a possibility. It may be impossible to imagine such change without central heating (or rolled-steel joists, in the case of open-plan living), but there is no way that central heating on its own determines the form that these rooms take. Other things were also required: we needed changes in social manners for one thing, more informality, a different sense of childhood and so on.

Looking across the twentieth century and into the twenty-first, it is not hard to see that technology is allowing some of the most significant changes to take place. We've already seen how the computer has been party to changes in teenage bedroom culture. But what about the notion of the house and its place in our lives: has the computer altered this in significant ways? Here it is worth looking at a few sheets of typewritten paper written in 1984 by Michael Aldrich. Aldrich was chief executive of Rediffusion Computers. More importantly, he pioneered what today we call internet shopping. He was also Margaret Thatcher's IT consultant. His description of computer technology in the house is worth looking at, as at one level it seems prescient while at another it shows us how limited our predictions are likely to be.

The speculative essay is called 'Home: The Command Base' and begins by showing us how our pleasurable experiences of home are related to the way that technology connects us to a set of services:

> The connection of basic services – piped energy such as gas and electricity, piped water and sanitation and piped communication such as telephone and television – means that the attractions of the home are greater, more things can be accomplished there and we enjoy spending more time there. We have more time to spend at home because of the continued decline in the working life through more formal education, longer holidays, earlier retirement and greater life expectation.[5]

Aldrich shows us one way of thinking about how we can become home bodies: our houses have become convenient to us both in terms of bodily comforts (heat, sanitation etc.) and social connections (telephones, televisions). Shockingly, he shows us that our energy consumption is, by 1984, staggering:

A 1984 home has about the same installed horsepower as a turn of the [previous] century textile mill. Domestic appliances are in abundance – cookers, washing machines, clothes dryers, vacuum cleaners, hair dryers, toasters, refrigerators, freezers, food-mixers, electric kettles and irons, pressure cookers, dish-washers, coffee machines, deep-fat fryers and the rest. For information, education and entertainment, there are transistor radios, hi-fis, static and portable televisions, video cassette recorders, audio cassette players and even Citizen Band radios.[6]

Aldrich knew that computer technologies would drastically alter our lives as communicative beings. His question, though, and a question that is still very much at the heart of thinking about housing and computers, is: how would this alter us? 'It is, of course, possible', writes Aldrich, 'that instead of "homo communicator" we will have Bunker Bill, locked into his Command Base, antisocial, antipathetic and antiseptic – existing in the last redoubt of the micro-hermit. However, we may find people have more time to do the things they really enjoy doing and thus become more liberated, more caring and happier.'[7] The good dream of computer homes might include images of happy home-working adults, liberated from endless commuting, of children learning all sorts of fascinating things as they are guided by their carer, who is fully versed in internet protection software. The bad dream of computer homes is everyone as a micro-hermit.

Aldrich is more interested in the good dream. In his dream of the future the computerised home will need a centre:

the command centre for the home is likely to be the kitchen. Appliances will tend to be built into fitted units and control panels will be built into a console. A master console will permit, for example, interrogation of the deep freeze for a list of contents and allow central control of appliances and security in the home. The kitchen will have a considerable amount of cabling. As the command centre, the kitchen will be larger than at present.[8]

It is always interesting to look back on predictions and see what it was that was so hard to extrapolate from the contemporary scene and push into the future: the 1980 imagination couldn't foresee the miniaturisation of power supplies that would allow for mobile phones, laptops and such like that would make the need for a static command centre unnecessary.

The mobility of commuter technologies limits some of the predictions that Aldrich makes, though it still makes his predictions interesting precisely because of the distance between them and our current experiences of fiddling about with some form of work-related computer housekeeping while watching TV. So, if the kitchen is a command centre, the house as a unit is the command base and is now not just a place for conducting our private life but also the centre of our work life and our educational life. For Aldrich the line between work and non-work will be maintained within the geography of the house:

The Command Base itself will continue to be divided into living and sleeping areas. There will be work and play areas. In the past we have termed these work and play areas, the study and the sitting room. The work area will be a quiet place where a television/computer terminal is used to ship, to bank, to send messages and to interact with communication and information systems and services worldwide. The computer buff will be able to roam the world's telecommunication networks as today the ham roams the radio networks, provided, of course, one can afford the tariffs from the network operators. The real cost of telecommunications has to fall consistently over a number of years for such a scenario to be economically viable. The work area is for interactive information processing where the worker is engaged in actively using the machine or machines.[9]

This sense of distinct places designated as work areas or play areas would now seem incompatible with the fact of mobile technology, which can make any room an office, shop or playroom, often simultaneously.

The sense of expertise has also changed. Today, of course, everyone could be wafting around on the internet and you certainly don't need that much in the way of buff-ness to do this. The machines themselves have succeeded mainly on the basis that they have de-buffed themselves. But the question of whether the computer user will become a micro-hermit rather than a liberated social animal is not just about the relationship between the household and the outside world, but also about the relationships within a household. Aldrich's imaging of family play in a computer age seems wonderfully naive:

> In the play area by comparison, the emphasis will be more on the passive watching of television or various forms of video. Participation will be probably limited to zapping 30 plus TV channels perhaps only to find that there isn't anything that catches the interest or imagination. Both in the work and play areas, the computer-based televisions or terminals will be used for games. Socially gaming is important. It will bring people together. Instead of Scrabble or Space Invaders, all the members of the family will be able to join in elaborate games that will often have a strong educational content.[10]

At this point all you have to do is mention first-person shooters or social networking sites to see how a good deal of technology allows you to be much more sociable with people you definitely aren't sharing physical space with.

These aspects of the computer house are like people's imaging of TV in its early days. But it is the financial operations that Aldrich gets so right, as we sit at home doing our banking or buying our shopping. People's homes are filled with household-ers 'working' on the computer. Of course, we don't always call it work. But this might be a mistake. In a fantastic analysis of changes in housework Ruth Schwartz Cowan shows how, in the change from the house as a centre of production to a centre of consumption, labour practices may well increase. Her point is that, during an era when a woman (or a man, though that seems unlikely) undertook an annual round of jam, marmalade and chutney-making, this was a one-off, labour-intensive act performed just once a year. When, instead of that, we have shop-ping, we shouldn't just imagine that labour is not happening. For Cowan not only is this a form of labour but it is a form of fairly constant labour. And this is where Aldrich is on the money:

> The consumer will be able to purchase products, manage financial affairs, communicate with business and personal acquaintances, work and learn – from home. The economic result of such activity will be to transfer more productive work to the home. If one takes as an example a retail transac-tion involving a householder and a local store, the transaction will be logical rather than physical. Communication will be electronic, payment will be by electronic funds, transfer and delivery will be by electronic mail or physical mail. The direct labour in the system belongs to the consumer and the delivery man in the case of physical goods only. Labour cost will be largely externalised from retailer and banker to consumer.[11]

The problem with this is that, instead of being tools of

convenience, such tools exert pressure on us to be constantly interacting with these machines in an almost ceaseless form of labour. Of course, what stands in the way of an image of the future where we are forever labouring to sustain ourselves through machines is the real possibility that we will run out of the resources that fuel these machines and the networks they are plugged into. If fossil fuels do run out, then all our technological advancement in the home could seem futile: instead of computer skills, we would require survival skills. Our homes would become places for the older arts of cooking and caring, of husbandry and horticulture.

The future of the future

The island of Unst is the northern-most inhabited bit of Britain. It is the second largest island of Shetland and lies on the same latitude as southern Greenland. It is home to puffins and guillemots and a retired couple from Wiltshire. Michael and Dorothy Rea have built a house there and are planning to grow old together on the island. The house itself is nothing much, architecturally speaking: it is a standard 'kit' house made from off-the-shelf frames.

Like many of the Shetlands and the Hebrides, Unst is experimenting in renewable energies, and one of the things that Unst has in abundance is wind. When Michael and Dorothy's house was being assembled, one of the heavy roof sections was caught by a gust of wind and smashed on to the ground. The island is home to gale-force winds on a regular basis. 'I have been waiting 24 years for this house to be built', says Dorothy. 'It is just a standard house, an honest house, nothing fancy. It's a serious project in renewable design and energy efficiency, an experiment in joined-up technology, but it is also a house we intend to grow old in.'[12] The house is designed to be a zero-carbon house that uses some under-used technology as well as harnessing some of the free wind power that is whirling about. It is super-insulated with 'Celotex' (an expanding foam insulator), and the double-glazing is filled with argon. But the house uses a heat pump that 'sucks in air to take the heat out of the ambient air temperature' – quite a feat on an island that far north of Aberdeen.

The couple claim that 'If we can do this here, anyone can do it anywhere. It's just an ordinary house. It could be in Edinburgh; it could be in Chigwell.'[13] It could be anywhere, but it isn't. Like many 'off-the-grid' projects, it isn't located in a terraced house in Edinburgh or Chigwell. There are good reasons for that, of course: some of this technology (wind turbines) needs space and planning permission. Terraced houses are perhaps just too gridded. Many of the 'off-the-grid' housing projects look how you might imagine hippie counterculture housing to look: yurts and benders predominate. As we search for the house of the future, this sort of portable 'light' housing may well become more common. Certainly as a 'new vernacular' style it might seem much more possible than the various experimental super-hi-tech housing that was being imagined in a time of unlimited energy expansion in the 1960s. When the experimental architects declared that 'we are in pursuit of an idea, a new vernacular, something to stand alongside the space capsules, computers and throw-away packages of an atomic/electronic age', it was imagined that electricity would become 'too cheap to meter'.[14] In an era where planetary resources are running out, where peak oil production has been reached and where the over-consumption of fossil fuels is causing all sorts of unpredictable problems, then the house of the future has a planetary obligation to try to tread more lightly on the ground.

The terraced house has proved amazingly durable. Partly this is because it constitutes the majority of our urban housing stock. It has adjusted to changing circumstances pretty well – it has had to. Much of the housing we now occupy wasn't initially attached to any 'grids' – it was built before networks of electricity, gas and communications could be imagined. In the history of housing in Britain the idea of the 'mains' – be that mains electricity, mains water, mains sewage – has been a relatively recent idea. The challenge to the ordinary house isn't going to be to cope with the future of technological communication (which is often what 'future-proofing' seems to amount to) but to cope with a different cosmology of dirt and cleanliness. For the terraced house to sit more lightly on the ground may require a house like this terraced house in Sydney, Australia:

> The house runs on solar power collected from roof panels, with any excess going back into the grid. Potable water is collected from the roof and filtered using sophisticated carbon technology. All waste water from the house flows into a Dowmus waste system, which uses earthworms and micro-organisms to break down and filter human effluent, gray water, and food scraps. This waste management system sits outside the back door. It looks like a long garden seat (and that is another function) running along the length of the tiny backyard. Inside worms manage the household waste. At the end of the system, water, which is mostly free of pathogens, is pumped through a compact ultraviolet light disinfector to ensure that is completely sterile. This water is then used to wash clothes and flush the toilet, with any excess pumped into a reed bed at the bottom of the garden.[15]

Of course, some of this would require more than the pocket-handkerchief backyards you find in many terraces. But the idea of sitting 'out the back' of an evening, wearing clothes that had been washed in grey 'toilet water', sitting on a large wormery that is busy devouring the household faeces, seems like a future that would transform our sense of home in quite profound ways. Total ecological living may well become a reality for only a minority – primarily because it would require new buildings. It does seem likely, though, that we will all be altering our lifestyles to something more sustainable. What this will do to our houses will most likely be gradual – like the introduction of recycling and water metering.

The ordinary house has gone through some amazing transformations in the last hundred years. Who, in the early years of the twentieth century, could have predicted the teenage bed-sit? And how many would have imagined that nearly every house would by the end of the century have an indoor toilet, hot water on tap and central heating. It is, of course, impossible to predict how the ordinary house will alter in the future. Given the evidence, it would be foolhardy indeed to imagine that it would stay the same.

And finally what of our Martian anthropologist? What report did it take back to its planet?

Habitat Report
Species: Human
Location: mainly consists of a large island
Climate: cold and wet

These animals primarily live in segmented boxes that are fitted together in rows that do not interconnect. During the day many of the occupants travel to work to earn the money to pay for these small boxes. When they aren't working they are often found in these boxes – eating, sleeping, talking, cooking, having sex, washing and so on. In the evening they can often be seen huddled together or separately looking at screens watching other people cook, eat, talk, have sex and buy segmented boxes.

ACKNOWLEDGEMENTS

I carried out the initial research for this book in three archives: the archives of the Museum of Domestic Design and Architecture (MoDA) in Colindale; the Victoria and Albert, Archive of Art and Design, in Blythe House, Olympia; and the Mass-Observation archive at the University of Sussex. Thanks to all the archivists involved for their kind assistance. I also want to thank Daniel Crewe and Cecily Gayford at Profile for editorial advice throughout the writing of this book, and Matthew Taylor for copy-editing.

While I was working on this book, my father died. I think he would have liked the book. It was much more his thing than anything else I've written. I dedicate it to his memory, as someone who took inordinate pleasure in being a homemaker.

LIST OF ILLUSTRATIONS

While every effort has been made to contact copyright-holders of illustrations, the author and publishers would be grateful for information about any illustrations where they have been unable to trace them, and would be glad to make amendments in further editions.

NOTES

 Welcome Home

1. *Ideal Home Householders' Guide*, vol. 1 (London: Odhams Books, 1966), p. 5.
2. Mass-Observation began in 1937, kept going through the war, fell into decline in the late 1950s and was revived again in 1981 and is still going strong today. It is, as the name suggests, a large-scale collection of observations, opinions, reminiscences and anecdotes. Mass-Observers (usually numbering between 500 and 1,000 at any one time) respond to directives soliciting their feelings about all sorts of subjects, from political events to eating habits.
3. Humphrey Spender, in *The Long Summer* (Channel 4, May 1993).
4. Sue Bowden and Avner Offer, 'Household Appliances and the Use of Time: The United States and Britain since the 1920s', *Economic History Review*, 47:4 (1994), p. 729.
5. June Freeman, *The Making of the Modern Kitchen: A Cultural History* (Oxford: Berg, 2004), p. 5. The figure of 63 per cent owner occupation has remained fairly constant since 1996 but has now (2012) gone down to 61 per cent as a result of the global financial crisis.
6. Stuart Hall, 'The "West Indian" Front Room', in Michael Millan, *The Front Room: Migrant Aesthetics in the Home* (London: Black Dog, 2009), p. 19.
7. Richard Hoggart, *An Imagined Life: Life and Times, 1959–1991* (Oxford: Oxford University Press, 1993), p. 84.
8. Hoggart, *An Imagined Life*, p. 85.

2 **Please Come In**

1. C. L. R. James, *Letters from London* (Port of Spain: Prospect Press, 2003 [first published 1932]), p. 59.

2. Mary Gilliatt, 'Furnishing with Flair', *Good Housekeeping* (January 1968), p. 25.

3. Department of the Environment, *Homes for Today & Tomorrow* (London: Her Majesty's Stationery Office, 1961), p. 9.

4. Caroline Clifton-Mogg et al., *The Complete Home Decorator* (New York: Portland House, 1991), p. 62.

5. Lesley Hoskins (ed.), *The Papered Wall: The History, Patterns and Techniques of Wallpaper* (London: Thames and Hudson, 2005), p. 154.

6. *The Crown Wallpaper Magazine* (formerly *The British Wallpaper Magazine*), 15:1 (1938), p. 3.

7. *Daily Mail Ideal Home Exhibition* (London: Associated Newspapers, 1957), p. 219.

8. F. J. Camm, 'Our "Do It Yourself" Policy', *Practical Householder*, 1:1 (October 1955), p. 15.

9. Terence Conran, *The House Book* (London: Mitchell Beazley, 1974), p. 175.

10. Conran, *The House Book*, p. 175.

11. David Sylvester, *Memoirs of a Pet Lamb* (London: Chatto & Windus, 2002), p. 7.

12. Sylvester, *Memoirs*, p. 65.

13. Charles R. Perry, 'The British Experience, 1876–1912: The Impact of the Telephone during the Years of Delay', in *The Social Impact of the Telephone*, ed. Ithiel de Sola Pool (Cambridge, MA: MIT Press, 1977).

14. Advert in *Daily Mail Ideal Home Exhibition* catalogue (London: Associated Newspapers, 1932), p. 240.

15. *Daily Mail Ideal Home Exhibition* catalogue (1932), p. 232.

16. Perry, 'The British Experience, 1876–1912', p. 79.

17. *Daily Mail Ideal Home Exhibition* catalogue (1932), p. 233.

18. *Ideal Home and Gardening*, 67:4 (April 1953), p. 50.

19. *The House That Made Me* (Channel 4, December 2010).

20. *Good Housekeeping*, 92:4 (October 1967), p. 128.

21. *Good Housekeeping*, 92:4 (October 1967), p. 107.

22. Mass-Observation, 'Things about the House', summer directive 1988, T1575, female.

3 **Take a Seat**

1. Unidentified child with speech bubble, *IKEA Catalogue 2004*, p. 23.

2. Mass-Observation, autumn 1983, L796, female.

3. Mass-Observation, autumn 1983, 406, male.

4. Mass-Observation Archive, Topic Collection, Housing 1938–48, TC 1/6/6/G (from report October 1941).

5. Osbert Lancaster, *Here, of All Places* (London: John Murray, 1959), p. 170.

6. *Housewife* (May 1946), p. 2.

7. *The Housewife's Book* from 1937, reproduced in Mike Brown and Carol Harris, *The Wartime House: Home Life in Wartime Britain, 1939–1945* (Stroud: Alan Sutton, 2001), p. 56.

8. The classic account of working-class housework in pre-First World War London is Maud Pember Reeves, *Round about a Pound a Week* (London: Virago, 1979 [first published 1913]).

9. Mass-Observation, *People's Homes* (London: John Murray, 1943), pp. xii–xiii.

10. Conran, *The House Book*, p. 187.

11. *Our Homes and Gardens*, 1:1 (June 1919), p. 1.

12. *Our Homes and Gardens*, 1:2 (July 1919), p. 33.

13. *Our Homes and Gardens*, 1:1 (June 1919), p. 5.

14. Mass-Observation, *People and Paint* (Slough: Imperial Chemical Industries, 1949), pp. 60–61.

15. Roger Fry, *Vision and Design* (Oxford: Oxford University Press, 1981), pp. 47–48. *Vision and Design* is a collection of Fry's writings from the first two decades of the twentieth century and was first published in 1920.

16. Fry, *Vision and Design*, p. 48.

17. The classic accounts are situated outside of Britain: for the US there is Vance Packard's *The Status Seekers*, from 1959; for France there is Pierre Bourdieu's *Distinctions: A Social Critique of the Judgement of Taste*, from 1979. For a British example, see Denis Chapman, *The Home and Social Status* (London: Routledge & Kegan Paul, 1955).

18. Fry, *Vision and Design*, p. 48.

19. Mass-Observation, autumn 1983, A008, female.

20. Mass-Observation, 'Objects about the House', summer 1988, W1480.

21. Mass-Observation, 'Objects about the House', summer 1988, P1500, female.

22. Alison and Peter Smithson, *The Charged Void: Architecture* (New York: Monacelli Press, 2001), pp. 190–91. The 'appliance house' was a concept that they started working on in 1956.

23. Mass-Observation, 'Objects about the House', summer 1988, L1444, female.

24. Gordon Russell, in Council of Industrial Design, *Design '46* (London: His Majesty's Stationery Office, 1946), p. 94.

25. Sir Stafford Cripps in Council of Industrial Design, *Design '46*, p. 94.

26. *New Statesman and Nation* (28 September 1946), p. 220.

27. Mass-Observation, 'Britain Can Make It' files, 1946, F40 C.

28. Lancaster, *Here, of All Places*, p. 160.

29. Ian Cox, *The South Bank Exhibition: A Guide to the Story It Tells* (London: His Majesty's Stationery Office, 1951), p. 72.

30. 1960s' G-Plan catalogue, facsimile in Basil Hyman and Steven Braggs, *The G-Plan Revolution: A Celebration of British Popular Furniture of the 1950s and 1960s* (London: Booth-Clibborn, 2007), pp. 96–97.

31. Lawrence Wright, *Home Fires Burning: The History of Domestic Heating and Cooking* (London: Routledge & Kegan Paul, 1964), p. 192.

32. W. H. Auden, 'Letter to Lord Byron' (1936), in *Collected Poems*, ed. Edward Mendelson (London: Faber & Faber, 1994), p. 89.
33. *The Daily Mail Ideal Home Exhibition* (1937), p. 52.
34. Cox, *The South Bank Exhibition*, p. 72.
35. Gordon Russell, in Council of Industrial Design, *Design '46*, p. 94.
36. Conran, *The House Book*, p. 196.
37. John Braine, *Life at the Top* (Harmondsworth: Penguin, 1965 [first published 1962]), p. 34.
38. Department of the Environment, *Homes for Today & Tomorrow* (London: Her Majesty's Stationery Office, 1961), p. 26.
39. Bowden and Offer, 'Household Appliances and the Use of Time, p. 729.

4 Put the Kettle On

1. Terence Conran, *The Kitchen Book* (London: Mitchell Beazley, 1977), p. 98.
2. *Everyday Things* (London: Royal Institute of British Architects, 1936), p. 5.
3. 'From War to Peace' (press release for 'Britain Can Make It' exhibition, 1946, London, V&A archive).
4. *Our Homes and Gardens*, 1:1 (June 1919), p. 27.
5. *Our Homes and Gardens*, 1:1 (June 1919), p. 27.
6. *The Housewife's Book* (London: Syndicate, 1937), p. 78.
7. Roger Smithells (ed.), *News of the World Better Homes Book* (London: News of the World, 1954), p. 93.
8. *Our Homes and Gardens*, 1:7 (December 1919), p. 206.
9. *Our Homes and Gardens*, 1:7 (December 1919), p. 206.
10. *Our Homes and Gardens*, 1:7 (December 1919), p. 205.
11. *Our Homes and Gardens*, 1:5 (October 1919), p. 144.
12. Mass-Observation, *People's Homes*, p. 99, citing a survey from 1941.
13. Adie Ballantyne, *Choose Your Kitchen: A Book for a Housewife* (London: Faber & Faber, 1944), p. 6.
14. Ballantyne, *Choose Your Kitchen*, p. 5.

15. 'Modern Homes Exhibition', Mass-Observation Archive, University of Sussex, item 2360 (Box 9, Housing 9/A), pp. 6–7.

16. 'Modern Homes Exhibition', Mass-Observation Archive, University of Sussex, item 2360 (Box 9, Housing 9/A), n.p.

17. Mass-Observation, 2 March 1946, F35C.

18. Mass-Observation, 2 March 1946, F50B.

19. Mass-Observation, 'A Report on "Britain Can Make It" Exhibition: Section C', December 1946, p. 33.

20. 'Britain Can Make It', V&A archive.

21. From an advert, *c.* 1920, in Anthony Byers, *The Willing Servants: A History of Electricity in the Home* (London: Electricity Council, 1981), p. 11.

22. 'British Electrical Development Association', *Daily Mail Ideal Home Exhibition* (London: Associated Press, 1954), p. 35.

23. Mass-Observation, 'A Report on "Britain Can Make It" Exhibition, Section C', December 1946, p. 35.

24. *Daily Mail Ideal Home Exhibition* (1956), p. 97.

25. *Daily Mail Ideal Home Exhibition* (1956), p. 97.

26. *Daily Mail Ideal Home Exhibition* (1956), p. 32.

27. *Furnishing with Formica*, produced by *Good Housekeeping* in association with Thomas de la Rue & Co., undated and unpaginated, *c.* 1955. Museum of Domestic Design and Architecture (MoDA), London, BADDA 4144.

28. *Daily Mail Ideal Home Exhibition* (1956), p. 98.

29. *Daily Mail Ideal Home Exhibition* (1954), p. 32.

30. Ruth Schwartz Cowan, 'How the Refrigerator Got Its Hum', in *The Social Shaping of Technology*, ed. Donald MacKenzie and Judy Wajcman (Milton Keynes: Open University Press, 1987), p. 214.

31. Elizabeth Shove and Dale Southerton, 'Defrosting the Freezer: From Novelty to Convenience', *Journal of Material Culture*, 5:3 (2000), pp. 301–19.

32. June Freeman, *The Making of a Modern Kitchen: A Cultural History* (Oxford: Berg, 2004), p. 146.

33. Elizabeth Shove, Matthew Watson, Martin Hand and Jack Ingram, *The Design of Everyday Life* (Oxford: Berg, 2007), p. 22.

34. Mass-Observation Archive, Topic Collection, Housing 1938–48, TC 1/6/6/G (from report 11 June 1942).

35. Mass-Observation Archive, Topic Collection, Housing 1938–48, TC 1/6/6/G (from report 16 June 1942).

36.   Mass-Observation, summer 1988, B1756, male.

37. *The Housewife's Book*, p. 78.

38. Frances Short, *Kitchen Secrets: The Meaning of Cooking in Everyday Life* (Oxford: Berg, 2006), p. 9.

39.   Short, *Kitchen Secrets*, p. 125.

40. Short, *Kitchen Secrets*, p. 128.

41. Mass-Observation, autumn 1983, H266, female.

42. *Good Housekeeping: The Best of the 1940s* (London: Collins & Brown, 2007), p. 121.

43.   Eileen Candappa and Harry Haas, *The Spice of Happiness*, cited in Rohan Candappa, *Picklehead: From Ceylon to Suburbia (A Memoir of Food, Family and Finding Yourself)* (London: Ebury Press, 2007), pp. 208–09.

5 Mind Your Manners

1.   Stefan Muthesius, *The English Terraced House* (New Haven, CT, and London: Yale University Press, 1982), p. 95.

2.   Jane Hamlett, '"The Dining Room Should Be the Man's Paradise, as the Drawing Room Is the Woman's": Gender and Middle-Class Domestic Space in England, 1850–1910', *Gender & History*, 21:3 (2009), p. 583.

3.   Isabella Beeton, *Mrs Beeton's Book of Household Management* (abridged) (Oxford: Oxford University Press, 2000 [first published 1861]), p. 28.

4.   Beeton, *Mrs Beeton's Book of Household Management*, p. 21.

5.   Beeton, *Mrs Beeton's Book of Household Management*, p. 23.

6.   Judith Listowel, *Manual of Modern Manners* (London: Odhams Press, 1959), p. 105.

7.   Jilly Cooper, *Class: A View from Middle England* (London: Mandarin, 1994 [first published 1979]).

8. *Ideal Home Householders' Guide*, vol. 3, p. 194.

9. Wendy Godfrey, *The Sainsbury Book of Entertaining* (London: Cathay Books, 1982), p. 18.

10. *Ideal Home Householders' Guide*, vol. 3, p. 194.

11. Grace Lees-Maffei, 'Accommodating "Mrs. Three-in-One": Homemaking, Home Entertaining and Domestic Advice Literature in Post-War Britain', *Women's History Review*, 16:5 (2007), pp. 723–54.

12. Anne Murcott, 'Women's Place: Cookbooks' Images of Technique and Technology in the British Kitchen', *Women's Studies International Forum*, 6:1 (1983), p. 34.

13. *Good Housekeeping*, 93:3 (March 1968), p. 32.

14. *The Good Food Guide Second Dinner Party Book* (London: Hodder & Stoughton, 1979), pp. vi–vii.

15. Beeton, *Mrs Beeton's Book of Household Management*, p. 367.

16. Nicola Humble, *Culinary Pleasures: Cookbooks and the Transformation of British Food* (London: Faber & Faber, 2005), p. 24.

17. Lizzie Collingham, *Curry: A Biography* (London: Chatto and Windus, 2005), p. 115.

18. Collingham, *Curry*, pp. 141–42.

19. *Wife and Home: The Married Woman's Magazine* (January 1954), p. 44.

20. *Wife and Home: The Married Woman's Magazine* (January 1954), p. 45.

21. Richard Llewellyn, *How Green Was My Valley* (Harmondsworth: Penguin, 2001 [first published 1939]), p. 10.

22. Llewellyn, *How Green Was My Valley*, p. 11.

23. Candappa, *Picklehead*, p. 61.

24. Candappa, *Picklehead*, pp. 66–67.

25. W. Somerset Maugham, *Of Human Bondage* (London: Vintage, 2000 [first published 1915]), p. 16.

26. H. J. Jennings, *Our Homes and How to Beautify Them* (London: Harrison and Sons, 1902), p. 173.

27. Hamlett, "'The Dining Room Should Be the Man's Paradise'", p. 580.

28. Charles Eastlake, *Hints on Household Taste in Furniture, Upholstery and Other Details* (New York: Dover, 1969 [first published London, 1868]), p. 72.

29. Mass-Observation Archive, Topic Collection, Housing 1938–48, TC 1/6/6/I (from report 25 March 1942).

30. Eastlake, *Hints on Household Taste in Furniture, Upholstery and Other Details*, p. 84.

31. Mass-Observation, 'A Report on "Britain Can Make It" Exhibition: Section C', December 1946, p. 41.

32. Mass-Observation, 'Objects about the House', summer 1988, 1277, female.

33. Mass-Observation, 'Objects about the House', summer 1988, 466, male.

34. Conran, *The House Book*, p. 226.

35. Conran, *The House Book*, p. 222.

36. Mass-Observation, autumn 1983, 058, female.

37. Bryan Magee, *Clouds of Glory: A Hoxton Childhood* (London: Pimlico, 2004), p. 219.

38. Shaun Moores, '"The Box on the Dresser": Memories of Early Radio and Everyday Life', *Media, Culture & Society*, 10 (1988), p. 8.

6 Ups and Downs

1. Paul Nash, *Outline* (London: Columbus Books, 1988 [first published 1949]), p. 25.

2. Nash, *Outline*, p. 26.

3. Nash, *Outline*, pp. 27–28.

4. Nash, *Outline*, p. 33.

5. Barbara Vine [Ruth Rendell], *The House of Stairs* (Harmondsworth: Penguin, 1989), p. 76.

6. Richard Wollheim, *Germs: A Memoir of Childhood* (London: Black Swan, 2005), p. 48.

7. Mass-Observation, *People's Homes* (London: John Murray, 1943), p. 150.

8. *Protect and Survive* (London: Her Majesty's Stationery Office, 1980), p. 11.

9. Mass-Observation Archive, Topic Collection, 'Britain Can Make It' exhibition, September 1946, TC 26/2/C (female 28 C, tailor).

🏠 7 Now Wash Your Hands

1. Llewellyn, *How Green Was My Valley*, p. 9.

2. Siegfried Giedion, *Mechanization Takes Command* (New York: W. W. Norton, 1969 [first published 1948]), pp. 686–87.

3. Chicago building company from 1944, cited in Giedion, *Mechanization Takes Command*, p. 705.

4. Mass-Observation, *People's Homes*, p. xiii.

5. Joan Littlewood, *Joan's Book: The Autobiography of Joan Littlewood* (London: Methuen, 1994), p. 12.

6. W. J. Turner, *Exmoor Village (British Ways of Life)* (London: Harrap & Co., 1947), p. 39.

7. Mass-Observation, *People's Homes*, p. 111.

8. Giedion, *Mechanization Takes Command*, p. 682.

9. George Orwell, *The Road to Wigan Pier* (Harmondsworth: Penguin, 1962 [first published 1937]), p. 57.

10. *The Times*, cited in Lawrence Wright, *Clean and Decent: The Fascinating History of the Bathroom and the Water-Closet* (London: Penguin, 2000 [first published 1960]), p. 264.

11. Cited in Tony Rivers, Dan Cruickshank, Gillian Darley and Martin Pawley, *The Name of the Room: A History of the British House and Home* (London: BBC Books, 1992), p. 95.

12. Orwell, *The Road to Wigan Pier*, p. 15.

13. Linda Small, cited in Michael Millan, *The Front Room: Migrant Aesthetics in the Home* (London: Black Dog, 2009), p. 25.

14. Giedion, *Mechanization Takes Command*, p. 700.

15. Anthony Byers, *The Willing Servants: A History of Electricity in the Home* (London: Electricity Council, 1981), pp. 82–83.

16. Anthony Ridley, *At Home: An Illustrated History of Houses and Homes* (London: Heinemann, 1976), p. 121.

17. Wright, *Clean and Decent*, p. 259.

18. Mass-Observation, *People's Homes*, p. xiv.

19. Mass-Observation, *People's Homes*, p. xiv.

20. Mass-Observation, *People's Homes*, p. 120.

21. Mass-Observation, *People's Homes*, p. 118.

22. Wright, *Clean and Decent*, p. 2.

23. Giedion, *Mechanization Takes Command*, p. 680.

24. Creda advert, *Picture Post*, 34:1 (4 January 1947), p. 3.

25. Gleason cited in Elizabeth Shove, *Comfort, Cleanliness and Convenience: The Social Organization of Normality* (Oxford: Berg, 2004), p. 104.

26. Jill Murphy, *Five Minutes' Peace* (London: Walker Books, 1986), n.p.

27. Claire Rayner, *Housework: The Easy Way* (London: Corgi, 1967), pp. 87–88.

28. *Daily Mail Ideal Home Exhibition* (1972), p. 8.

29. *Daily Mail Ideal Home Exhibition* (1972), p. 8.

30. *Daily Mail Ideal Home Exhibition* (1972), p. 8.

31. Conran, *The House Book*, p. 301.

32. Anthony Snow and Graham Hopewell, *Planning Your Bathroom* (London: Design Council, 1976), p. 6.

33. Snow and Hopewell, *Planning Your Bathroom*, p. 31.

34. Snow and Hopewell, *Planning Your Bathroom*, p. 32.

35. *The Daily Telegraph* (23 October 2010); http://www.telegraph.co.uk/property/propertynews/8080653/Death-of-the-bidet.html

36. Douglas Adams, *Life, the Universe and Everything* (London: Pan, 1982), p. 4.

37. D. W. Winnicott, *The Child, the Family, and the Outside World* (Harmondsworth: Penguin, 1964), p. 42.

38. Magee, *Clouds of Glory*, p. 15.

39. Wollheim, *Germs*, p. 110.

40. Christina Hardyment, *Dream Babies: Child Care from Locke to Spock* (London: Jonathan Cape, 1983), p. 194.

41. Stopes 1939, cited in Hardyment, *Dream Babies*, p. 128.
42. W. H. Auden, 'The Geography of the House', cited in *About the House* (London: Faber and Faber, 1959), p. 27.

🏠 8 Put the Light Out

1. IKEA catalogue (2004), p. 185.
2. Michel Leiris, 'The Sacred in Everyday Life', in *The College of Sociology, 1937–39*, ed. Denis Hollier, trans. Betsy Wing (Minneapolis, MN: University of Minnesota Press, 1988 [first published 1938]), p. 24.
3. Braine, *Life at the Top*, p. 8.
4. Braine, *Life at the Top*, p. 9.
5. *Housewife's Book*, p. 31.
6. The problem is that no one can find the original headline: all you can find are old references to the headline and cartoons mocking it. So it might be that it only exists as a parody of the sort of imperialist presumption that was characteristic of pre-war Britain.
7. Mass-Observation Archive, Topic Collection, Housing 1938–48, TC 1/6/6 (from report 11 June 1942).
8. Mass-Observation, *People's Homes*, p. 81.
9. Mass-Observation, *People's Homes*, pp. 82–83.
10. *Habitat Catalogue 1980/81*, p. 75.
11. *Good Housekeeping*, 92:4 (October 1967), p. 13.
12. *Good Housekeeping*, 92:4 (October 1967), p. 195.
13. *Good Housekeeping*, 92:4 (October 1967), p. 12.
14. *Good Housekeeping*, 92:4 (October 1967), p. 44.
15. *Good Housekeeping*, 92:4 (October 1967), p. 22.
16. *Good Housekeeping*, 92:4 (October 1967), inside cover.
17. *Habitat Catalogue 1974*, p. 10.
18. *Habitat Catalogue 1978/79*, p. 68.
19. Mike Taylor, letter, *Daily Telegraph* (21 January 2013), p. 19.
20. *Habitat Catalogue 1978/79*, p. 68.

21. Dr Graham in 1783, cited in Lawrence Wright, *Warm and Snug: The History of the Bed* (London: Routledge & Kegan Paul, 1962), p. 200.

22. Lydia Syson, *Doctor of Love: James Graham and His Celestial Bed* (Richmond: Alma Books, 2008).

23. Marie Stopes, from *Enduring Passion* (1928), cited in Hilary Hinds, 'Together and Apart: Twin Beds, Domestic Hygiene and Modern Marriage, 1890–1945', *Journal of Design History*, 23:3 (2010), p. 290.

24. E. M. Delafield's *The Way Things Are* (1927), cited in Hinds, 'Together and Apart: Twin Beds, Domestic Hygiene and Modern Marriage, 1890–1945', p. 278.

25. Rivers et al., *The Name of the Room*, p. 102.

26. Marie Stopes, *Married Love* (London: Putnam & Co., 1940 [originally published 1918]), p. 88.

27. Stopes, *Married Love*, p. 92.

28. Stopes, *Married Love*, p. 95.

29. Stopes, *Married Love*, pp. 77–78.

30. Stopes, *Married Love*, p. 73.

31. Stopes, *Married Love*, p. 96.

32. Alex Comfort, *The Joy of Sex: A Gourmet Guide to Lovemaking* (London: Quartet, 1972), p. 14.

33. Comfort, *The Joy of Sex*, p. 29.

34. Comfort, *The Joy of Sex*, p. 29.

35. Comfort, *The Joy of Sex*, p. 71.

36. Comfort, *The Joy of Sex*, p. 55.

37. Tim Lott, *The Scent of Dried Roses* (Harmondsworth: Penguin, 1997), p. 40.

38. Arthur Conan Doyle, *The Adventures of Sherlock Holmes* (London: Folio Society, 1993 [first published 1892]), p. 204.

39. Turner, *Exmoor Village*, p. 28.

40. Eastlake, *Hints on Household Taste*, p. 202.

41. Joyce Lankester Brisley, *More of Milly-Molly-Mandy* (London: George G. Harrap, 1929), p. 10.

42. *Everyday Things,* exhibition catalogue (London: Royal Institute of British Architects, 1936), p. 27.
43. Maurice Collins, *Eccentric Contraptions* (Newton Abbot: David & Charles, 2004), p. 10.
44. Byers, *The Willing Servants,* p. 85.
45. Byers, *The Willing Servants,* p. 86.
46. Byers, *The Willing Servants,* p. 86.
47. Wright, *Warm and Snug,* p. 223.
48. Maugham, *Of Human Bondage,* p. 13.
49. Mass-Observation, 'Objects about the House', summer 1988, V1116, female.
50. Eastlake, *Hints on Household Taste,* p. 206.
51. Conran, *The House Book,* p. 262.

 **9 No Entry**

1. Wright, *Warm and Snug,* p. 325.
2. Magee, *Clouds of Glory,* p. 128.
3. Magee, *Clouds of Glory,* p. 128.
4. Mass-Observation, *People's Homes,* p. 72.
5. Orwell, *The Road to Wigan Pier,* p. 51.
6. Ian Macrory, *Measuring National Well-Being: Households and Families, 2012* (London: Office of National Statistics, 2012), pp. 1–8.
7. J. M. Barrie, *Peter Pan* (London: Hodder & Stoughton, 1971 [first published 1911]), p. 23.
8. Barrie, *Peter Pan,* p. 20.
9. Watson from 1928, cited in Hardyment, *Dream Babies,* p. 175.
10. Hardyment, *Dream Babies,* p. 128.
11. Hardyment, *Dream Babies,* p. 190.
12. Brereton, 1927, cited in Hardyment, *Dream Babies,* p. 191.
13. Hardyment, *Dream Babies,* p. 192.
14. Mass-Observation, *People's Homes,* p. xi.
15. Macrory, *Measuring National Well-Being,* p. 6.

16. Department of the Environment, *Homes for Today & Tomorrow*, p. 11.
17. Hanif Kureishi, *The Buddha of Suburbia* (London: Faber and Faber, 1990), pp. 13–14.
18. Jon Henley, 'Why Our Children Need To Get Outside and Engage with Nature', *The Independent* (16 August 2010).
19. Conran, *The House Book*, p. 298.
20. Conran, *The House Book*, p. 298.
21. Conran, *The House Book*, p. 298.
22. Sonia Livingstone, 'From Family Television to Bedroom Culture: Young People's Media at Home', in *Media Studies: Key Issues and Debates*, ed. Eoin Devereux (London: Sage, 2007), p. 304.
23. Livingstone, 'From Family Television to Bedroom Culture', p. 311.
24. Will Self, 'Diary', *London Review of Books*, 34:21 (2012), p. 47.
25. Livingstone, 'From Family Television to Bedroom Culture', p. 314.
26. Livingstone, 'From Family Television to Bedroom Culture', p. 314.
27. Griff Rhys Jones, *Semi-Detached* (Harmondsworth: Penguin, 2007), p. 154.
28. Mass-Observation, autumn 1983, 058, female.
29. *IKEA Catalogue 2004*, p. 187.
30. *IKEA Catalogue 2004*, p. 187.

10 Mind Your Step

1. Neil Wilson, *Shadows in the Attic: A Guide to British Supernatural Fiction, 1820–1950* (London: British Library, 2000).
2. M. R. James, 'The Haunted Dolls' House', *Collected Ghost Stories* (Ware: Wordsworth Editions, 2007 [originally published 1931]), p. 265.
3. Gaston Bachelard, *The Poetics of Space* (Boston, MA: Beacon Press, 1969 [first published in French in 1958]), p. 18.
4. C. S. Lewis, *The Lion, the Witch and the Wardrobe* (London: Grafton, 2002 [first published 1950]), pp. 11–12.

5. Maxwell Hutchinson, *Number 57: The History of a House* (London: Headline, 2003).

6. R. L. Stevenson, *The Strange Case of Dr Jekyll and Mr Hyde and Other Stories* (London: Everyman, 1992 [first published 1886]), p. 109.

7. Virginia Woolf, *Mrs Dalloway* (Harmondsworth: Penguin, 1969 [first published 1925]), p. 31.

8. Felix Walter, *House Conversion and Improvement* (London: Architectural Press, 1956), p. 166.

9. Walter, *House Conversion and Improvement*, p. 12.

10. Sally Coulthard, *The Ten Best Ways to Add Value to Your Home* (Harlow: Pearson, 2008), p. 29.

11. Coulthard, *The Ten Best Ways to Add Value to Your Home*, p. 60.

12. 'Teleworking: The Myth of Working from Home', *BBC News Magazine* (27 February 2013); http://www.bbc.co.uk/news/magazine-21588760.

13. 'Teleworking: The Myth of Working from Home'.

14. Mass-Observation, autumn 1983, D156, female.

15. Martin Postle, Stephen Daniels and Nicholas Alfrey, *The Art of the Garden* (London: Tate, 2004), p. 9.

16. Oscar Wilde, *The Happy Prince and Other Tales* (Ware: Wordsworth Editions, 1993 [first published 1888]), p. 38.

17. Frances Hodgson Burnett, *The Secret Garden* (London: Penguin, 1987 [first published 1911]), p. 69.

18. C. H. Middleton, *Your Garden in War-Time* (London: Aurum Press, 2010 [first published 1941]), p. 5.

19. Middleton, *Your Garden in War-Time*, p. 5.

20. Middleton, *Your Garden in War-Time*, p. 118.

21. Middleton, *Your Garden in War-Time*, p. 12.

22. Turner, *Exmoor Village*, p. 47.

23. Rachel Carley, *The Backyard Book: Ideas and Resources for Outdoor Living* (London: Cassell, 1988), p. 9.

24. Mass-Observation, A2464, male, aged thirty-eight, cited in Mark Bhatti and Andrew Church, 'Cultivating Natures: Homes and Gardens in Late Modernity', *Sociology*, 35 (2001), p. 378.

25. Harriet Gross and Nicola Lane, 'Landscapes of the Lifespan: Exploring Accounts of Own Gardens and Gardening', *Journal of Environmental Psychology*, 27 (2007), p. 234.

26. Bhatti and Church, 'Cultivating Natures: Homes and Gardens in Late Modernity', p. 376.

27. Julian Barnes, *Metroland* (London: Picador, 1980), p. 44.

28. David Leibling, *Car Ownership in Great Britain* (London: RAC Foundation, 2008), p. 4.

29. 'Accommodating the Small Car', *Our Homes and Gardens*, 1:3 (August 1919), p. 94.

30. *Our Homes and Gardens*, 1:3 (August 1919), p. xli.

31. Michael Young and Peter Willmott, *Family and Kinship in East London* (Harmondsworth: Penguin, 1990 [first published 1957]), pp. 158–59.

32. Young and Willmott, *Family and Kinship in East London*, p. 158.

33. Young and Willmott, *Family and Kinship in East London*, p. 159.

34. Gareth Jones, *Shed Men* (London: New Holland, 2004); Gordon Thorburn, *Men and Sheds* (London: New Holland, 2003).

35. Frank Hopkinson, *The Joy of Sheds: Because a Man's Place Isn't in the Home* (London: Portico Books, 2012); C. T. Grey, *Fifty Sheds of Grey* (London: Boxtree, 2012).

11 Do Come Again

1. *The Daily Mail Ideal Home Exhibition* (1958), p. 163.

2. Simon Pepper, 'Housing at Roehampton', *Modern Britain: The Cambridge Cultural History*, ed. Boris Ford (Cambridge: Cambridge University Press, 1992), p. 279.

3. Jack Lynn in 1962, cited in Alan Powers, *Britain* (London: Reaktion Books, 2007), p. 113.

4. Mass-Observation, *People's Homes*, p. 219.

5. Michael J. Aldrich, 'Home: The Command Base', unpublished manuscript, Michael Aldrich Archive, University of Brighton, March 1984, p. 1.

6. Aldrich, 'Home: The Command Base', p. 1.
7. Aldrich, 'Home: The Command Base', pp. 6–7.
8. Aldrich, 'Home: The Command Base', p. 4.
9. Aldrich, 'Home: The Command Base', p. 6.
10. Aldrich, 'Home: The Command Base', p. 6.
11. Aldrich, 'Home: The Command Base', p. 5.
12. Severin Carrell, 'The Island House That Powers Itself – with a Little Help from 100mph Gales', *The Guardian* (19 May 2008).
13. Carrell, 'The Island House That Powers Itself'.
14. Denis Crompton (ed.), *Concerning Archigram* ... (London: Archigram Archives, 1998), front cover.
15. Gay Hawkins, *The Ethics of Waste: How We Relate to Rubbish* (Sydney: University of New South Wales Press, 2006), pp. 124–25.

INDEX